THE WORLD OF
RŌZOME

THE WORLD OF
RŌZOME

WAX-RESIST TEXTILES OF JAPAN

Betsy Sterling Benjamin

KODANSHA INTERNATIONAL
Tokyo • New York • London

To Takeo Sano
1913–1995
Rōzome Master

NOTE TO THE READER: All Japanese names in the text are given in the Western order, given name followed by surname. Measures are expressed in the metric system first, followed by approximate equivalents in feet and inches. The size of the art works is expressed in terms of height first, then width. Temperatures are given in Celsius followed by approximate Fahrenheit equivalents.

Several of the interviews in this work originally appeared in slightly different versions in the following magazines, and are reprinted here by permission:
"Kageo Miura: A Master of Roketsu-zome Art." *Fiberarts Magazine* (Asheville, North Carolina), vol. 19, no. 5, March/April 1993.
"The Art of Shoukoh Kobayashi." *Surface Design Journal*, vol. 17, no. 3, Spring 1993.
"Life in Muromachi: Yusuke Tange, Kimono Artist." *Textile Fibre Forum Magazine*, vol. 11, issue 3, #35, 1992.

Distributed in the United States by Kodansha America, Inc., 114 Fifth Avenue, New York, N.Y. 10011, and in the United Kingdom and continental Europe by Kodansha Europe, Ltd., 95 Aldwych, London WC2B 4JF. Published by Kodansha International, Ltd., 17-14 Otowa 1-chome, Bunkyo-ku, Tokyo 112 and Kodansha America, Inc.

96 97 98 99   10 9 8 7 6 5 4 3 2 1

Library of Congress Cataloging-in-Publication Data Application Pending

ISBN4-7700-1774-X

CONTENTS

Foreword

I was delighted to be asked to write a foreword to Betsy Sterling Benjamin's book—the first in English—on Japanese wax resist, and marveled at the extraordinary coincidence that this request should occur so soon after the introduction of the "new" resist techniques coming from Scandinavia. Although there are recently developed chemical methods to keep one layer of dye from affecting another, it is the mechanical resist approaches like wax resist that are the most direct and reliable. Indonesian batik is probably the most familiar example of the style.

Japanese textiles, both past and present, continue to astonish, amaze and inspire. The aesthetic, intellectual and spiritual contributions of the countless and often anonymous Japanese textile artists are legend. They have for centuries dedicated themselves to the surface and structure of cloth, created to protect, enhance and exalt the body, as well as to transform domestic, regal and sacred spaces. Many books have been written on Japanese weaving, paste resist, stencil dyeing and, more recently, bound resist with Yoshiko Wada's masterful *Shibori*. Until now, little information has been available in English on rōketsuzome.

Betsy Sterling Benjamin's contribution is long-awaited and sure to find a prominent place in the library of anyone with a genuine love for textiles. The section on process clears up the mystery of technique and describes in detail how the unique effects of rolling, stenciling, stamping and spraying wax may be achieved. The history section is compelling and thorough, weaving together dates, places, events and legends into a colorful and factual chronicle. The interviews with contemporary rōketsuzome artists bring the process into the present, introducing us to fresh and vital visions of this ancient way of wax and dye.

This beautifully illustrated, scholarly book brilliantly reveals the secrets of a particular approach to materials and ideas. Once again we are reminded of the unlimited potential of human creativity to transmute light and color, texture, form and meaning.

Jason Pollen

Professor, Kansas City Art Institute
President, Surface Design Association

Introduction

"Liquid dye on thirsty cloth."[1] Molten wax. A steady hand. These are the basic elements of wax resist.

Many cultures consider fabric dyeing an art form. Western culture has honored weaving, while the countries of Asia have shown equal respect for resist dyeing. In its simplest form, resist dyeing was a quick substitute for more time-consuming woven cloth patterns and was used to decorate clothing and add color and interest to everyday life. In some Asian cultures resist-dyed clothing designated rank or status in the community. In its most exalted form, it was found in palaces, temples and churches, where it became ritual cloth, created to celebrate or commemorate important rites of passage. As soft, hanging wall paintings, resist-dyed textiles narrated old stories of religion and myth, depicting honored royalty and even deities.

The beauty of kimono and the magic of wax resist first brought me to Japan more than fourteen years ago. Here wax resist is not called batik but rōketsuzome or the shortened form of the word, rōzome. Although modern European and American batik have been inspired by the wax-resist fabrics of Indonesia, Japan has its own historical source that flowed from the Asian continent and inspired the textile treasures stored in the Shōsōin repository of Nara for more than twelve hundred years. Japanese rōzome, like the batik of Indonesia, is produced using wax, cloth and dye, but the Japanese process has many distinctive techniques and is a product of Japanese inventiveness.

I first became interested in wax resist in elementary school when I saw our simple wax crayon drawings transformed as they received a layer of colored paint. Watching the wax crayon strokes resist the water-based paint was pure magic. I saw my first contemporary batik in 1971 while living in Iceland, where a few artists were working with wax and the European cold-water dyes. After returning to the United States, I focused on learning this wax-resist process and dye chemistry and on mastering the exotic Indonesian tool, the *canting*, used to draw fine lines in wax. A short stay in Yogyakarta increased my technical knowledge, but it was the wonderful, controlled Japanese dyeing technique of rōketsuzome to which I was most drawn. American batik of the sixties and seventies was based on the Indonesian method of brushing wax on fabric and dipping it into a vat of dye for color. This method produced flat, even tones of color, but I found that the fabric quickly became saturated with dyestuff after three or four overdyeings. The Japanese rōzome method used a variety of wax application methods and brush dyeing that controlled and even allowed for shaded dye applications. Multiple colors were possible on one piece of cloth. This was the kind of control I had been searching for in my own work. In 1981 I moved to Japan to master resist-dyeing techniques and to study kimono history and design.

Years later, while traveling to England, Australia, New Zealand and my native United States to lecture on Japanese textiles, I encountered audiences who had never seen the work of Japanese rōzome artists. This book is for those who wanted to see more of the Japanese work that is so rarely exhibited in the West. Its focus is broad, encompassing historical background as well as interviews with contemporary artists and descriptions of various Japanese rōzome techniques.

At the heart of this book is an interview section in which seventeen artists speak about their work and their lives as artists. Because of space considerations, these seventeen must represent the large number of other, equally talented artists who are also committed to their work and who also regularly exhibit work worthy of notice. These particular artists were chosen primarily because of the strength of the work that they have consistently produced. Other factors were technical innovativeness, the human interest associated with their life stories, and their interest in this project and willingness to talk with a stranger about their work. The artists are grouped into categories of Innovation, Technique, Tradition and Style, which are a means of organization only. Each artist works with his or her own personal imagery and combination of techniques, while some are more notable for innovative methods or have an unusual life story. Like other modern Japanese, most rōzome artists live in large cities, with the majority clustered around the cultural and textile center of Kyoto. A large number say that they enjoy working with wax resist because it is something they can do entirely by themselves, independently and in their own studios, unlike other Japanese traditional resist processes, most of which require support. This quality of rōzome seems to attract artists of a particularly independent and less traditional nature. The artists interviewed range from old masters of eighty to others in midlife and a few as young as thirty-four. Most of the artists in this book produce some kimono every year; this remains the traditional canvas of Japanese textile artists. However, all produce their exhibition work as large paintings, panels or folding screens. A few occasionally do three-dimensional work as well. It was the powerful work of these and other rōzome artists, and my desire to see it presented to the West, that pushed me to put aside my own creative work and write this book.

In Japan, rōzome has a history dating back to the seventh and eighth centuries, when it was called by its ancient name, rōkechi. Written documentation tells that it was produced by workers who stamped wax on fabric, in a manner assumed to have come from China. None of the actual blocks used for stamping remain in existence, so our knowledge must come from the textiles themselves. Some of the most complex patterns are seen on very fragmented fabrics; these have been redrawn here, enabling us to see what the design must have looked like when freshly stamped on the ancient fabric. During the Heian period, which followed, the process died out and wax-resist fabrics were not seen again in Japan until the early seventeenth century, when imported *sarasa* arrived from India. *Sarasa* was greatly admired and sought after as tea-ceremony textiles, but in Japan the Indian wax-resist textiles were adapted as stencil-and-paste designs on fabric. It was not until the early twentieth century that interest in rōzome reawakened. The accessibility of the Shosoin *rōkechi* collection, the return of textile artists and technicians from travels in India, Germany and Paris, where Indonesian batik was in vogue, and the availability of native as well as imported waxes all allowed a return to this resist process, which had been ignored since the eighth century.

The seventh-century wax-resist textiles I studied in Japan led me to search for their antecedents. Early volumes on batik have erroneously cited the Shosoin *rōkechi* screens as the oldest existing wax-resist textiles in the world, but this is far from true. Archaeological excavations in the past 150 years have uncovered resist textiles in the Near East, Central Asia and China, some of which date back to the fourth century B.C. It is extremely difficult to be certain whether wax, mud or paste was used as a resist to create some of the ancient textiles. In the Antiquities section I have included those textiles that have been assumed by scholars to be of wax-resist technique and those that exhibit the characteristics of textiles patterned with hot wax. Conclusive evidence may come later with more advanced technology.

My approach here has been from the point of view of an artist who has worked with the process for almost twenty-five years. Delving into the hazy beginnings of wax-resist textiles and looking for that familiar stroke left by wax on fabric centuries old has been a consuming project. The days spent with Japanese textile masters as they talked of their work and their motivation gave me a special glimpse into a contemporary Japan I am still discovering. I came away from most interviews charmed by the artists' willingness to share their stories despite their initial shyness, and awed by their talent and commitment. It is hoped that not only textile artists and enthusiasts, but also those interested in Japan, contemporary art and modern lifestyle will find this book of value.

Japanese resist textiles have grown out of the area of ethnology and the decorative arts, and into the area of fine arts where they also justifiably belong. As with most work on cloth, photographs do not do justice to the subtlety of dye, color and texture. Rōzome deserves to be seen and I hope that people around the world will have more opportunities to do so in the future.

Betsy Sterling Benjamin

Definitions

Wax on cloth resists the penetration of dye. The Japanese method of controlling the application of wax and dye results in something not seen in the batik work of other cultures. This work, known as *rōzome* or *rōketsuzome*, is created with craft materials, yet presented as art to be displayed in museums and galleries.

It is the word "rōketsuzome" that most clearly describes the technique (resist) and the materials (dye and wax) used in the process as well as the art that results. The Japanese word rōketsuzome is composed of the elements *rō*, or wax, *ketsu*, or resist (block-out) and *-zome*, the noun form of the verb *someru*, to dye. Wax resist textiles have come to be known around the world by the Javanese word, batik, from the verb *ambatik* (to mark with spots or dots), but the very unique qualities of rōketsuzome suggests the need for a term that describes it more clearly than "Japanese batik."

Indonesian batik is created with special tools, specifically, the *canting* tool, used to create lines and the *cap*, or metal stamp. Color is added to the fabric by immersion in various dye baths, alternating with additional applications of wax. The result is a multicolored fabric with detailed, linear motifs. While cracks are unacceptable in the finest Java batik, these weblike patterns are considered a natural characteristic of international batik.

By contrast, rōketsuzome is predominantly created with brushes in controlled wax and dye applications. Techniques of half-resist and brush trailing for textural effects are included and, while linear patterning is possible using a thin brush, this style is not typical of Japanese rōketsuzome. Most contemporary artists use the wax as a strong block-out, blending wax formulas that will not allow any cracking of the wax surface. Dye is brushed on in a very controlled manner using many techniques of dye shading. The startling results include a luminosity of color rarely seen in batik work from other countries.

Rōketsu, rōketsuzome and rōzome can each be translated into English, but artists do not always agree on the subtle shadings of these words even in Japanese. All agree, however, that a fourth term, *rōkechi*, is the one used for ancient wax-resist textiles from seventh- and eighth-century Japan. *Kechi* is not a Japanese word but comes from a Japanese reading of the Chinese ideogram *-jie*, to block out or resist. The word "rōkechi" is associated with stamped resist cloth of ancient times, something quite different in style, motif and technique from contemporary work. The process was called *shin-rōkechi* ("new wax resist") when the technique was reintroduced early in this century, and soon became *rōketsu* in modern terminology. Later the word for "dyeing" was added and the term rōketsuzome was coined. *Rōzome* arose as a shortened or contracted form of this word. Some artists like to use the term rōzome, since it contrasts with the word for traditional *nori-zome*, or paste resist. Currently, the variations of wax resist have grown to include the use of pigment rather than dye, and artists working in this manner prefer the term rōketsu, rather than rōzome, to describe their work.

Individual artists continue to debate the exact meaning of these terms for themselves. Many like the term rōketsuzome because it clearly describes the process. Others prefer rōzome, and say that rōketsuzome sounds to them like the old process used to create commonplace, functional textiles such as *furoshiki* (wrapping cloths) or *noren* (cloth door hangings). They feel that the word rōzome best suits the art they create; the culmination of their artistic expression. Rōkechi, rōketsu, rōketsuzome, rōzome; these trace the evolution of a word from its seventh century Chinese derivation to a term for the work of contemporary artists working with wax resist to create art.

Chronology

JAPAN

PREHISTORIC
Jōmon ca. 10,000 B.C.–ca. B.C. 300
Yayoi ca. 300 B.C.–ca. A.D. 300
Kofun ca. 300–600

ANCIENT
Asuka 552–710
Nara 710–794
    Tenpyō 729–748
Heian 794–1185

MIDDLE AGES
Kamakura 1185–1333
Muromachi 1392–1573

PRE-MODERN
Azuchimomoyama 1573–1600
Edo 1600–1868

EARLY MODERN
Meiji 1868–1912

MODERN
Taishō 1912–1926
Shōwa 1926–1989
Heisei 1989 to present

CHINA

Early (Western) Han 202 B.C.–ca. A.D. 8
Later (Eastern) Han 25–220

Three Kingdoms 220–280
    Jin 265–420

Southern and Northern Dynasties 439–589
    Early Song 420–479

Sui ca. 581–618

Tang 618–906

Five Dynasties 907–960

Song 960–1279

Yüan (Mongol) 1271–1368

Ming 1368–1644

Qing ca. 1644–1912

Plate 1 **Child's Linen Tunic** Blue resist-dyed garment found at the burial field of Akhmim. Patterned with blocks stamps and resist material believed to be wax. Sixth century A.D. and of foreign, possibly Syrian, origin. Victorian and Albert Museum. (inv. 1522–1899)

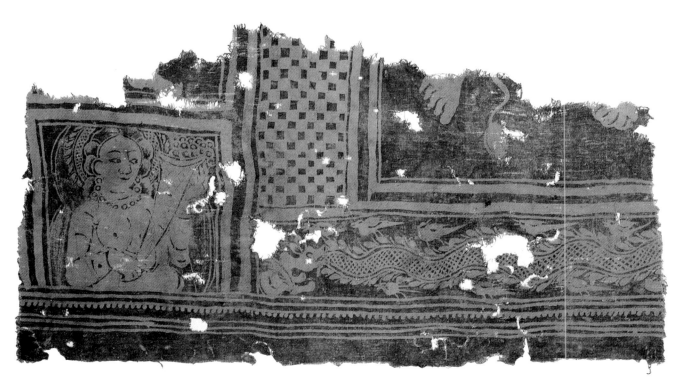

Plate 2 **Niya Bodhisattva** Resist-dyed cotton fragment of a human figure holding a cornucopia within a frame. To the right of the figure is an elongated dragon with birds and patterns of stripes, checks and dots that show this section to be a corner border design for a much larger panel. From Tomb 1 at Niya, Minfeng County, first century. 45 x 86 cm./17⅝ x 33⅞ in. Uighur Autonomous Region Museum, Urumchi, Xinjiang.

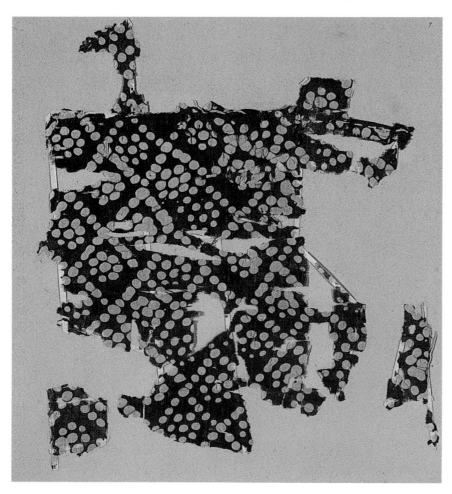

Plate 3 **Diamond Lattice** Fragments of a blue and white resist-dye dot lattice pattern on silk and polychrome figured weave; the entire cloth may have been used as a face-cover for a corpse. Found in Tomb 2 of Area 6, Astana, ca. 364, Stein Loan Collection, Victoria and Albert Museum, London. (Ast. vi. 2.04)

Plate 4 **Birds in a Cage** Fragment of silk wax-resist on a blue ground. White and brown design of two birds and small rosettes surrounded by an enclosing vine pattern or cage; stamped- or brushed resist process. Excavated from Tomb 2 of Area 9, Astana of the sixth to eighth centuries. 6 x 11 cm./2¼ x 4¼ in. National Museum, New Delhi. (Ast. ix 2.012)

◄ Plate 8 **Ram Screen** Design stamped and brushed with wax on yellow *ashiginu* silk dyed brown and retouched with green malachite pigment. Inscribed as tax payment in the year 751. This 163.5 x 56.5 cm. panel/64¹/₂ x 22¹/₄ in. shows a ram with curling horns posing under a tree surrounded by vegetation. The ram's neck-band of linked-pearl design and distinctive pose indicate a Persian Sassanid influence. Mid-eighth century. From the treasures of the Shōsōin.

Plate 9 **Parrot Screen** Stamped and brushed with wax on yellow silk with brown ground; patterns of a parrot under a tree a phoenix, the mythical animal known as the *kirin*, a small fawn, a hunter and vegetation. Mid-eighth century. 163 x 56 cm./64¹/₄ x 22 in. From the treasures of the Shōsōin.

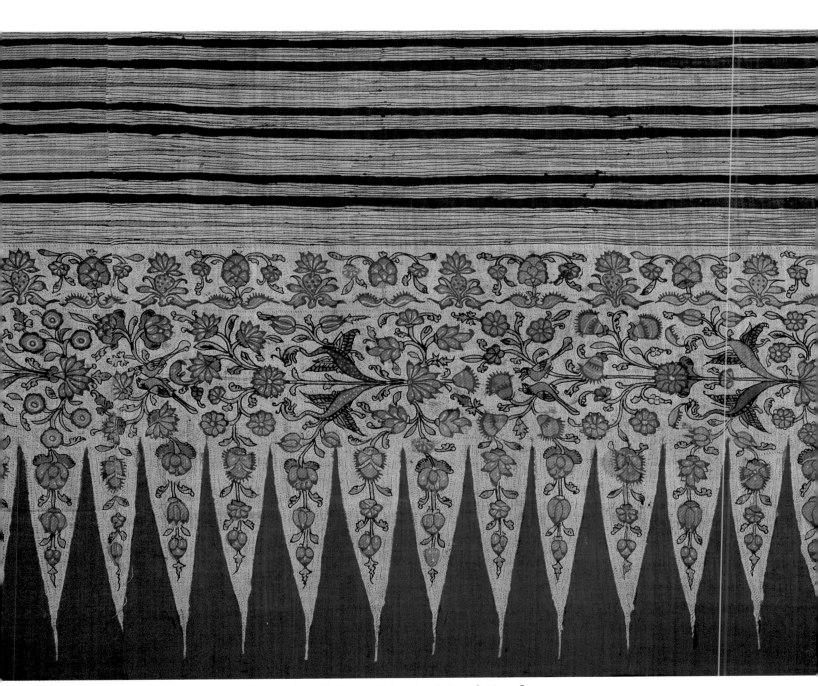

Plate 10 **Seventeenth-century Imported** *Sarasa* (Detail) Cotton cloth with a design of stripes, flowers, birds and a sawtooth pattern on a white ground. Wax-resist, mordant-printed and painted. This kind of cloth was made in India for tea-ceremony use as *fukusa* (display cloths) or *shifuku* (cloth bags used to protect tea caddies) and collected by high ranking lords and wealthy families. Seventeenth century, from the Konjaku Nishimura Collection.

Plate 11 Tomonosuke Ogō. *Sangetsu byōbu* (Mountain Moon Screen). Wax resist on paper. 170 x 185 cm./67 x 73 in., 1946. Photo: Yusuke Tange. From the Moto-haru Koyama collection.

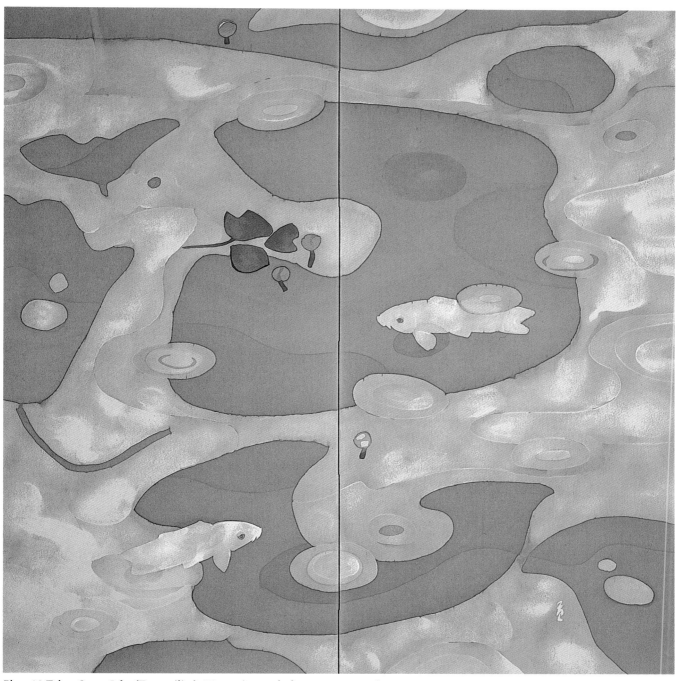

Plate 12 Takeo Sano. *Jaku* (Tranquility). Wax resist on cloth. 161 x 157 cm./
63$^1/_2$ x 61$^3/_4$ in., 1977. Kyoto Municipal Museum of Art.

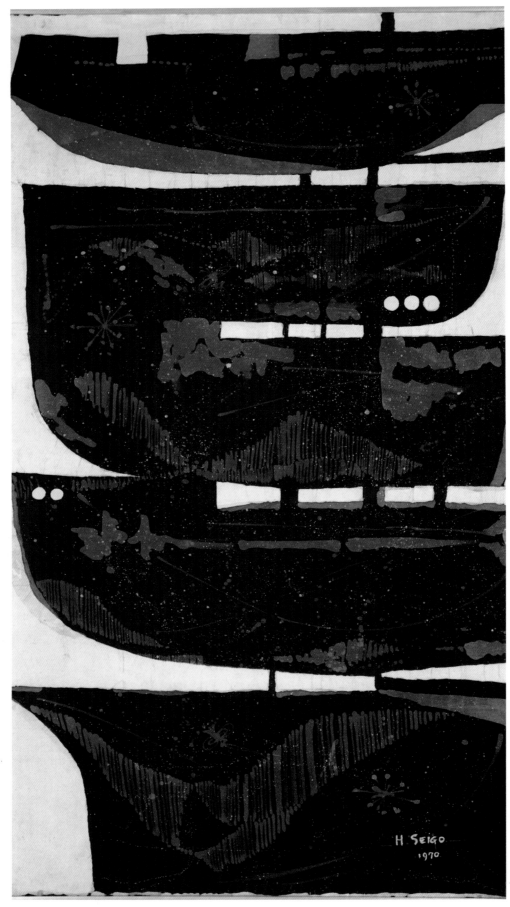

Plate 13 Seigō Hirokawa. *Sora no patân* (Sky Pattern). Wax resist on cloth. 145.5 x 79.5 cm./57¼ x 31¼ in., 1970. Suntory Museum.

Plate 14 Tōichi Motono. **Drama: D.** Wax resist on cotton. 210 x 150 cm./82³/₄ x 59 in., 1989. Photo by Murai Art Photo Studio.

Plate 15 Yasuhiko Tanaka. *Sabaku* (Sands). Wax resist and wax roller on cotton. 44 x 34 cm./17¹/₂ x 13¹/₂ in., 1985. Photograph by the artist.

Plate 16 Gekka Minakawa. *Kujaku no zu* (Peacocks). Wax resist on silk, 333 x 170 cm./131 x 67 in., 1961. (Commissioned for use on a Gion Festival float.)

Plate 17 Taizō Minakawa. **Istanbul.** Wax resist on linen. 210 x 175 cm./
82³/₄ x 69 in., 1982. Photo by Masami Sugimoto.

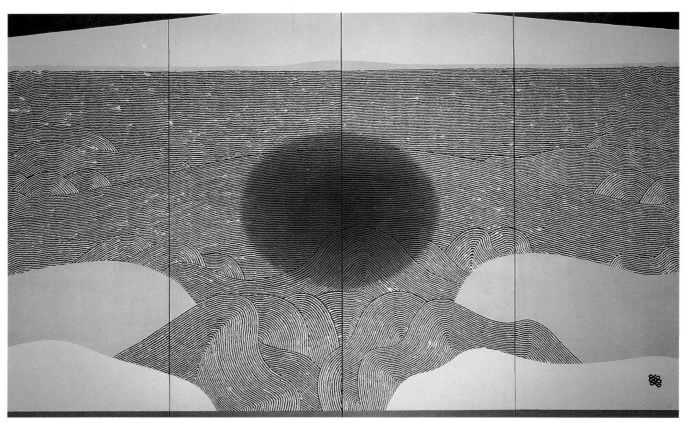

Plate 18 Shōsaku Teraishi. **Horizon.** Wax resist on cotton. 170 x 280 cm./67 x 110¹/₄ in., 1992. Photograph courtesy of the artist.

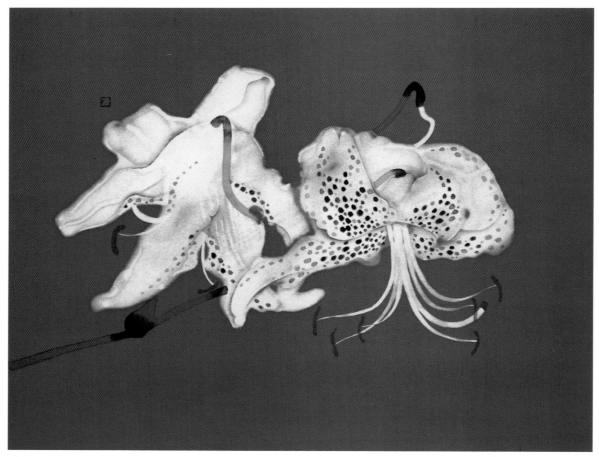

Plate 19 Shōsaku Teraishi. *Oniyuri* (Tiger Lily). Wax resist on cotton. 26 x 30 cm./10¹/₄ x 12 in., 1990. Photograph by Wako.

Plate 20 Teiji Nakai. *Mokkon* (Soul of the Tree). Wax resist on linen with indigo dye. 172 x 172 cm./67^3/$_4$ x 67^3/$_4$ in., 1990. Photo: New Color, Inc.

Plate 21 Kageo Miura. *"Botan no zu"* (Peony Folding Screen). Wax resist on silk. 180 x 178 cm./ 71 x 70 in., 1979. Photograph courtesy of Senshoku to Seikatsusha.

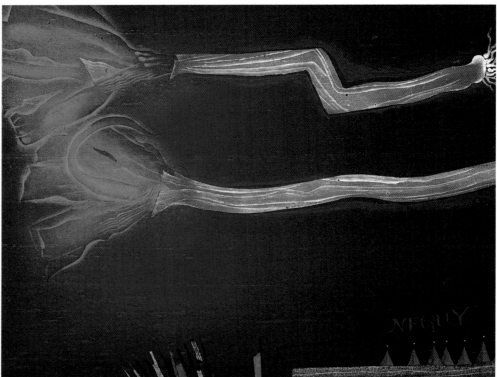

Plate 22 Kageo Miura. *"Neguy"* (Green Onion). Wax resist on silk with dye and pigments. 80 x 100 cm./31¹/₂ x 39¹/₄ in., 1992. Photograph by Shōkandō.

Plate 23 Tsukio Kitano. *"Kakure kirishitan"* (Hidden Christians). Wax resist on *gasenshi* paper with pigments. 170 x 168 cm./67 x 66 in., 1974. Photograph by New Color, Inc. Collection: Kyoto Prefecture.

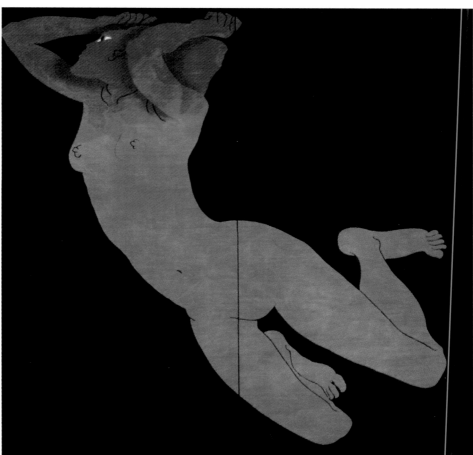

Plate 24 Tsukio Kitano. *"Oyogu onna"* (Bathing Woman). Wax resist, natural dyes and *sumi* ink. 168 x 170 cm./66 x 67 in., 1982. Photograph by Ikuo Terashima. Collection: Fukui Prefectural Museum.

Plate 25 Tadayoshi Yamamoto. *"Haru"* (Spring). Wax-resist tie-dye (*rō-shibori*) and photographic serigraphy on silk. 180 x 300 cm./71 x 118 in., 1985. Photo by New Color, Inc.

Plate 26 Kohrow Kawata. *"Noren"* (Doorway Curtain). Linen cloth with wax and paste resists. 190 x 180 cm./75 x 71 in., 1990. Photograph by Isao Nishikawa.

Plate 27 Shigeki Fukumoto. *"Tomoe"* (Whirl). Wax resist on cotton.
177 x 180 cm./69³/₄ x 71 in., 1989. Photograph by the artist.

Plate 28 Shoukoh Kobayashi. *"Hibiki"* (Rhyme). Wax resist and acide dye on silk.
164 x 360 cm./65^1/$_2$ x 141^3/$_4$ in., 1991. Photograph by Junichi Kanzaki.

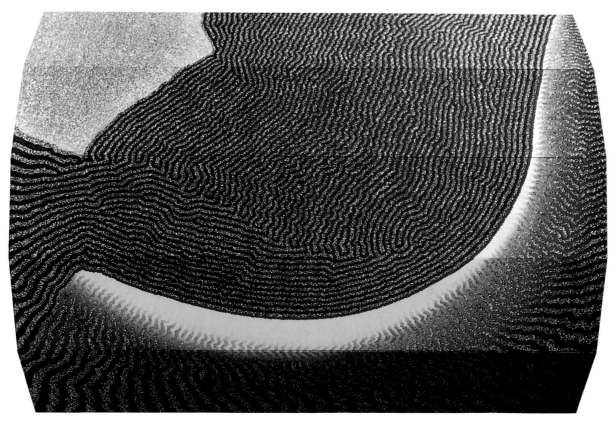

Plate 29 Shoukoh Kobayashi. "Kyō" (Echo). Wax resist and acid dye on
silk. 132 x 170 x 30 cm./52 x 67 x 12 in., 1992. Photo by the artist.

Plate 30 Mitsuo Takaya. *"Seiza"* (Constellations). Wax resist on silk. 170 x 170 cm./67 x 67 in., 1993. Photograph by the artist.

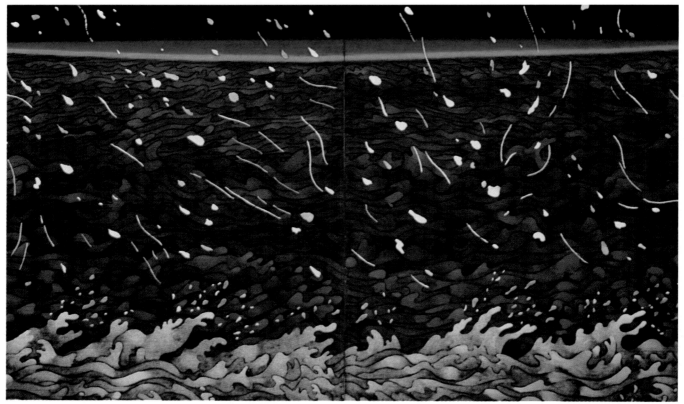

Plate 31 Mitsuo Takaya. Detail from *"Fuyu no hotaru"* (Fireflies in Winter). Wax resist on silk. 170 x 170 cm./67 x 67 in., 1991. Photograph by the artist.

Plate 32 Chie Ōtani. "Center of Thinking." Wax resist on silk. 190 x 160 cm./75 x 63 in., 1991. Photo by K. Tateoka.

Plate 33 Chie Ōtani. "The Sound of the Sea." Wax resist on silk. 185 x 170 cm./73 x 67 in., 1985. Photo by K. Tateoka.

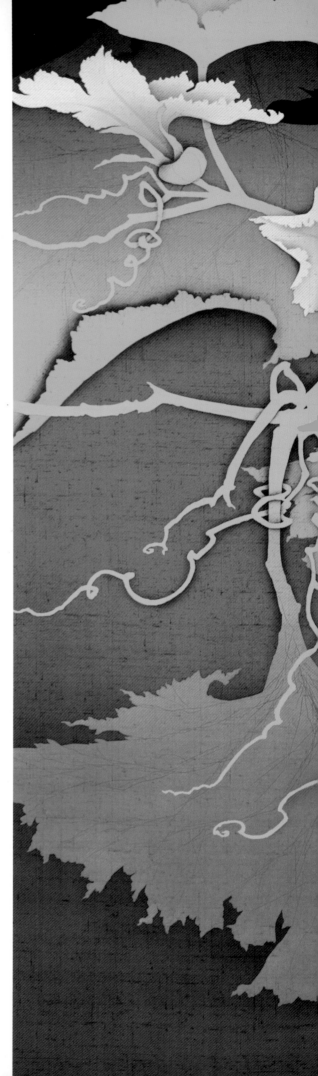

Plate 34 Yusuke Tange. *"Natsu no sakari"* (Height of Summer). Wax resist on silk. 180 x 170 cm./71 x 67 in., 1994. Photograph by the artist.

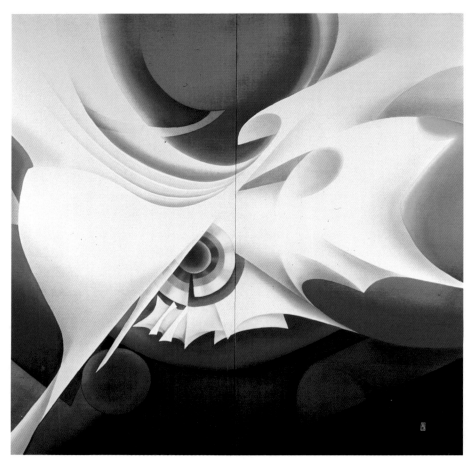

Plate 35 Yoshito Tanino. "*Kōkyō: Fūjin*" (Symphony: The Wind God). Natural and acid dyes on silk. 190 x 180 cm./75 x 71 in., 1991. Photograph by New Color, Inc.

Plate 36 Yoshito Tanino. "*Kōkyō: Umi*" (Symphony: The Sea). Natural dye on silk. 190 x 180 cm./75 x 71 in., 1993. Photograph by New Color, Inc.

Plate 37 Katsuji Yamade. *"Hira bosetsu"* (Evening Snow, Mt. Hira). Wax resist
on cotton. 180 x 170 cm./71 x 67 in., 1990. Photograph by the artist.

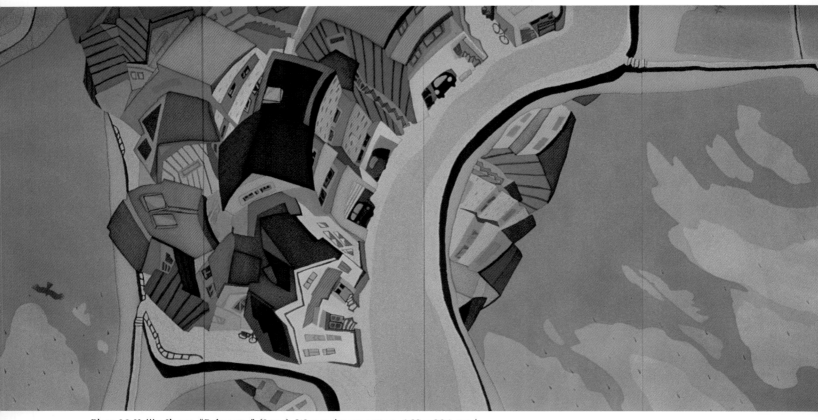

Plate 38 Keijin Ihaya. *"Rokugatsu"* (June). Wax resist on cotton. 162 x 324 cm./
64 x 127$^1/_2$ in., 1993. Photograph by New Color, Inc.

Plate 39 Midori Abe. *"Natsubi"* (Days of Summer). Wax resist on hemp cloth.
220 x 180 cm./86¹/₂ x 71 in., 1987. Photo by Ikkō Nagano.

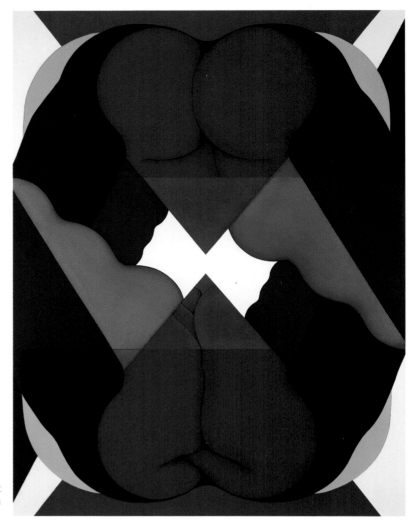

Plate 40 Yukiko Komori. *"Hana"* (Flower). Wax resist on cotton. 162 x 152 cm./64 x 60 in., 1991. Photograph by Hidefumi Morimiya.

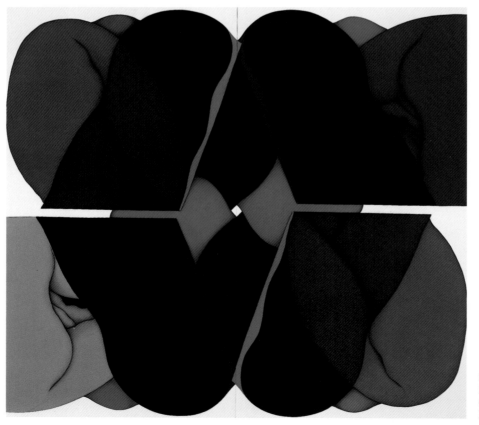

Plate 41 Yukiko Komori. *"Hana III"* (Flower III). Wax resist on cotton. 167 x 222 cm./ 65³/₄ x 87¹/₂ in., 1992. Photograph by Hidefumi Morimiya.

Plate 42 Yasuko Iyanaga. *"Minami no shima kara no okurimono"* (Gift from a Southern Island). Wax resist on silk. 210 x 160 cm./ 82³/₄ x 63 in., 1989. Photograph by Takahiko Sakurai.

Plate 43 Yasuko Iyanaga. *"Minami no shima kara no okurimono: Minami kaze"* (Gift from a Southern Island: Southern Wind). Wax resist on silk. 210 x 160 cm./82³/₄ x 63 in., 1992. Photograph by Takahiko Sakurai.

Plate 44 Naomaru Ōkubo. *"Kurete yuku"* (Night Falls). Wax resist on cotton.
175 x 160 cm./69 x 63 in., 1993. Photograph by New Color, Inc.

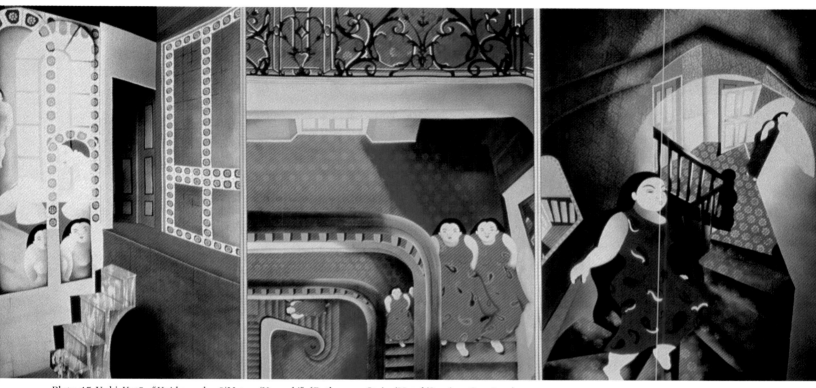

Plate 45 Yuki Katō. *"Kaidan yokusō/Hoteru/Yo asobi"* (Bathroom Stairs/Hotel/Staying Out Late). Wax and *dakku* resist on silk. 133 x 180 cm./52$^1/_2$ x 71 in., 1993. Photograph by New Color, Inc.

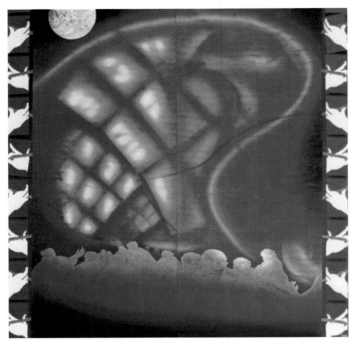

Plate 46 Hiroshi Hashida. *"Hiire no kei: Danjiri Matsuri"* (Lamplighting: The Danjiri Festival). Wax resist on cotton. 180 x 180 cm./71 x 71 in., 1991. Photograph by Eisaku Fukui.

Plate 47 Masahisa Nakagawa. *"Sou"* (Twins). Wax resist on silk. 180 x 172 cm./71 x 67³/₄ in., 1991. Photograph by the artist.

Plate 48 Seiya Hashida. *"Sekisō"* (Layers of Earth). Wax resist on cotton. 183 x 169 cm./ 72 x 66¹/₂ in., 1987. Photo courtesy of New Color, Inc.

Plate 49 Minoru Tabata. *"Botan"* (Peony). Wax resist on silk. 215 x 180 cm./84³/₄ x 71 in., 1986. Photograph courtesy of Gendai Kōgei Bijutsuka Kōkai Kinki Kai.

Plate 50 Hiroyoshi Yamashita. *"San sen gōryū, I"* (Three Streams Meet, 1). Wax resist on silk. 150 x 100 cm./59 x 39¹/₄ in., 1989. Photo by the artist.

Plate 51 Harumi Horiuchi. *"Sakura-Sakura"* (Cherries Everywhere). Wax resist
on cotton. 170 x 160 cm./67 x 63 in., 1993. Photograph by the artist.

Plate 52 Masaji Yamamoto. *"Maru to sen"* (Circles and Lines). Wax
and silk-screen printing on silk. 180 x 150 cm./71 x 59 in., 1991.
Photograph by Jō Satō.

Plate 53 Akihiko Okada. *"Neian no machi kado"* (Quiet Street Corner). Wax resist on silk. 140 x 174 cm./55 x 68$^1/_2$ in., 1989. Photograph by Yusuke Tange.

Plate 54 Mikako Ujiie. *"Kawara-bei"* (Clay Roof Tiles). Wax resist on silk.
150 x 140 cm./59 x 55 in., 1993. Photo by Kōichi Nishimura.

Sekidashi Process

Plate 55

The drawing is transferred to the fabric, and areas that will remain white are covered with wax.

The background is dyed a yellow ocher.

After the dye has dried completely, wax is applied to the background to "reserve" this color. Note that since the wax mixture has a yellow cast it temporarily darkens the color of any dyed area over which it is painted.

Next, all areas of the leaves and stem are brushed with an olive green dye.

At this stage, leaves that are to remain olive green have been brushed with wax, and a second, brighter green has been applied to other areas.

The final forest green dye is brushed on, covering the darkest leaf and stem areas.

After the wax is removed and the piece is steamed to set the dyes, the true dye colors emerge.

To dye the flower area, the background section is covered with wax. The fabric is dampened and a pale gray dye brushed on the center. The flower petals are then dyed in the same "layering" method as was used for the leaves. That is, the petals in the foreground are dyed a very pale color and then receive a coating with wax. Next, the petals behind them are dyed a deeper shade.

Wax has been removed a second time and the cloth has been steamed to set the various colors. Details of the stamens and pistil have been added with *gofun* (crushed oyster shell) and other pigments.

The completed stem area shows the strong color contrasts that can be produced with the layered application of dye in the *seki-dashi* technique.

The finished work.

RESIST-DYED TEXTILES FROM ANTIQUITY

Humans have spun fiber and woven cloth since the seventh millennium B.C. The desire to add color and pattern to the cloth must have arisen not long afterward. Dyed fiber has been found in Anatolia that dates from as early as the sixth millennium B.C. Mordants, the chemicals used to bond dye permanently to fabric, were known in India from 2000 B.C. Evidence from the Egyptian wall paintings of the Khnemhotep Tomb at Beni Hasan (1900 B.C.), the frescos, figures and vases of second millennium–B.C. Crete and the later seventh century–A.D. caves in Ajanta, India, all show that ancient people wore beautifully patterned garments. Knowledge of how to pattern cloth with resists such as wax, resin, mud or paste could have been discovered easily when an accidental spot of pitch or grease on fabric refused to take on color in a dye bath. However, the exact date at which people began to use resist-dyeing processes is unknown.

Scholars have suggested that resist textiles originated in countries as far apart as India, Peru, China, Syria and Egypt—or, in Dr. Alfred Büghler's opinion, in all those diverse places simultaneously.[2] Some scholars assume that wax-resist dyeing originated in Asia and spread down to the Malay archipelago, while others feel that resist textiles are indigenous to India and that the knowledge traveled along trade routes throughout, first, Asia and, later, the Western world (Robinson 39). The most famous wax-resist textiles, the batiks of Indonesia, seem to be part of an ancient tradition, yet the first written record of Javanese batik does not appear until 1518 (Elliott 22), and most scholars believe that the knowledge was carried to Java by early Indian or Chinese settlers. Although India has long been assumed to be one of the earliest sources of dye and printing knowledge, no resist-dyed textiles dating from before the sixteenth century have been found there, probably because the wet climatic conditions did not allow any to survive. However, the patterns decorating printed and resist-dyed textiles found in Fustat, Egypt, suggest that these may be of Gujarati origin (Gittinger 33). The very early Greek geographer Stabo (63 B.C.–A.D. 20) mentions printed textiles from India[3] and notes that travelers who visited India from the first century onward reported "flowered garments made of the finest muslin and cloths painted with a pencil."[4] These fabrics are believed to have incorporated some form of resist dyeing.

Until recently, the earliest reference to the use of a wax-resist process on dyed textiles has been accepted as Plinius the Elder's (A.D. 23–79) description in *Natural History* of the magic of the Egyptian dye pot:

> In Egypt they also color cloth by an exceptionally remarkable kind of process. They first thoroughly rub white fabrics and then smear them not with colors but with chemicals that absorb color. When this has been done, the fabrics show no sign of the treatment, but after being plunged into a cauldron of boiling dye they are drawn out a moment later dyed. And the remarkable thing is that though the cauldron contains only one color, it produces a series of different colors in the fabric, the hue changing with the quality of the chemical employed, and it cannot afterwards be washed out. Thus the cauldron which, if dyed fabrics were put into it, would undoubtedly blend the colors together, produces several colors out of one, and dyes the material in the process of being boiled; and the dress fabrics when submitted to heat become stronger for wear than they would be if not so heated (XXXV: 42).

This reference was thought to describe wax resist, especially since it followed a lengthy discussion of the use of wax in art and, specifically, heated wax applied by brush (XXXV: 41). However, these applied substances are likely to have been colorless chemical mordants that would each react with a dye and produce different colors in a single dye bath; in some cases these may have been used together with wax. Most textile scholars agree that some resist substance (either wax or mud) was also used, in addition to mordant patterning, in first-century Egypt, though no clear description of the wax-resist process is available.[5] A summary of various resist-dyed textile discoveries gives us an overview of possible developments in various geographical areas prior to the introduction of resist textiles in Japan. While it remains impossible, even with technological analysis, to draw definitive conclusions as to the exact resist materials used on ancient textiles, this history will highlight those fabrics that have historically been accepted as wax resist and those that display visual characteristics suggestive of the use of wax. Future technological advances may help further illuminate the field.

The Mediterranean and the Near East

One of the earliest textile finds assumed to be an example of wax-resist cloth is from the cluster of mounds known as the Seven Brothers Kurgans, located opposite Kertch (or ancient Pantikapaion) on the northern coast of the Black Sea where Greek colonies were established from the seventh century B.C. (Figures 1a–1b). In

Figures 1a/1b **Kertch Cloth** At right, fragments from a wax-resist cloth used to cover a sarcophagus from Kurgan 6 of the Tombs of the Seven Brothers near Kertch, Crimea, early fourth century B.C. Courtesy of the Hermitage Museum. Above, a reconstruction of the fragments by D. S. Gertziger, from the collection of the Hermitage. (inv. S. Br. VI, 16)

1875, fifty wool fragments were found draped over a wooden coffin, presumed to be the remains of a funeral blanket or sarcophagus shroud. Reconstruction revealed both the vast size of the original piece and a surprising resist "painting" of Greek mythology in multiple friezes created by fourth century–B.C. artists. This large wool covering was made from eleven woven strips, each 30 centimeters wide and 3 meters long (1 foot by 10 feet), sewn together with wool thread (Gerziger 51). A mended section suggests that the covering may have been used and repaired even before being placed in the tomb.

The Kertch cloth, now in the collection of the Hermitage, is tricolored and appears to have been painted with a liquid wax resist (Gerziger 51). The orange, or buff-colored, silhouettes in the cloth are outlined in black and dark red on a background that appears to be either black or dark blue. Speculation on the process suggests either that the original woven panels were first dyed an orange-buff color or that this was the natural color of the aged fabric.[6] It appears that hot wax was next painted onto the faces of the figures and onto the outlines of the garments and design motifs, and that the cloths were then immersed in a red dye. Additional waxing would reserve those areas to be kept a red color, and, finally, a dipping in indigo would give the cloth its striking, almost black appearance. Alternatively, after the wax was removed by scraping, washing and/or boiling, a final overdye of orange could have been responsible for darkening the indigo nearly to black and changing the natural fabric color to the orange buff now evident.[7]

There are two groups of resist-dyed motifs on the large cloth: mythological scenes and ornamental patterns of "waves, meanders, squares, dotted rosettes, braids and checkers" (Gerziger 55). The mythological scenes are composed of upper and lower parts and surrounded by a patterned strip. There are four exclusively ornamental sections of crosses, palmetto and lyre shapes repeated.[8] These are likewise surrounded by additional patterned strips. The mythological scenes may have alternated with the ornamental sections.

All the mythological scenes or motifs are similar to those found on Greek vase painting of the sixth through fourth centuries B.C. The two-dimensional figures, which appear to be women fleeing with arms aloft and their patterned clothing fluttering, show strong emotion in both gesture and expression.[9] Above the figures are fragments of names referring to mythical figures such as Athena, Nike and Dionysus.[10] Water nymphs or Neptune's maidens are shown on another segment, along with warriors and carriages similar to those seen in terra cotta of the fourth to fifth centuries B.C.,[11] and L. Stephani dates the textile fragments as fourth century B.C. on the basis of their iconography.

Textile historian E. J. W. Barber suggests that the variety of textiles found in the Seven Brothers Kurgans indicates that the process of patterning cloth had already undergone a long period of development. She believes that such painted fabrics may have been widely available, and cites references made by the Greek historian Plinius the Elder (XXXV: 150) and fifth-century philosopher Herodotus (I: 203) to Caucasus Mountains inhabitants to the south who painted their clothing with colorfast designs half a century before the date customarily assigned to the Kertch cloth. However, it is not clear whether the "painted clothing" to which they referred would have been patterned with a resist.

Barber also refers to early resist fabrics that appeared in Italy from the earlier Bronze Age: "From the Lago di Ledro excavations, Peroni reports some remains of textiles that had been printed in some way with a resinous substance (Peroni 100). He does not say, however, what sort of design had been used, nor have we any way of knowing whether the 'resinous substance' had been used as dye or as a resist medium.[12] Nonetheless it is intriguing to have even this much direct evidence for printing cloth in early Europe" (Barber 226).

In addition, some resist-dyed pieces dating from the early second century A.D. have been found in the Mons Claudianus site in ancient Egypt. As with many textile finds, the exact nature of the resist is not clear, but beeswax is known to have been readily available at this time, from Plinius's frequent references to its medicinal as well as artistic uses (XI: 6–9, XXI: 49, XXXV: 39–41). The Mons Claudianus resist fragments are all wool, like those of Kertch. The designs are not clear, but at least one is identified as an organic motif, probably a vine (Bender Jorgensen 10).

Further, several fragments from the Roman period that appear to be resist-dyed have been found at the At-Tar Caves in Iraq. The site served as a western outpost of the Silk Road where trade goods including pile carpets and embroidered and patterned twills went east, and spices and silks came west (McDowell 60). Cotton resist-dyed cloths from At-Tar show a pattern in a natural color against a background dyed dark blue, but the fragmented quality of the cloth makes it difficult to discern a clear pattern. Japanese archaeologist Hideo Fujii has suggested that this particular site dates from between the third century B.C. and the third century A.D. A number of cotton resist-dyed pieces have been found in Palmyra, Syria, an important junction of trade routes to the east. The largest fragment shows a pattern of four-petaled rosettes and dots in roundels and lines as a resist on red-dyed cotton in a more elegant version of a petal-and-dot design that appears at a later date in Central Asian tombs (Pfister 16).

A complete child's linen tunic with a resist design was found by the German archaeologist Forrer in the late nineteenth century at the burial fields of Akhmim on the banks of the Nile[13] (see Plate 1). The garment was in extraordinarily good condition due to the location's very dry conditions. This textile, with its white lozenge pattern on an indigo blue background, is accepted as an example of a wax-resist textile from the sixth century. Its simple resist pattern appears to be a combination of three carved blocks: a rod-shaped pattern creating two sides of the lozenge, a dot pattern placed at the junction of the two sides and a simple flower or star shape stamped in the center of each lozenge. The pattern does not continue across the seams, so the garment is thought to have been sewn from pre-printed fabric. Several wooden blocks were found at the same site and these are assumed to have been used for fabric printing. Schaefer suggests that these were used to stamp wax patterns onto fabric that was then dipped into a dye bath but, on the other hand, the blocks could have been used to stamp pigment or ink (917). Despite these related finds, some scholars feel that the tunic may be of Persian, Syrian or possibly Indian origin, because of its unusual cut.[14]

A sixth-century resist fabric has also been found in Europe, in the tomb of St. Caesarius, Arles, France (502–543). The fabric shows a white resist pattern of dots, rings and circle motifs on blue cloth. Schaefer has queried its presumed European origin, however, saying that the question of "whether this printed fabric was native work or imported from the Orient cannot be determined" (917).

Coptic Curtains

Those studying resist-dyed fabrics of pre-seventh-century origin take special interest in the more than ten known Coptic curtains painted on indigo by a resist process. The curtains, or hangings, appear to come from a fifth- to sixth-century transition period in Egypt, marked by the blending of pagan and Christian iconography and predating the Christianized Coptic period, which continued through the twelfth century.[15] These fabrics were narrative tapestries assumed to have served as wall decorations in the homes of the wealthy or as curtains to divide sections of the early churches.[16] The production of such resist-dyed curtains was less costly and much less time-consuming than making one of the famous Coptic tapestry weavings of similar design. All these resist curtains were discovered centuries later in necropolises, where they had served a secondary function as burial shrouds and wrappings.

The resist-painted designs were drawn primarily from classical mythology as well as Old and New Testament biblical scenes. They were separated by bands of geometric motifs similar in design to the smaller wool tapestry strips that ornamented the linen garments of sixth-century Egypt. Curtains may have been acceptable for the purpose of church decoration, but church officials were quite vocal about extravagance in garments. As early as the fourth century, St. Basil and St. Ambrose commented on the wastefulness of the figured fabrics and the frivolous people "who wear the gospels on their mantles instead of their hearts and look like painted walls."[17]

One of the most spectacular of the resist-dyed curtains, known as the *Veil of Antinoopolis*, was found by Albert Gayet in 1905 in Antinoopolis and is now at the Louvre Museum in Paris (Figures 2a–2b). It was discovered twisted into a rope

Figures 2a/2b **Veil of Antinoopolis** Above, a resist-dyed linen fragment found in a tomb in Antinoopolis, fourth century A.D. One of the earliest Coptic curtains, this very large fragment shows three designs: a procession of large figures including Dionysus and his mother at the bottom; a scroll of vines and birds in the middle and a series of scenes depicting Dionysus' childhood at the top 1.30 x 3.47 m./approximately 4 x 11 ft. Louvre Museum, Paris. (inv. 11102). Below, a reconstruction of the curtain, held by the Abegg-Stiftung Bern (Riggisberg). Reconstruction drawing by Regula Schorta.

and wrapped around a female mummy to hold the shroud in place (Kendrick Vol. I: 15). To the textile artist, the humble, recycled use of this cloth as funerary wrapping is at odds with its grand proportions (1.30 by 3.47 meters/approximately 4 by 11 feet; incomplete) and its vivid imagery that was revealed only after the cloth was restored.[18] Divided into two parts and banded by design motifs, the lower panel depicts a procession of maenads, sileni and satyrs accompanying Dionysus and his mother, Semele, in what has been called "an orgiastic dance." The upper band shows the birth and childhood of the young god Dionysus (Rutschowscaya 28). The figures appear to have been painted with a brush using a liquid resist medium. The separating bands of grapevine scrolls, birds and floral motifs could have been created with various stamps dipped in a resist medium, or they might have been applied with a brush and resist medium. While the Coptic curtains are generally accepted as wax-resist textiles, scholars prefer to reserve judgment on the exact type of resist used, until definite confirmation is possible.

Figure 3 **Nativity** Resist-dyed linen fragment found in Akhmim and dating from the fifth or sixth century. The figure on the right is Maria with the letters MAPIA (Maria) above, while on the left is the Archangel Gabriel. 47 x 92.5 cm /18¹/₄ x 36 in. Victoria and Albert Museum. (inv. 1103–1900)

The *Veil of Antinoopolis* dates from the fourth century and was possibly commissioned by a wealthy individual or group of people during a period of pagan opposition to the new and increasingly popular Christian religion (Rutschowscaya 82). Several motifs illustrating the life of Dionysus, such as the nativity and washing of the infant, have been compared to Christian iconography. The bacchanalian figures, however, are similar to those seen on fourth-century Sassanian silver vases. According to Dr. Marie-Helene Rutschowscaya, curator of Egyptian antiquities at the Louvre Museum, the large panel may have been considered "uninteresting or worthless" at a later date and discarded, and taken up again later for use in a necropolis (82). Dr. Rutschowscaya is now preparing an extensive study of this important early resist fabric, which should provide further illumination.

Smaller pieces, possibly altar cloths or curtains, with Old and New Testament themes known as the *Annunciation* (Figure 3), *Nativity, Judas, Miracles of Christ* and the *Thomas, Mark and Peter* are now housed at the Victoria and Albert Museum. They all show the variety of strokes, thick and thin lines and the free patterning that are possible with a fluid resist. These same patterns are evident in the tripartite composition of the Cleveland Museum curtain of Old and New Testament stories.[19] In another large curtain, the goddess *Artemis* stands on a stepped portico with bands of mythological heroes and hunting scenes to either side (Figure 4). The 6 by 1.94 meter (approximately 20 by 6 foot) curtain was restored by the Abegg-Stiftung Foundation in Berne, and the figure drawing with its powerful stance, elaborate costume detail and complex composition shows the freedom that could be achieved with this resist medium. A smaller design at the Staatliche

Figure 4 **Artemis** Resist-dyed linen fragment depicting the goddess Artemis on a stepped portal. The large composition shows a multilevel collection of mythological heroes and hunting scenes divided by floral motifs. From Ashmunein, fourth century. 6.00 x 1.94 m./236 x 76¼ in. Abegg-Stiftung, Bern (Riggisberg). (inv. 1397)

Museum in Berlin seems to be a Christian figure, while the figures in the two fragments at the Textile Museum in Washington, D.C.[20] appear to be mythological. While few of the figures in the fragments can be clearly distinguished, strong stylistic connections to the larger curtains are evident, and it is possible that a number of these smaller fragments could be related.

All the existing fragments of Coptic curtains show white patterns on blue-dyed linen (indigo) and share a style similar to that of Coptic art of the fifth through sixth centuries. Marked stylization of the features, enlarged, staring eyes, heads that are often haloed, short, curly hair, formalized poses (often a frontal or side view) and elaborate definition of garments are also seen in the carved ivory sculpture of the period.[21] In many cases the sculpture and the painted curtains also have spirally fluted columns separating the figures and are composed of horizontal band motifs (Shepherd 67); the curtains, however, show a degree of freedom and spontaneity not seen in the more formalized ivories.

There seems to be no stylistic difference between mythological and Christian motifs. Although Christian themes seem to outnumber the mythological, it is sometimes difficult to decipher the theme with precision because of the fragmentary condition of some pieces (Trilling 102). The curtains in the Louvre, the Victoria and Albert, the Cleveland and the Washington, D.C., textile museums all have Greek inscriptions that identify the figures within the compositions.

It is interesting to note the large number of similarities between the resist pieces known as Coptic curtains of the fifth and sixth centuries A.D. and the Kertch cloth of the fourth century B.C. The *Veil of Antinoopolis* and *Artemis* curtains are both done on a grand scale, like the Kertch piece. All the curtains, and the Kertch cloth too, share a similar compositional form, of bands of gesturing figures separated by strips of naturalistic or geometric motifs, obviously inspired by classical Greek forms. Both have inscriptions designating mythological or biblical personages. All appear to have an indigo ground color with a brush-applied resist that afforded a degree of freedom and spontaneity not seen in the woven or block-printed work of their respective eras.

Central Asia and China

During the first millennium, great overland trade routes connected the world of the Mediterranean and Europe with Central Asia and China, profoundly transforming the cultures of both East and West. Termed the "Silk Road" in the nineteenth century by German geographer Baron von Richthofen, this road actually consisted of two routes dating from the second century B.C. that passed to the north and south of the treacherous Taklimakan Desert (Bonavia 18). Originally home to nomadic tribes of Indo-European and Turkish ancestry, the area spanning the oasis towns of Khotan, Loulan, Niya, Kashgar, Urumqi, Turfan and Dunhuang, along with Anxi in the neighboring Gansu Corridor, saw a flourishing of art and culture. Islam from Arabia, Zoroastrianism from Persia and Nestorianism from Assyria influenced the religious thinking and iconography of the art. Some of the strongest influence seen in Central Asia, however, came from India and its first-century Buddhist missionaries. With the introduction of Buddhism came an artistic style called Gandharan, which combined the influences of ancient Greek, Roman, Persian and Indian art and is evident in the distinctive sculpture, frescos and textiles found in the many "Thousand Buddha Caves" scattered along the Silk Road.

The Silk Road was primarily a textile route, facilitating the exchange of Chinese silks, Palmyra (Syria) wools, Sassanid (Persia) tapestries and Indian cottons. Additional exchanges came by sea, with official envoys to the reigning Chinese emperor. An example of this far-reaching exchange between countries can be seen in the gift of Indian and Gandharan textiles to the Chinese court in the fifth century, made not by an Indian envoy, but by an Indonesian diplomatic mission.[22] Weaving techniques, dye technology and the various methods of patterning cloth were also part of the international exchange in the first millennium.

Expeditions along the Silk Road by British, Swedish, German, French, Japanese and American explorers in the early part of the twentieth century resulted in the discovery of ancient towns, Buddhist caves and tombs that have increased our knowledge of, while raising new questions about, the world of Asia of two thousand years ago.[23] Results from continued excavations by Chinese archaeologists in the latter part of this century have shown the cross-fertilization of art and culture in Asia and added to our store of knowledge on textile development.

Resist dyeing was done in China more than two thousand years ago. Ancient Chinese documents refer to wax-resist textiles as products of a "western country." This has been thought, at various times, to mean India, Syria or Greece. The process of dyeing "blue and white cotton cloth with wax printing" is described in the ancient Chinese text *Ling wai daida*:

> First, carve two wooden plates with the same pattern with holes bored through; second, place a piece of cotton cloth between these plates; next, fill the engraved wooden plates with liquid wax; take off the plates; place this cotton cloth in indigo dye; and finally, take the wax off by heating. Then you will see a beautiful, fine blue and white cotton cloth in wax-printing.[24]

Dr. Min Wu, Director of Textile Research at the Uighur Autonomous Region Museum, reports that this cloth was called "stained or spotted cloth" and was referred to in classical Tang literature. The literary reference calls the work very fine and says that it was done by the Yao-zu people in what is now Yunnan Province.[25]

Many of the non-Chinese minority tribes (Miao, Ge, Dong and Buyi) that now live in Guizhou Province in southwestern China have legends that claim they are the ancestral originators of *laran*, or wax-resist dyeing. Since the Early Song dynasty (420–497), the Miao have been known as the "indigo nationality," and various historical reports also tell of their skill in wax dyeing and embroidery.[26]

Most of these ethnic groups are known to have produced wax-resist textiles before coming under Chinese rule. The present-day minority tribes create geometric motifs with beeswax on indigo-dyed cotton using handmade metal tools (*ladao*), as well as brushes made of bamboo, hair or feathers (*labi*), as they have for centuries. The use of clamped wooden plates or stamps, as described in the *Ling wai daida*, however, no longer continues.[27]

The most elaborate example of resist-dyed textiles from the early period comes from a tomb in ancient Niya opened by Chinese archaeologists in 1959. The site is in the desert north of Minfeng, where the dry climate and geographical conditions probably contributed to the degree of preservation. Two large blue and white cotton fragments with related designs, one depicting a large human figure called the *Niya Bodhisattva*, were found inside a tomb, covering a wooden bowl that contained sheep bones. Both fabrics are border designs from a much larger cloth. The stripes and sawtooth patterns used to separate the other ornamental motifs on each fragment are universal patterns similar to those found on both Indian cotton textiles and the work of the minority tribes of southwest China. The smaller piece (50 by 80 centimeters/20 by 31½ inches) shows geometric patterns such as circles and dots as well as resist lines painted horizontally, vertically and diagonally that create an elaborate basket-weave motif. The thick and thin stripes or bands of resist organize the various patterns into segments and appear to have been painted with a brush or possibly with a metal tool dipped in a fluid resist.

The larger piece (45 by 86 centimeters/17⅝ by 33⅞ inches) contains one of the finest examples of what appears to be wax-resist iconography yet to be discovered in Central Asia from such an early period (see Plate 2). Chinese textile scholars originally thought it to date from the Eastern Han period (A.D. 25–221) but now believe that it may be even older (A.D. 3).[28] The large human figure fills a corner square of the fabric and shows a female head and torso. The figure is wearing a sheer garment as well as a beaded necklace and earrings and is holding a cornucopia of flowers. Since her head is surrounded by a double halo, some have called the image a bodhisattva; however, it is now suggested that the figure could actually be a female deity of a local cult and is not necessarily of Buddhist origin.[29] Her three-quarter pose and averted eyes are similar to the figurative style of Greco-Roman tapestry and Turkestan cave paintings. To the right of the figure is a square geometric pattern, and below, a border design of an elongated dragon with birds. All the patterns appear to be resist designs applied with a brush and/or a metal tool, rather than a resist stamp. Above the border panel is a small section of a very large human foot motif and a catlike paw and tail, but this is the only piece that survives. From the size of the foot, it is assumed that this substantial fragment was part of a very large cloth, most likely a hanging panel. Although found in a Central Asian tomb, the unusual iconography, together with the fiber content, have

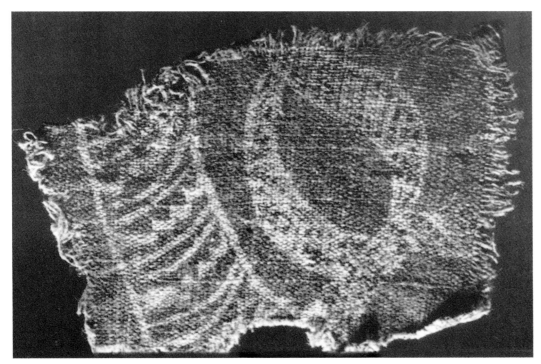

Figure 5 **Fragment from Yudian** Blue and white resist-dyed cotton fragment, showing flowing lines and geometric patterns; the resist appears brush-applied. Found in Yudian, China of the Northern Dynasties (386–581 A.D.) 7 x 11 cm./2³/₄ x 4³/₈ in. Uighur Autonomous Region Museum, Urumchi, Xinjiang.

led scholars to believe that these cotton pieces are not of Chinese origin.[30] Finds at Niya by Sir Aurel Stein early in the twentieth century as well as more recent dated discoveries by Chinese experts suggest that two to three thousand years ago, a race of people other than ethnic Chinese may well have inhabited the area where the *Niya Bodhisattva* was discovered.[31]

The 1972 discovery by Chinese archaeologists of a slightly older tomb (ca. 168 B.C.) in Mawangdui, Changsha, revealed a vast number of well-preserved Western Han–dynasty textiles including resist-dyed clothing and fragments. Although none appears to have been produced with wax resist, the padded robes with printed patterns and single lengths of cloth with stenciled or dye-stamped motifs show some remarkable similarities in design to the wax-stamped cloth (*rōkechi*) that existed in Japan as early as the seventh and eighth centuries. Flowering trees, meandering vines and birds either facing one another or in flight are all motifs that appear on Shōsōin *rōkechi* fabrics and the Mawangdui tomb discoveries. An unusual gold and silver paste rhomboid of a cloud or feather motif stamped on silk gauze may be a harbinger of the wax stamps that would be used in Japan six centuries later. Evidence that fabric was actually printed with blocks or stamps has been supported by the discovery of two bronze blocks found in a tomb known to date from the second century B.C. in south China that bear patterns very similar to the Mawangdui rhomboid pattern.[32]

Another striking pattern can be seen in a piece of indigo-dyed cotton cloth found at a Yudian site (Figure 5). Although it is only a small fragment (7 by 11 centimeters/2³/₄ by 4³/₈ inches), the flowing lines and geometric patterning appear to have been done with a brushed resist coming from a tradition different from that of the stamped or stenciled wool pieces with which it was found (Hsio-yen 317). Since cotton was not commonly seen in China until after the eleventh century, most of the excavated cotton pieces are thought to have come from border areas or to have been imported from elsewhere.

Figure 6 **Fragment from Astana** Blue and white resist-dyed ramie fragment; this piece of a larger cloth shows a leaf motif inside a circle below, and a complex pattern above. The resist process is brush- or stamp- applied. Excavated from a tomb in Astana, eighth century. 38 x 4.2 cm./15 x 1⅝ in. Ryūkoku University Library, Kyoto.

Additional resist fragments were excavated in Astana by a little-known team of Japanese explorers who were among the first to open the important Astana tombs in 1912. The discovery of textiles was secondary to this predominantly religious mission organized by the Reverend Kozui Ōtani, an adventurous Japanese priest whose interest in Central Asia was piqued during his days as a student in London at the turn of the twentieth century. While attending the meetings of the Royal Geography Society, Ōtani met well-known explorer Sir Aurel Stein and learned of the wealth of Buddhist sutras that Stein and others had recently excavated.[33] When Ōtani was just twenty-six, before he became head of the powerful Nishi-Honganji Temple in Kyoto, he organized the first of three expeditions for the purpose of finding documents that would verify the path Buddhist doctrine traveled from India to the east (China and Japan).[34] Along with the many sutras and artifacts brought back from the long explorations (1902–04, 1908–09 and 1910–14) was a cache of woven, painted and resist textiles typical of the Tang dynasty. Unfortunately, Ōtani's expeditions were personally financed and never backed by a large research institution; with his early resignation from temple leadership in 1914, personal misfortune, political instability in Asia and the ensuing war in the Pacific, the well-intentioned priest was never able to have the collection fully studied before it was dispersed. The collection is now scattered among the Beijing and Lushan Museums, the National Museum in Seoul, the Tokyo National Museum and Ōtani's home institution, Ryūkoku University in Kyoto.

Of the twenty-five known textiles from the Ōtani collection in Japan, an unusual ramie resist-dyed indigo piece excavated from Astana and now housed in Ryūkoku University is most relevant to this study. A small piece (38 by 4.2 centimeters/15 by 1⅝ inches) torn from a much larger fabric of coarsely woven ramie, the resist pattern shows an upper and lower design, each enclosed in a roundel pattern (Figure 6). A leaf motif is clearly visible in the lower design. The fragment is not large enough that the upper motif can be deciphered, but the resist is very strong and a certain variation of line is evident. While the leaf (palmetto) design imitates printing by a stamp due to its segmented design, the other part of the design suggests the quality of a brush resist. The piece has not been tested for wax residue and shows no obvious cracking of the applied resist, but it does have the fluid stroke quality often seen in wax-resist pieces. Like the cotton Niya figure and the Yudian fragment, this ramie piece suggests a strong influence from sources beyond the typical Tang-dynasty textile field.

Continued excavation of a number of sites near Astana has revealed a large number of silk textiles that suggest a knowledge of the wax-resist process in Central Asia by at least the sixth to eighth centuries. A group of six fragments sharing the same lattice dot pattern, a small silk fragment of facing birds and a green and white cloth of mountains, sages and birds in flight may well be three early examples of wax-resist textiles. All have patterns that appear to be stamped rather than brushed on, and exhibit obvious breaks in the surface of the resist where dye has seeped through to color the cracked pattern. This pattern of cracks is typical of the way in which hardened wax breaks, but it would not be provident to make an absolute conclusion on process until chemical analysis can confirm this visual evidence.

The *Diamond Dot Lattice* patterned silks consist of a central flower form with seven dot petals inside a lozenge or lattice with five dots creating each of the side bars (see Plate 3). This simple pattern must have been a popular design, especially for clothing, as numerous examples have been found in a variety of fourth- and fifth-century tombs in Astana and Loulan.[35] One example forms part of a woman's skirt, and there are also two other pieces which Yamanobe has suggested may be "decorative cuffs" from some kind of miniature garment (144). Another fragment of the same design was incorporated into a Buddhist ritual banner. The fragments available are not large enough to determine conclusively what process was used, but the pattern appears to have been created by a single carved block dipped in hot wax and then stamped on cloth. Variations in the printing, however, suggest that single-dot block, repeatedly stamped, might have also been used. A matrixed wooden plate with cut holes, clamped onto folded fabric with hot wax poured through, as described in the ancient Tang text *Ling wai daida*, has also been suggested. All the fragments are so small, though, that it is not possible to tell by analyzing the repeat prints whether a clamped plate was used. From the characteristic cracking of the surface of the resist area, it appears that all of the six or more fragments may have been patterned with hot wax before being dyed with indigo.

The piece known as *Hermits Riding Cranes* was discovered by the Chinese excavation team at Astana in 1973 and appears to date from the Tang dynasty

Figure 7 **Hermits Riding Cranes** Fragment of a silk coat; resist dyeing on a green ground. The pattern depicts hermits or sages riding cranes, in addition to motifs of mountains, flowers, a phoenix and other birds. Excavated from Tomb 191 in Astana, Xinjiang Province. 53 x 29 cm./21 x 11½ in. Uighur Autonomous Region Museum, Urumchi, Xinjiang.

(Figure 7). The 53 by 29 centimeter (21 by 11½ inch) fabric resembles the wax-stamped fabrics found in the seventh- and eighth-century works housed in Japan's Shōsōin. The motif of a hermit riding a crane is an ancient symbol of the Taoist beliefs prevalent during the Tang era. Birds in flight, a phoenix with wings outstretched, standing ducks, stylized cloud scrolls, two different mountain motifs and two flowering tree patterns make up the total design. This silk fragment, presumed to be part of a coat, is figured with approximately ten different blocks. Chinese authorities have suggested that this is resist-dyed by means of a clamp-resist process called *jiajie* (board-jamming). The designs form a generally consistent pattern that is more randomly spaced than might be expected from a board-jamming process and implies the use of individually stamped blocks. Cracking and dye veining are obvious in small sections. Printed on thin silk fabric, the large sample is very similar in style, motif and process to the *rōkechi* of Japan's seventh- and eighth-century Shōsōin collection.

The smaller fragment of facing songbirds surrounded by an arabesque design with meanders is referred to as *Birds in a Cage* and was discovered by Stein in a cave in Astana dating from between the sixth and eighth centuries.[36] The design appears to be a combination of blocks, stamped onto a brownish yellow cloth that was then dyed blue (see Plate 4). The random stamping of additional circle rosettes in white indicates that these may have been resist stamped on the original white fabric before the cloth was dyed brownish yellow. While the image shows a strong resist pattern in most places, there are, however, some breaks, likely from the dye's partial penetration of the resist and from cracks in the resist that suggest improper handling. These cracks seem to point to a hard wax surface. Again, the fragment is too small to tell whether a clamped resist might have been used, rather than carved blocks, but the less-than-precise arrangement of images may indicate hand-stamping with blocks.

These three textiles—the *Diamond Dot Lattice*, *Birds in a Cage* and *Hermits Riding Cranes*—appear to be strong suggestions of a wax-resist process in pre-seventh-century China. An additional six-point medallion roundel with a bird enclosed comes from the same Astana tomb as the *Cranes* and is said to have been done with a process that in modern technical terms might be called bleaching or discharge dyeing.[37] The steps involved in applying pattern to this brown silk fragment of a woman's skirt are described as, "First, dye the background cloth. Then print the image using a patterned block and a strong alkaline chemical. This chemical will draw out the color of a red or black dye and result in a bright yellow pattern left" (Xinjiang 185). There is some unevenness in the printing that shows either the incomplete penetration of alkaline bleach or an imperfectly applied resist stamp.

This fabric is similar to a group of alkaline-patterned silk gauze fabrics with simple rosettes, tested by the Xinjiang Cotton Weaving and Dyeing Factory. At first, these ten pieces were thought to be wax-resist fabrics, but chemical analysis later revealed the presence of an alkaline solution used with stamps and printed on "hard" silk. Whereas some alkaline stamps were printed on top of dyed fabric to bleach out the image, these pieces were produced using an alkaline paste stamp to degum the "hard" silk that was later washed in a mild acid solution and dyed. The degumming of the printed areas allowed for a different amount of dye penetration and a slight change in color, in order to highlight the stamped design.[38]

Most of these Chinese fabrics show iconography and resist technology very similar to that of the early wax-resist work of seventh- and eighth-century Japan. The similarity between seventh-century Japanese wax-resist textiles and Tang-dynasty fragments leads us to believe that at least some of the Chinese pieces were created with an advanced wax-resist process. Chinese authorities have not been able to duplicate this controlled wax stamping on silk. This inability to reproduce the effect has led them to believe that clear patterns could not be produced on silk with wax resist.[39] There is, however, little doubt that the wax-resist process known in ancient times as *rōkechi* came to Japan via Tang China.

The exchange of fabrics and techniques from early Greece, Egypt, Persia and India with Central Asia, Turkestan and China are all part of the heritage that influenced the textiles that became known in Japan as *jōdai gire* (ancient fabrics) and are part of the treasure found in the Shōsōin repository in Nara.

SHŌSŌIN RŌKECHI

Background

Japan is unique among the countries of the world for its wealth of ancient textiles. These treasures were not buried in tombs with important figures who had died, nor sealed into caves where they would be vulnerable to looting and plundering; rather, they were dedicated to the Buddha and placed in huge storage boxes in a storehouse for over a millennium. This is the vast Shōsōin storehouse at Tōdaiji Temple in Nara. The Shōsōin is a raised rectangular structure divided into three sections, with its north and south wings built of Japanese cypress in a unique triangular timber style known as the *azekura* style. While earthquakes, floods and wars decimated many structures throughout the country and other buildings within the same temple compound were destroyed by fire, this storehouse survived. For centuries the collection was left alone, virtually ignored. In the late nineteenth century the importance of the collection was recognized and a massive process of checking, classification and restoration was begun. One hundred years later, however, a full inventory has yet to be completed because of the fragility of the many articles and the sheer vastness of the holdings. Access to the Shōsōin repository has always been highly controlled, and yet over the centuries some pieces have disappeared or been borrowed and not returned. A box marked "ceremonial costumes of Emperor Shōmu and Empress Kōmyō" is empty (Hayashi 60), and one hundred suits of armor with splendid *nishiki* woven trimming are described in great detail in the temple records of items held, but are in fact missing.[40] Nevertheless, such unique items as the delicate writing paper of an eighth-century emperor, the costume of an ancient dancer and the elegant screens of dyed silk used in the palace have survived and are just a few of the many artifacts that can now be seen by the public in annual fall exhibitions at the Nara National Museum. Included among the textiles are over 100 costumes, 570 screens, 250 scrolls, approximately 600 albums of mounted fragments, 300 glass mounts and about 200 boxes of unclassified fragments.[41] This represents an unrivaled collection of textiles from the seventh and eighth centuries, some imported from the Asian continent and others produced by textile craftsmen in Japan. The great majority reflect a strong influence by Tang China as well as the aesthetic sensibility of the eighth-century ruling class of Japan.

Fragile textiles break down quickly due to climatic changes, and yet more than 180,000 textiles and fragments have survived at the Shōsōin under conditions that were ideal for preserving cloth. Nara, located in central Japan, is not known for its dryness; however, annual fluctuations in humidity are minimal, and the Shōsōin stands above the ground on stilts, allowing for ample ventilation. Originally this unique construction was thought to be responsible for the collection's exceptional preservation, but tests have shown that the treasures were stored in sturdy chests covered with lids five centimeters (two inches) thick, and that these chests should be credited, rather than any special quality of the building itself.[42]

Many of these ancient textiles were created for one spectacular event that was years in preparation: the 752 dedication of the gilt-bronze Daibutsu (Great Buddha statue) by Emperor Abdicant Shōmu at Tōdaiji Temple in Nara. Records tell that ten thousand people participated, including priests from throughout the Eastern world, foreign ambassadors and court personnel as well as hundreds of masked dancers, performers and court musicians. Tao-hsuan, the great Tang priest, came from China, and the high priest of Buddhism, Bodhisena of India, also participated. Textiles were an essential part of this ceremony. Elaborately embroidered inaugural banners of all sizes, and decorative resist-dyed streamers attached to *keman* (Buddhist ornaments) cascaded from temple rafters and fluttered from trees. Documents say that elaborate costumes of purple, lavender, grass green, Indian red, safflower yellow, light blue and crimson added to a veritable sea of rainbow colors that flooded the temple grounds.[43]

Four years later in 756, upon Shōmu's death, the dowager empress dedicated all her husband's worldly goods to Buddha and established a storehouse for these artifacts that became the Shōsōin repository that we know today. Several groups of additional donations were made over the following years of objects that included medicines, screens, carpets, musical instruments and various objects that the former empress said were "handled by the late emperor in bygone days . . . [and] remind me of him and caus[e] me bitter grief."[44] Agate cups, faceted glassware, huge silver vessels and red lacquer chests from China, Persia and Syria that had originally been offered at the dedication of the Buddha were also included, together with Shōmu's own personal items. More than one hundred costumes and accessories worn by musicians and dancers at the ceremony and made of chiffon, silk twill, brocade and hemp cloth, a variety of Buddhist regalia and implements, temple ornaments, musical instruments, banners, cushions and other dyed and woven fabrics, along with ritual banners from the memorial service were also placed in the storeroom.[45] The empress dowager also divided a large number of similar pieces among eighteen other temples, though most of these items were lost over the ensuing centuries. It is these seventh- and eighth-century textiles bequeathed to Hōryūji Temple and some older textiles that were already in that temple's holdings, as well as the treasures stored at the Shōsōin, that make up the group of textiles known in Japan as *jōdai gire,* or ancient fabrics.[46]

Textiles

The 180,000 textiles in the collection, composed of greatly varied pieces including costumes, tiny fragments and 2.75 meter (9 foot) ritual banners, are made from silk, ramie, wool and hemp fibers. The fibers themselves can help us identify the origin of many of the textiles. The scores of felted wool rugs are believed to be imported and some even bear labels of the Unified Silla dynasty (668–918; Korea). Cotton patterned weave fragments, originally preserved in Hōryūji Temple and later dispersed among several collections, are also presumed to be foreign, since cotton was not grown in Japan until after the fifteenth century. Archaeological finds and ancient written chronicles show that ramie and silk, however, were produced in Japan from as early as the Yayoi period (ca. 200 B.C.–A.D. 250).[47]

The woven pieces in the Shōsōin collection include silk called *ashiginu* and monochrome plain-weave ramie. In addition, monochrome patterned weave in silk such as *aya* (figured twill), *ra* and *sha* (twist-weave silk gauze) and polychrome nonpattern plain weave in silk and ramie are also found. The most numerous of the examples, however, are of a silk polychrome patterned weave or brocade called *nishiki.* These include tapestry weave (*tsuzure* and *shokusei*), warp *nishiki,* weft *nishiki,* float-patterned *nishiki,* double weave and even *kanton nishiki,* resist-dyed warp *kasuri* (ikat) patterns.[48] Much of the study of the Shōsōin textiles has focused on this extensive collection of patterned weave fabrics. However, in this volume, discussion of weaving will be limited to matters that are specifically relevant to resist dyeing.

Compared to *nishiki,*[49] there are far fewer pieces of dye-patterned textiles among the ancient fabrics. Dyed textiles fall into three distinct categories of resist technique: *kyōkechi,* clamp or board-jamming resist fabrics; *kōkechi,* bound and tie-dyed fabrics known now as *shibori;* and *rōkechi,* wax-resist fabrics (known as rōketsuzome or rōzome in modern Japanese). These three ancient resist processes are often called *sankechi.* The largest number of resist fabrics were done by the *kyōkechi* process, in which fabric was folded and clamped between elaborately carved boards and various dyes were poured through specific holes in the wood frames, resulting in a colorful, controlled design. Japanese wax resist, *rōkechi,* used brushes and patterned stamps dipped in hot beeswax and stamped onto fabric that was then dyed. As is also seen in ancient resist work, the wax created a strong barrier for the dyes and resulted in a brightly patterned cloth. It was *kyōkechi*, however, that best suited the taste of the Nara court. The controlled, multicolored *kyōkechi* may have resembled to some extent the widely loved *nishiki* weaving that was much more time-consuming and expensive to produce; this may have been one reason for *kyōkechi*'s popularity. Surprisingly, *kyōkechi* fell into disuse along with wax resist and did not undergo a revival until much later in history. Of the three resist processes, only *kōkechi* tie-dye enjoyed an unbroken history from ancient through modern times.

Sources of the Ancient Fabrics

Controversy continues concerning the origin of the *jōdai gire*, or ancient fabrics of the Shōsōin and Hōryūji Temple. Without a doubt, both the Sui and Tang dynasties of China had a strong influence on Japan during the Nara period. Groups of up to one hundred envoys were sent regularly to China, often accompanied by craftsmen and artisans. They returned with knowledge of new techniques and with samples that could later be studied and used as prototypes. Given this exposure and influence, it is not surprising that many Shōsōin fabrics show techniques and even patterns similar to work discovered in China and already documented as Tang products. Yet while some artifacts and weavings did come from Asia, it would be wrong to assume that all the materials in the Shōsōin collection are of foreign origin. In fact, there is very little documentation to prove that any are imports.[50]

> When the Japanese of the Tenpyō period (710–794) first encountered the marvels from the Tang court, they were astonished by their superb quality and almost certainly seized with a desire to fashion such objects for themselves. Most of the Tang objects exhibit a degree of technical excellence that sets them apart from work produced by Tenpyō artisans, but some articles are scarcely distinguishable from their Tang prototypes, and Tenpyō craftsmanship cannot be lightly dismissed. Tenpyō craft arts developed under the remarkable tutelage of Tang art and, taken as a regional idiom, cannot be considered substantially different. For these reasons, the arts of Tang and Tenpyō are normally assigned to the same family and treated concurrently, but as further study of treasures in the Shōsōin clarifies these differences, the history of Tenpyō craft arts will have to be rewritten (Hayashi 32).

Though some feel that the Japanese lacked the technical expertise to produce such work, the long history of textile development in Japan disputes this. The development and growth of the weaving industry in Japan is attributed to the large numbers of Chinese and Chinese-trained Korean weavers who immigrated to Japan in the fourth and fifth centuries. Frequent references to the Nishiki-*be*, a clan of textile specialists, tell of the welcome by Emperors Ōjin and Yūryaku and the fiefdoms and hereditary clan status that were conferred on the weavers. Besides the large number of talented immigrants, artisans who came to Japan to teach technique brought sample cloths that were first carefully analyzed and then copied or modified to suit Japanese tastes. In 701 an Office of Textiles (Oribe no Tsukasa) was established that produced high-quality patterned weaves. It is obvious that the techniques and resources were probably available to produce the majority of textiles found in the Shōsōin; however, the question of whether this is a collection of Chinese textiles or a reflection of the best of work on the Tang model produced in Japan, continues to be debated. Until scientific analysis of fibers is able to clearly identify Chinese and Japanese fibers of the seventh and eighth centuries, as Dr. Junrō Nunome has done with Han-dynasty silks, individual textiles should be assessed separately as to origin.

In the absence of conclusive scientific analysis of the textiles, Kaneo Matsumoto, former textile curator of the Shōsōin collection, has formed criteria for judging whether pieces were made abroad or in Japan. Acknowledging Chinese and other foreign influence, Matsumoto states in his book *Jōdai-gire: Seventh and Eighth Century Textiles in Japan from the Shōsōin and Hōryūji* that he would identify approximately ten textile items or groups of items that are examples of rare designs or unusual techniques he feels are foreign fabric.[51] All of these are woven or embroidered pieces, with the exception of a single leather box with grapevine scrolls and landscape scenes done in brushed wax and dyed leather. Most of the group of textiles dyed with the *sankechi* techniques were done on plain weave, which was often used at the Nara court; for this reason it is generally agreed that this category was all produced in Japan by Japanese artisans, possibly working under émigré supervision. Further agreement on this point has come with the discovery that a number of these pieces, including some that look the most foreign, have ink inscriptions noting that the weaving was done in Japan as *corvée*, or labor performed as payment of tax. Matsumoto, who has done perhaps more research than anyone else on the subject, believes that all of the Shōsōin *rōkechi* pieces were probably created in Japan.[52]

Rōkechi

Within the documents of the Shōsōin there is reference to the *rōkechi-dokoro*, a workshop for creating the wax-resist patterned fabrics known as *rōkechi*. The archives refer to *rōkechi* craftsmen as "stampers," since the majority of *rōkechi* fabric was created with stamps of various patterns that were pressed onto cloth after being dipped in wax.[53] The phrase *oshi-rōkechi*, or pressed wax resist, in ancient texts refers to this process of stamping. While recent chemical analysis of Tang textile fragments generally thought to be wax resist in fact points instead to the use of

Figure 8 **Ramie Bag Design Stamp Pattern** Reconstruction of an original floral patterned block used to stamp wax on ramie cloth dyed blue. The cloth was sewn into a bag 35 cm. (14 in.) long that is one of the treasures of the Shōsōin.

a paste stamp or an alkaline paste stamp, the overwhelming number of ancient Japanese references to wax stamps and wax fabrics leaves little doubt among Japanese textile historians that these pieces are, as has always been assumed, *rōkechi;* this view is further confirmed by simple visual assessment.[54] Wax-resist dyed cloths were used in costumes and screens and to decorate the interiors of court and temple buildings. In many ways, *rōkechi* was a freer, more flexible way of patterning white fabric than the more laborious *nishiki* weave. This freedom is reflected in the spontaneous *rōkechi* designs and random stamping of some patterns.

Cloth

The fabrics used for *rōkechi* were predominately *ashiginu* and *aya,* which are both forms of silk weave. Since the collection reflects the preferences of the ruling class of eighth-century Japan, it is not surprising that the furnishings and garments were usually made of silk, with few examples of more utilitarian fabrics.

A typical *rōkechi* design produced on silk is called *Floral Lattice* and includes a design of birds and fish overlain with a diagonal lattice of small flowers and lines called *kasumi,* meaning mist (Plate 5). Prepared as a wrapping cloth or *furoshiki* to cover three boxes of priests' robes, this cloth was donated by Empress Kōmyō to Tōdaiji Temple in 756. The wrap was made in two layers, consisting of a lining of

Figure 9 **Flower Grass Fragment** Figured twill (*aya*) with wax-resist designs of flowering plants on a purple ground. Mid-eighth century. 149 x 57 cm. (58³/₄ x 22¹/₂ in.). From the treasures of the Shōsōin.

pale green *ashiginu* and a covering with a yellow-and-white *rōkechi* pattern on a green *ashiginu* ground. The fabric measures 145 by 102 centimeters (57 x 40¹/₄ inches). This design of birds and fish with floral latticework was quite popular; there are at least three other variations of the pattern in the Shōsōin collection and still others in various public and private collections.[55] One of the other pieces in the Shōsōin includes an inscription showing that the fabric was produced as a form of tax payment in 748.[56] Matsumoto concludes that this pattern originated in eighth-century Japan and was used exclusively for *rōkechi* dyeing; he says that he knows of no similar extant textiles with this distinctive design produced in China (*Jōdai gire* 232).

Ramie was a strong, durable cloth favored by the upper class in the Nara period for undergarments as well as work clothes; a few pieces have also been found that were used as a ground for wax dyeing. One rare ramie piece, sewn into a bag shape 35 centimeters (14 inches) in height, shows a floral stamped motif on a blue-dyed (indigo) ground (Figure 8). Matsumoto is intrigued by the contemporary look of this design and observes that "the cool colors and simplicity of the patterns [are] in keeping with the rough texture of the ramie, leav[ing] us with almost the feeling of a modern example" (222).

Aya was rarely used for *rōkechi* patterns because it is itself a patterned weave. When the fabric is moved, the pattern can seem to appear and disappear, according to the play of light over it. One unusual example in the collection of *aya*, however, features two simple flowering grass stamps in *rōkechi* on a purple-dyed silk with a woven arabesque pattern[57] (Figure 9). Most of these *aya* samples are identified as stand covers that may have been used in temple buildings.

Ra, or silk gauze, is not ideal for use in wax resist either, because of its thinness. However, it was used extensively in the folded/clamped process known as *kyō-kechi*. There is at least one example of *rōkechi* on *ra* among the *jōdai gire*, in the lining fabric of an incense case.[58] It is not known whether the fabric was folded in half before stamping, but if studies confirm that it was, Matsumoto indicates that the assumption "that folding the cloth in half and dyeing is unique to *kyōkechi* may have to be reassessed."[59]

Perhaps the most unusual ground for *rōkechi* found in the Shōsōin collection is paper. A 30 by 35 centimeter (11¾ by 13¾ inch) wrapper for a *Kegon-kyō* sutra, one of the Buddhist scriptures, made of hemp cloth with a border of paper patterned and dyed in a *rōkechi* style, has been found. Neither the paper ground nor the simple dotted-and-splashed style are typical of the collection. Further examination has revealed that the reverse or lining papers are actually fragments of Unified Silla–dynasty census registers dating from the year 755. This wrapper is exceptional since it appears to contain both rare examples of early Korean official documents and eighth-century paper *rōkechi* from Korea, a country not known previously for wax-resist artifacts.

Dyes

The bright colors of the *jōdai gire* textiles are surprising, given the age of the pieces. Red, purple, green and blue are the predominant ground colors of the *rōkechi* articles. However, orange, light pink, yellow, pale and deep green, a reddish purple, three different shades of blue and various browns are also seen. During the Nara period, knowledge of vegetable dyes increased tremendously and dyestuffs were imported from throughout Southeast Asia, China and India. The use of mordants to bond or "fix" dyes chemically was known. Iron, ash lye and vinegar made from the fruit of the recently imported *ume* (plum) were also used for this purpose.

Dyes came from a variety of sources and often had medicinal uses as well. For red color, the native *akane* (*Rubia cordifolia* L., var. *Mungista Miq.*, Japanese madder) and *benibana* (*Carthamus tinctorius* L., safflower) imported from China in the fifth century were used. The brilliant scarlet (*hi iro*) color is vivid even twelve hundred years later, as are the light pinks. Both were probably produced from madder dye, since *benibana* tends to fade with age to a tan color. Lac (*Lakshadia chinensis*), or *enji* in Japanese, which has been found among the medicines stored in the Shōsōin, was also used to dye deep reds that faded in time to a reddish brown color (Hayashi 168). *Suō* (*Caesalpinia sappan* L., sappanwood) was imported during the Nara period and often top-dyed over yellow to produce an orange-red, or over indigo for a purple shade. Yellow came from three sources: lemon yellow was obtained from the native *kihada* (*Philodendron amurense Rupr.*), mustard yellow from the *kariyasu* (*Miscanthus tinctorius Hackel*) and warm yellow from the gardenia *kuchinashi* (*Gardenia jasminoides Ellis f. grandiflora Makino*). The native *murasaki* or gromwell (*Lithospermum erythrorhizon Sieb. et. Zucc.*) provided shades of purple; and indigo (*tade ai*), first imported during the fourth or fifth century, was used to dye three distinct shades of blue. Grass green, moss green, and olive were obtained by overdyeing yellow with indigo. *Tsurubami* was a brown color prepared from acorns (*Quercus acutissima carruth.*). Black was derived from chestnuts; however, chestnuts and acorns were often mixed together with an iron mordant to produce a stronger black dye.[60]

Most of the *rōkechi* dating from the Nara period were done with one or two dye baths. Fabric was stamped with hot wax and then either dipped into a dye bath or brushed with dye by hand. In some instances, a second waxing was done and the fabric was dipped into an additional dye, thus producing two dye colors with the original fabric color. While the poured-dye *kyōkechi* pieces boast as many as eight colors on a single piece, it is rare to see a *rōkechi* piece with more than three colors. Because of the dip-dyeing process, the fabric quickly became saturated with color and further dyeing only produced muddy colors. Very skilled modern artists can overdye many different colors, but the process of controlled color-layering was either unknown or too time-consuming for the intended purposes of ancient *rōkechi*.

Some unusual pieces do attempt three to four dyes on a single fabric and use the innovative technique of stamping on both the front and back sides of the fabric for multiple shades. One *ashiginu* stand-cover fabric is stamped with at least four different blocks of waves, seaweed, fish and ducks and includes four colors.[61] The design is composed on a reddish purple ground with a horizontal pattern of waves and seaweed stamped on cloth that was first dyed yellow. After overdyeing (perhaps with *suō*) to produce an orange-red, the diagonal lattice pattern of paired fish was stamped on the top of the fabric and two duck stamps were applied to the back. The result is a lighter shade where the stamps overlap each other. The final dye bath was probably indigo, producing a purple-red over the *suō* dye (see Plate 6). There are slight hints of a pleasing green around some of the sea-grass and wave motifs. I believe this is accidental, where small amounts of the first wax resist broke down on the edge of the stamped area and allowed some indigo to color the area dyed yellow. When a detail of this piece is examined, the printing looks quite random, but an overview shows a complex plan of four motifs done in horizontal and diagonal bars on both sides of the silk. The thick and thin stamping of some patterns seems to point to a struggle to control the amount of wax during repeat stampings with the same block. This piece was backed with a *kōkechi* patterned green silk and padded with ramie to be used as a stand pad. It has survived in particularly fine condition and retains much of its original vivid color.[62]

Uses

Rōkechi in the Shōsōin collection had a wide variety of uses: as wrapping cloths, bags, standing screens, leather box covers, stand covers, linings, costumes, socks, banners, *keman* or pendants, decorative covers for *nageshi* (ceiling beams) and floor coverings. Patterns used in lining cloths were often stamped in a free and random manner; sometimes old and damaged stamps with missing parts were used for this seemingly casual work. However, far greater care and control is obvious in the production of costumes, banners and standing screens.

■ Screens

Perhaps the four screens used by Emperor Shōmu in the Imperial court are the best known of all Japanese *rōkechi*, though they are not really representative of the collection. Screens were valuable assets for the court or private living quarters since they provided division of the interior space, gave necessary privacy and acted as attractive barriers against drafts. Ten *rōkechi* folding screens, each with six panels, are listed in the *Kokka chinpō chō* (Record of Rare Treasures of the Nation) and their colors and specific designs were recorded later when the treasures were reexamined in 856.[63] Only four panels remain of the original sixty and each has been remounted within the past hundred years.[64] The four depict an elephant, a parrot, a ram, and a pairing of a wild boar and an eagle; each is posed under a tree in the style typical of Sassanid Persia.

The elephant screen and the ram screen were made from the same bolt of silk, since a fault in the weaving can be seen running up the right side of both panels. Although the use of the exotic elephant and a curly-horned ram wearing a Sassanid-style beaded collar were historically thought to suggest that these pieces were imported treasures, recent renovations have revealed an ink inscription stating that the cloth had served as payment to the government in 751 of a *chō*, or tax.[65] Since it seems unlikely that cloth would have been woven in Japan for payment of tax and then sent abroad for design work and returned, the screens are now considered to be native to Japan.[66]

The ram panel—with its main figure sporting curling horns and a beaded medallion collar or breastplate—is the boldest and most artistically successful of the four screens (see Plate 8).[67] Matsumoto feels that this figure was applied by brush, which is understandable given the size of the figure. However, there are various reasons to think instead that the figure may have been produced with a large stamp.[68] Surrounding the bold ram, an asymmetrical tree with flowering leaf details and monkeys stamped in malachite pigment add a balance and charm not seen in the other panels.

By comparison, the parrot with tree panel has interesting Persian- and Chinese-inspired motifs but a less integrated composition consisting of separate sections (see Plate 9). In the upper half, birds fly over a stylized tree. On one side of the tree, a phoenix raises its wings and on the opposite side a small figure plays a *sho*, or mouth organ. All these motifs are stamped. In the lower half, the parrot sits on a stump with a flower and a leaf spray in its beak, a typical Persian motif. In the immediate foreground below the main parrot motif is a miniature fawn and mounted archer chasing a fleeing deer through stamped vegetation. Various designs were included in this panel, with what appears to be relatively little concern for the final outcome or the relationship between the units.

The four screens, each measuring approximately 163 by 57 centimeters (64 by 22½ inches), have a wide number of stamps and hand-drawn motifs painted with wax on yellow *ashiginu*. It appears that the panels were dyed brown with an extract of acorn (*tsurubami*) and that then, once the wax had been removed, various pigments were added to heighten the color.[69] White pigment (possibly *gofun*, crushed oyster shell or a white lead compound) was painted on the elephant, and a fine-grained green malachite pigment was carefully stamped on the leaves and fern patterns of the ram screen.

A few of the stamps were used on all four panels. The shrub in the foreground of the elephant and parrot panels appears, with brushstrokes added, as the background tree of the ram piece.[70] All four panels share a common fern pattern stamped randomly in the foreground, although the foliage of each tree is produced with its own unique stamp. A small fawn is printed on both the parrot and ram screens. A monkey stamp was used within the tree of the ram panel while a hand-drawn monkey rests in the branches of the elephant screen. A tiny wild boar is stamped in the foreground of the elephant screen and appears to one side of the hawk screen paired with a *kirin* (a Chinese mythical animal). Along with the various stamps, hand-drawn images have been added using a brush dipped in wax, to complete the composition and link the various stamps in landscape-style designs.

■ Costumes

Three coats (*ōshi*) for musicians, decorated with exquisite stamped patterns, are in fragmented but recognizable condition. One round-necked, long-sleeved silk coat in pale red contains an inscription indicating that it was "worn by a flute player who played *gigaku* music"[71] and has a wax-resist floral design (Figure 10). Another *ōshi* coat has a beautiful, ornate pattern of paired ducks within a wreath of leaves (Figure 11). The *Tōdaiji yōroku* (Record of Accounts of Tōdaiji) gives the names of two people who led the musicians at the dedication of the Great Buddha of Tōdaiji in 752, and it is assumed that one of these men wore this elaborate garment on that occasion.[72] One *ashiginu* silk costume with *rōkechi* dyeing is assumed to be a child's dance costume because of its small size.[73] Another red fragment shows an excellent example of a *rōkechi* stamp pattern taken from a popular weaving design

Figure 10 **Eight-lobed Floral Design Stamp Pattern** Reconstruction of original block pattern used on silk dyed light green. This fabric was used in a long *ōshi* coat that was part of a musician's costume and that is included among the treasures of the Shōsōin. The cloth is inscribed as tax payment (743 A.D.). It was later dyed and tailored into a garment.

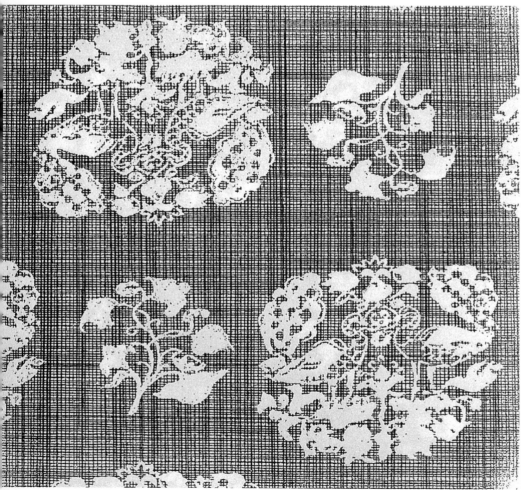

Figure 11 **Facing-Ducks Stamp Pattern** Reconstruction of a wax-resist stamp pattern found on fragments of a brown dyed plain weave silk *ōshi* coat documented as a performer's coat. The main motif, approximately 19 cm./7^1/$_2$ in. in width, shows two peacocks atop a floral pedestal facing one another and surrounded by a roundel.

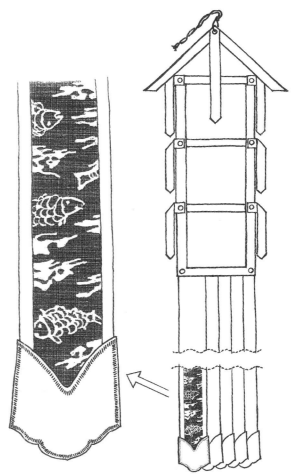

Figure 12 **Open-winged Phoenix Stamp Pattern** Reconstruction of a wax-resist stamp found on fragments of a dance costume that is one of the treasures of the Shōsōin. The pattern is of an open-winged phoenix surrounded by a grape roundel and a smaller, eight-lobed subordinate design. The phoenix was regarded by the Chinese as an auspicious bird, while the grape pattern is known to have come from the West. A similar phoenix may be seen on the Chinese Tang fragment found in 1973 at Astana. (See also *Hermits Riding Cranes* page 72.)

of the Nara period also seen in Tang China. The fabric, thought because of its cut to be part of a musician's costume, has a design of an open-winged phoenix surrounded by a delicate vine scroll roundel. This stamped motif alternates with a smaller but equally elaborate eight-pointed leaf and grape pattern (Figure 12). The phoenix symbol can also be seen in a woven *nishiki* brocade armrest and is surprisingly similar to a fragment of Chinese *nishiki* from the Tang dynasty found in Turfan.[74] All these musicians' costumes bear elaborate, detailed stamps, the most exquisite seen among the Shōsōin *rōkechi* pieces.

■ Buddhist Banners

The *rōkechi* and *kyōkechi* techniques were used to decorate many of the five hundred cloth *ban*, or Buddhist ritual banners, that are found in the collection. These banners have a triangular head, followed by three to five panels composing a body, with fabric strips called arms (*sui shu*) added to each body segment and four or five cloth legs (*ban kyaku*). They were finished with metal fittings that gave the cloth banners the weight they needed to hang properly (Figure 13).

Figure 13 **Buddhist Banner** Reconstruction of a banner used in Buddhist rituals. These banners consist of a triangular "head," a body of three segments, cloth strips, or arms, on either side, and five narrow panels at the bottom known as legs. Many such banners were displayed within the temple at the dedication of the Great Buddha of Tōdaiji in Nara. This reconstruction is modeled after a banner that had two "legs" patterned with *rōkechi* stamps of a fish-and-wave pattern that is one of the treasures of the Shōsōin.

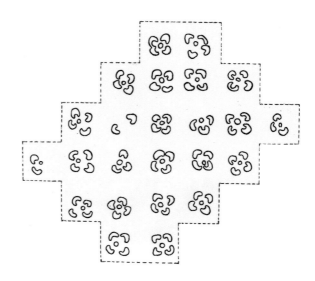

Figure 14 **Twenty-four Flower Stamp** At left, reconstruction of an original design found on fragments included among the treasures of the Shōsōin and showing a pattern of twenty-four flowers; some of the flower elements are missing. The block appears to have fitted together in a zigzag or stepped fashion, and was used for repeat patterns. At right, a single block.

One banner created for "the ritual to console the soul of the deceased Emperor" in 757 has two unusual 117 by 11.7 centimeter (46 by 4½ inch) banner legs made of *rōkechi* patterned silk. Delicate stamps of fish, waves and islands are freely stamped on the deep purple silk.

■ Floor Covers

A brilliant red silk *rōkechi* floor cloth is also among the ancient textile fragments housed in the Hōryūji section of the Tokyo National Museum; it was originally used as a cover for a rush mat. It measures 218 by 103 centimeters (86 by 40½ inches) and is believed to be the legendary *Ōmu-gata tandai* (floor cover with parrot design) used by Empress Regnant Kōken (see Plate 7). The exceptional design is described by Matsumoto as "an eight pointed *karahana* containing a pair of birds that face each other. The subsidiary motif . . . has a symmetrical flower/leaf spray with small butterflies at the top. Among *rōkechi* dyed textiles of the seventh and eight centuries whose designs are mostly linear in construction, this example displays an exceptionally broad application of wax resisted designs . . . [O]rdinarily among *jōdai gire* when a design has both main and subordinate motifs, they are arranged in a zigzag pattern across the field, but on this piece, the main and subordinate motifs are arranged alternately in vertical and horizontal rows. This is unusual" (*Jōdai gire* 225).

Stamps

The textile patterns on *rōkechi* were created from scores of different stamps made for this purpose. Simple four-petal flowers, vine-scrolls, flower medallions, pairs of ducks or parrots, a single stylized phoenix, birds in flight, and the combination of fish and waves are among the predominant motifs. Unfortunately, none of the stamps themselves have survived, so our knowledge of them comes only from the evidence provided by the printed fabric. The majority of the stamps were obviously made from a material that could be carved easily, such as wood; however, some of the delicate or curvilinear lines may have been produced by fabricated (constructed rather than cast) metal stamps.[75] Elaborately carved bronze seals exist from the eighth century that were used to stamp legal documents, and these may also have been used on fabric with wax. The fabricated metal stamp seems more likely, however, and may have preceded the 1840s development of the Indonesian *cap* or metal stamp by eleven hundred years.

Stamps were obviously considered precious and were not discarded even when they became damaged. The evidence of missing elements suggests that blocks were fragile enough to break off, suggesting that they were made of wood or constructed from metal as opposed to being cast. The actual line of the stamp can be seen as a darkened shadow in the fish-and-water-bird motifs stamped on the reverse of the fabric (see Plate 6). A number of contemporary rōzome artists have successfully reproduced the wax patterns of the Shōsōin collection using cast as well as fabricated metal,[76] but the exact materials of the *rōkechi* blocks remain a mystery.

The size and shape of the stamps varied, as did the number of motifs included on each. Some stamps, like those displaying a *karahana* medallion, used just one element. These were often printed with subordinate blocks with a single similar geometric design cut into it, with the two stamps being alternated across the fabric. As a rule, each stamp contained only a single design or multiple examples of the same pattern. The "floral lattice" stamp described earlier, however, is an exception, since it has both flower and mist lines. Visual analysis of the fabrics makes it apparent that two or three flower motifs were sometimes placed on one stamp or block, but occasionally as many as twenty-four of the same flowers may also be found on a single unit. It appears that most blocks were square in shape with straight sides. The placement of a stamp was often on an angle or zigzag (*chidori chirashi*), resulting in lozenge-style repeats. The "twenty-four-flower" block, with its unique stairstep, geometric shape and complex placement in an interlocking, puzzlelike configuration, is an exception (Figure 14).

Continental Influence on Style

The taste of the ruling aristocracy for natural patterns of flowers and animals dominates the designs of the Shōsōin *rōkechi,* but some motifs clearly show continental influences. The *karahana* medallions and phoenix-on-wing motifs both originated in China. The phoenix with outstretched wings is clearly similar to the phoenix seen in the Tang-period coat *Hermits Riding Cranes,* but the Chinese stamp seems less refined or detailed than the Japanese design that evolved later.

Karahana ("Chinese flower") is a twentieth-century term coined to denote the large, eight-point floral patterns seen in the *jōdai gire.* There are many variations on the flower medallion among the *nishiki* and *kyōkechi* textiles produced for the 752 dedication of the Daibutsu.[77] The medallion seems to have been inspired by an imaginary lotus flower or possibly the tree peony, and came to Japan via Tang China, where it can be found in the paintings and sculpture of the Dunhuang temple caves as well as in textiles. The flower medallion was extremely popular in eighth-century China (*Jōdai gire* 218). In Japan, pairs of animals and birds facing one another, typical of Sassanid Persian designs, were often placed in the *karahana* medallions. The musician and dancers' costumes prepared for the dedication of the Daibutsu provide excellent examples of *karahana rōkechi* designs.

The pearl-studded roundel or *renjū* collar of Sassanid Persia, like the motif of a bird or group of animals under a tree, are evident in seventh-century Tang weaving and resist dyeing, as well as in Japanese *kyōkechi* pieces. The grandest example is a series of animals under a tree done as a group of *rōkechi* screens. The stately ram panel of the Shōsōin, produced in mid-eighth-century Japan, seems to have a direct relationship to the weft-faced silk twill ram wearing a "Sassanian royal collar" of Iran of the late sixth century.[78] In addition, the Shōsōin ram panel bears a striking resemblance to Chinese flowering-tree-and-deer motifs. A silk brocade from the seventh-century Tang dynasty found in Xinjiang Province by the Ōtani expedition[79] has the same regal stance and beaded collar, and such a design may well have served as a prototype for the Shōsōin panel (Hayashi 120). While the original Persian pattern represented sacred trees and animals connected to the Iranian sky cult, the pattern originally became Sinicized and contrived and lost much of this original meaning when interpreted first by Tang China and later by Tenpyō Japan.

The *karakusa,* or grapevine arabesque, found on Japanese *rōkechi* stamps is said to be of Central Asian origin. Although *kara-* literally means "Tang," it was also used more broadly to denote anything foreign to Japan. The grapevine arabesque and palmetto pattern are both evident in many cultures and can be seen on the Coptic wax-resist linen *Veil of Antinoopolis* of the sixth century A.D. as well as the Seven Brothers Kurgans cloth of Kertch. It is possible that these floral designs arrived in Central Asia from Egypt, Greece and Rome along with the lotus motif from India between the fourth and sixth centuries (Hayashi 107). When these motifs were interpreted by the Japanese on Tenpyō *nishiki* and *rōkechi*, much of the original style was retained. Unlike the theme of the sacred animal under a tree, arabesques were based on patterns actually seen in nature, and the Japanese found them easier to adapt to their native design repertory (*Jōdai gire* 219). The simple arabesque pattern is called *nindō*, or honeysuckle, in Japanese, but actually portrays no particular species of vine. Dots on the designs seem to represent berries, possibly pomegranate or grape clusters; for unknown reasons, the arabesque is often coupled with the image of the phoenix on the wing on *rōkechi* stamped fabrics (Figure 12).

Inconsistencies

Those familiar with exquisitely woven *nishiki* and beautifully controlled *kyōkechi* sometimes disparage *rōkechi* work for certain inconsistencies in its stamping. Erratic stamping is seen less often on the standing screens and on the beautiful *ōshi* coats worn by the *komagaku* and *gigaku* performers, but there are very few examples of these, as compared to the wealth of other, less important *rōkechi* fabrics produced for use as stand covers and wrappers. In some of these latter kinds of fabrics, stamped patterns appear to be misaligned, misprinted or at times even stamped upside down. One *kesa* wrapper with a lattice pattern of flower alternating with fish and birds shows a bird where a fish stamp should be. This seems to show a casualness not seen in other textile examples.

To understand the possible reasons for these aberrations, it is helpful to understand the process. In *nishiki* weaving, if a mistake occurred and was caught, the section could be taken out and rewoven to correct the pattern. Mistakes were rare, although varying degrees of craftsmanship are apparent. Mistakes in *kyōkechi* were also unusual. Since the process is done with pre-carved blocks clamped to folded fabric with dye poured through color-coded holes, the only possible mistake would be in the folding of the fabric. This was extremely rare, since most *kyōkechi* patterns were simple mirror images requiring one or two simple folds. *Rōkechi was* the most immediate and fluid of the *sankechi* processes and raised numerous possibilities for mistakes in placement or wax application. Stamps were carved and thus the design was set; however, the combination of stamps and their placement, direction and pattern were not regulated and the craftsmen of the *rōkechi-dokoro* workshops made various decisions. Further, the temperature of the wax, the air temperature of the workroom (which varied with the season), the pressure placed on a stamp, and even the number of times a worker shook a stamp before stamping, could all influence the amount of wax that was transferred to the fabric and thus influence the cloth's appearance. *Rōkechi* involved many more variables than did other processes.

Matsumoto asks, in "Pattern Dyeing of the Shōsōin," if these inconsistencies were truly mistakes (17). He reminds us that the artisans of Tenpyō Japan were skilled craftsmen capable of creating sophisticated work that is hard to duplicate even today. He does not believe that such "artless technique" would have been tolerated, particularly since it clearly was not in other resist traditions, without a reason. Matsumoto calls this rōkechi's "shadowy element" and suggests that what seems random is actually a flexibility that added a surprising break from conformity. He suggests that what we may think of as irregular placement, stemming from a lack of technical skill, may have been a joyous, playful quality that accounted for the survival of rōkechi throughout the period as a fresh and experimental technique.

Playfulness is not closely associated with the Japanese character in general, but this trait was very much in evidence during the Nara period, and Matsumoto cites at least two examples of lightheartedness in the ancient arts. One concerns the blank space of a document related to the Sutra Copying Office in which a comical ink figure was drawn, showing a man arguing fiercely, his cuffs rolled up for emphasis. Above this figure are the Japanese kanji characters for "heated argument," suggesting that the drawing could possibly have been a quick doodle of an argument that had taken place in the office.[80] This irreverent sketch seems like a bit of whimsy, indicating that life was not all business for the sutra copyist of Tenpyō. In a second example, Matsumoto found maps of temple estates from the same period that include comical details added by the artist, apparently as a lark. In an otherwise proper, businesslike surveyor's map, details such as smiling ducks paddling across rivers of cresting waves would seem to point to some fun-loving nature or a desire to break monotony with humor.[81] Matsumoto concludes that such playfulness among map-makers and sutra copyists can likewise be seen in the work of the rōkechi-dokoro workers who might purposely add an incorrect or upside-down stamp in the complex pattern, wondering if someone would pick out the hidden "mistake." "It seems that the jovial attitude seen in the randomness of rōkechi may be common to ancient peoples."[82]

Demise of an Ancient Art

Following the exuberance of rōkechi development during the Tenpyō era, the process of patterning cloth with wax as a resist declined and later disappeared. The exact reasons for this are not known, but much can be surmised by examining the changes in the subsequent Heian period (794–1185). With the end of the Nara period, which had been dominated by religion, the new capital was moved twice, arriving in Heian-kyō, now Kyoto, in 794. Life in Kyoto revolved around the court and the ideals of refinement and aesthetics. The declining Tang dynasty of China continued to influence the early years of the Heian period, but emphasis was placed more on assimilation and adaptation of foreign aesthetics to suit the newly developed Japanese culture than on simple echoing of the Chinese mode. Isolationist thinking soon prevailed and imports on all fronts came to a stop. All things associated with foreign cultures declined, even in the arts. Textile design and probably specific processes that were viewed as foreign or echoing foreign styles also disappeared. *Rōkechi* seems to have been one of these.[83]

Other reasons for the demise of *rōkechi* during the Heian period may be related to materials and aesthetics. Large amounts of wax are known to have been imported for the lost-wax molds used to make Buddhist statues, and it is presumed that the same imported wax was used for *rōkechi*.[84] However, as imports decreased, it is likely that wax may have gradually become unavailable (Takada 87--88).

Aesthetic preferences were also changing as the aristocrats of Heian grew interested in both subtle shading and *kaori*, the creation of atmosphere using fragrance or scent. The *jūni-hitoe* (twelve-layer unlined *kosode*) and the importance of *kasane no irome*, layered clothing, show the extraordinary Heian sensitivity to color shading. The two processes that died out during the Heian period, *kyōkechi* and *rōkechi*, both embodied a Tang preference for distinct color change, large designs and strong color contrasts. Heian taste was subtler and more attuned to ambiguity, and thus the processes may have been rejected for aesthetic reasons. Some scholars also feel that the wax-resist pieces may have retained an odor of beeswax and that in an era of sensitive noses, a lingering wax smell in clothing or furnishings may have been unacceptable.[85]

Additionally, textile authorities also believe geography may have played a part in the lack of sustained production of *rōkechi* in Japan. Most of the ancient centers that produced wax-resist dyed fabric lay along the equator or in warm climates where molten wax could be applied in outdoor workshops and allowed to cool and harden without severe cracking.[86] Some have surmised that applying molten wax to textiles in cooler climates may have created unreasonable hardship. This line of thinking concludes that the climate of Japan was simply not conducive to sustained production of a resist process that relied on heated wax (Takada 87).

Antique textile collector Gai Nishimura suggests that many of the flamboyant clothing designs depicted in screens dating from the Kamakura and Momoyama periods could well have been made from textiles dyed in a wax-resist process. However, without extant fabrics or documentation, it is difficult to prove that ancient *rōkechi* survived beyond the eighth century.

SARASA OF EDO

From the eighth through sixteenth centuries, fabrics patterned with wax resist were virtually unknown in Japan. The *Engishiki* (927) reports that "*rōkechi* is not commonly used and the way to make it is not well understood, although a few examples still exist."[87] The extensive use of wax stamps during the Nara period and Tang-inspired motifs were apparently not known, or perhaps had been forgotten when the Shōsōin's doors were locked. Well-known textile collector Shōjirō Nomura tells us that there must have been some interest in the use of wax as a resist, since a crude imitation called *rōzuri* (wax rubbing) developed during the Heian period (794–1185; Minnich 112). This process involved first dotting or rubbing white cloth with wax and then rubbing flower or grass juices onto the surface.[88] Given the vast knowledge of dyes and dye theory that was available to Heian-period artists in the record of the *Engishiki*, it is surprising that Heian people should try to rub grass juice into fiber without a prepared dye bath, but Minnich suggests that immersion dyeing of wax-resist fabrics was not known (112). At the same time, silk was also laid on carved blocks and safflower (*benibana*) was rubbed over the surface to produce a dyed rubbing (Minnich 114). No examples of these Heian *rōzuri* survive, but "flower-rubbed robes" are often described in various literary works and themes and motifs from popular poems of the day were incorporated into designs. It was six hundred years later that wax-resist textiles were reintroduced to Japan by Dutch traders.

Imported *Sarasa*

The arrival of exotic wax resist and printed cloth from Asia in the late sixteenth century made a strong impression on the Japanese. The Momoyama period (1573–1616) signaled the beginning of political change as well as growth in foreign trade. A weaving center was reestablished at the Nishijin district of Kyoto with patronage by the ruling shogunate, and the tea cult blossomed under the influence of the powerful military leaders. At a time when Japanese trade and culture were flowering, the new cloth known as *sarasa* caught the eye of a society looking for change. "*Sarasa* (chintz), a term which sounds extremely exotic to Japanese ears, refers to madder-colored cotton fabrics which were produced in India from ancient times" (Yoshioka 92). The first written record of *sarasa* in Japan comes from the log of Captain John Saris of the British East India Company. Saris reports that Indian chintz was sent as a gift to a feudal lord of Hirano in 1613; however, an earlier reference to Indian *sarasa*, from Portugal in the year 1511, says that, "Ryukyuans (Okinawans) . . . took Bengali clothes to Japan for sale."[89] During the seventeenth century, Indian dyers covered the world market with resist-dyed cloths prepared especially for the varying tastes of Europe, Indonesia, Thailand and Japan. Reports by frustrated English traders say that Japanese were so interested in the novelty of their bright cloth that traders had trouble forecasting what would sell. Designs that sold briskly at first would be completely rejected in the next shipment as consumers constantly demanded fresh, new patterns (Gittinger 169).

Confusion as to the origin of this fabled *sarasa* cloth persists. Today the Japanese term *jawa sarasa* has become a generic term for batik from any country, because of a common feeling that all *sarasa* comes from Java. During the Edo period, however, the Indian fabric was mistakenly called "Siam cloth." Dyers who worked to imitate the cloth between 1670 and 1680 were called *shamuroshi* and shops selling it, *shamuro-ya*, using the Japanese term for Siam (*Shamu*). The confusion may have arisen because the early ships carrying the printed and resist-dyed cloth of India were known to be based in Thai ports, which means that the shipments had in fact arrived from Thailand (Minnich 255).[90]

Equally confusing is the derivation of the word *sarasa*. Japanese textile researcher Shinobu Yoshimoto, in his book *Jawa-sarasa*, traces the term's origin to sources in four different languages. The Portuguese term *saraca* means "cotton fabric made in India," as does the Spanish *saraza*. Yoshimoto also tells us that Surat is the name of a Gujarati harbor town that formerly exported cloth, and that *sarasah*, in old Javanese, means "various colors." The Spanish and Portuguese words, like the Japanese *sarasa*, are all foreign to these various languages (129–130). Mattiebelle Gittinger, in her excellent book on Indian textiles, *Master Dyers to the World*, supplies us with the most probable etymology, which is from the Gujarati *saras*, meaning "excellent" or "beautiful" (27–28). In Malay, this term was adapted as *serassah*, whereas in Japan it became *sarasa*. The earliest traders in these cloths were the Dutch, and their records clearly state that the cotton *sarasa* fabrics were "painted with foliage and birds" and came from the Coromandel Coast of east India.[91]

Cotton was not well known in Japan. Some nobility owned imported cotton pieces in the sixteenth century, but the plant was not widely cultivated in Japan

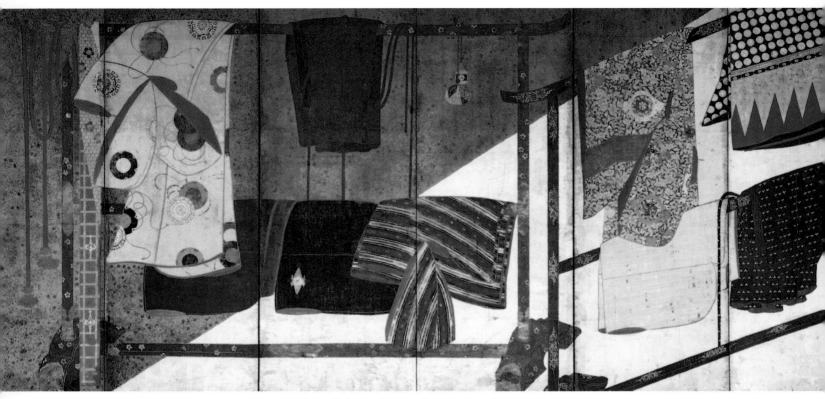

Figure 15 *Tagasode byōbu* (Screen depicting hanging *kosode*) *Sarasa* kimono appear on this seventeenth-century folding screen featuring popular designs of the period. Pigments on gold-leaf paper. Early Edo period (seventeenth century). 146.2 x 363 cm./57$^{1}/_{2}$ x 143 in., Museum of Art, Shizuoka.

until the eighteenth century, and the fabric was not available to the common people until still another century had passed (Brandon 39). The beautifully patterned and luxuriously colored *sarasa* became a precious, coveted fabric, widely collected by wealthy families for use in kimono and obi and as fabrics used in the tea ceremony (see Plate 10). Edo-period genre paintings such as *Scenes from the Pleasure Quarter* and *Tagasode byōbu*, the latter a screen depicting hanging garments (*kosode*), show many *sarasa* kimono (Figure 15).[92] Prints depicting women wearing obi patterned with a sawtooth design, obviously a fabric initially prepared for the Indonesian market and then apparently appropriated by the Japanese, are not unusual (Figure 16). For men, sword sheaths of *sarasa* as well as campaign coats, or *jin-baori*, worn over armor, were popular during the early Edo period.[93] Some textile scholars feel that the flowery style of the Indian cloth also influenced eighteenth-century traditional kimono designs (Takeda 171).

Every small piece of imported cloth was treasured, with the finest becoming fabrics for the tea ceremony. *Fukasa* display cloths, *shifuku* cloth cases used for tea caddies, and even covers for tea scoops were all made from special *sarasa*-patterned fabrics called *meibutsu gire* ("celebrated cloths") because of their special quality. Although *meibutsu gire* were considered rare and were highly coveted, an extraordinary range of patterns and designs came into the country during the late sixteenth through the seventeenth centuries. Four hundred and fifty different kinds of imported *sarasa* are included in the Tokyo National Museum collection, and the surprising number held in public and private collections also attests to the love of the exotic fabric.

Two different types of *sarasa* arrived in Japan during this time. One was a densely woven, fine cotton with minute patterns of wax-resist and mordant printing, dyed with red, subtle greens, yellows and indigos. Among this group are the

Figure 16 *Sarasa* **cloth** was used in the obi worn by the women depicted in this woodblock print by Shigemasa, dated 1777. The sawtooth pattern that was associated with Indonesian batik was especially popular. Tokyo National Museum.

Figure 17 *Meibutsu gire* **"Celebrated cloth"** Resist-dyed cotton from India was collected by many wealthy families during the sixteenth and seventeenth centuries. This example is held by the Tokyo National Museum.

geometric, floral and vine patterned *meibutsu gire* (Figure 17). A second group, the *oni-zarasa* (devil's cloth), was a thicker, more coarsely woven, block-printed cloth that was sold for floor coverings, wall hangings or cloth wrappers. A sixteenth-century explanation of an *oni* quality is "to be unmoving, showing fierce mien, yet (practice) possessing the quality of a flower."[94] Magnificent *oni-zarasa* were purchased or made to order for use on the historic Gion Festival floats, and one such hanging is dated 1684.[95]

Wa-sarasa—The Japanese Interpretation

Because of the great popularity of the fabric, European, Chinese, Javanese and Japanese versions of *sarasa* were soon available. Native dyers in Nabeshima, Sakai and Kyoto, and foreign dyers living in Dejima (in Nagasaki) competed to produce *wa-sarasa* or Japanese chintz, from the mid- to late seventeenth century. *Shamurō-zome*, or "Siamese cloth dyeing," is called an indigenous product of Yamashiro (the Kyoto area) in a volume published in 1645.[96] There were numerous problems in trying to duplicate the wondrous color of the imported *sarasa*. The Japanese had little experience dyeing cotton, a fiber that does not take dye as readily as does silk or wool. Native craftsmen also lacked the specialized knowledge of mordant technology and cotton production that the Indians had possessed since the second millennium B.C. (Gittinger 19).

The Japanese imitated the popular *sarasa* by a variety of substitute processes suited to the era. In Japan, the carved blocks and mordant stamping of Indian originals were substituted with paper stencils and rice paste. Minnich explains that Edo dyers felt that rice paste was more effective and durable on the native silks, despite evidence to the contrary from the early Shōsōin *rōkechi* (255). However, this explanation does not hold up when we consider that the cloth generally used in *wa-sarasa* was usually not silk but cotton, even when the technique was reproduced in Japan. Cotton was heavily imported beginning in the seventeenth century, and documents show that, by the late seventeenth century, 10 percent of all cotton from the Dutch Batavia factory alone was being sent to Japan.[97]

Stencils replaced blocks, paste replaced wax and pigments replaced dyes in the local *sarasa* chintz. Stencils and rice paste had been used to pattern silk fabric, as well as leather armor, since the Kamakura period (1185–1333). This was obviously the resist most familiar to dyers. Beeswax was still not readily available in the 1600s and the production of the native plant wax *mokurō* would not be developed until 1800.[98]

The brilliant reds that had attracted the Japanese were thought to be a madder dye unavailable in Japan. A native madder (*Rubia cordifolia* L.; var. *Mungista Miq.*) and stronger varieties (*Rubia tinctorium* L. and *Rubia cordifolia* Linn.) were used in Japan and are identical to the madders used in India. However, the miraculous red was actually a chay root (*Oldenlandia umbellata*) grown in calcium-rich Indian soil, providing a brilliant color superior to local Japanese madder. "The secrets of producing the brilliant fast red on cotton and linen eluded (even) European investigators until well into the eighteenth century" and appears to have eluded those in the Far East as well (Gittinger 21). In lieu of a permanent red, the Japanese relied on pigments that produced a less washfast product. Because of this, most *wa-sarasa* was primarily used for *furoshiki* wrapping cloths and *futongawa* (quilt covers) for the wealthy.

Sarasa benran, published in 1778, was one of the many manuals produced as a guide for making *wa-sarasa*. Printed woodblock illustrations showed the designs of Indian *sarasa* and designated appropriate colors and the traditional dye that was used. The technique section of the manual, however, was far from the traditional process of India, which used carved woodblock stamps, *kalam* pens, wax resist and mordant dyeing. The technique described was the Japanese process of *yūzen,* using a squeeze-cone (*tsutsu*) to apply rice paste as a resist, paper stencils and paste for repeat patterns and pigments to achieve the Japanese interpretation of Indian *sarasa.*

Yūzen, a method of creating a thin line with paste using a squeeze cone, or *tsutsu,* may well have received its impetus from the beautiful wax-resist line done with the Indian *kalam* pen that was very popular. Named for eighteenth-century Kyoto fan maker Yūzen Miyazaki, the *yūzen* process became the most fashionable way to apply design to fabric, a boon to the kimono industry of the time, and it is still very popular today. The relation between the wax line of the Indian *kalam,* the line of the Javanese *canting* (*tjanting*) and the *tsutsu* line of Japanese *yūzen* would make an interesting study. It is obvious that seventeenth-century resist-dyed fabrics of India had a strong impact on the Japanese textiles that were popular during the 250 years of the Edo period, and on the future of rōketsuzome that followed.

RŌKETSUZOME IN THE TWENTIETH CENTURY

The development of rōketsuzome in twentieth-century Japan was stimulated by diverse groups of artists, some from Tokyo and others centered in the more traditional former capital of Kyoto. Their revived interest in *sarasa*, Coptic curtains, Java batik, the Dutch Haarlem School and Chinese resists, as well as the opening of the eighth-century Shōsōin played some part in the revival of wax-resist textiles that produced the unique twentieth-century art known as rōketsuzome.

The West marks the passage of time in centuries, whereas Japan has traditionally divided time by the rule of emperors (for example, the Meiji, Taishō and Shōwa periods) or politically dominant families (including the Fujiwara clan of the Heian period and Tokugawa shogunate of the Edo period). The Meiji period (1868–1912) saw Japan transform itself from a feudal, isolated country into a modern, industrialized nation. In 1900, the West recognized the end of one century and the beginning of another with a world exposition in Paris, but in Japan the year was Meiji 33.

The Paris Exposition attracted displays from around the world. The craftsmen's associations of the towns of Arimatsu and Narumi near Nagoya sent workers to demonstrate the ancient art of *kōkechi*, now called *shibori* (tie-dye), winning recognition of their skills in the form of a bronze medal. Newly discovered Egyptian resist textiles known as the Coptic curtains were also on display, helping to awaken interest in the textiles of antiquity. However, the display of the Dutch East Indies, including demonstrations of Java batik and the brilliant costumes of Javanese puppets, caused the most excitement. Dutch textile companies had been established in Leiden and Haarlem as early as 1835, and native Javanese dyers were brought to Holland to train Dutch workers in the original wax-resist techniques (Robinson 41).[99] The Paris Exposition spurred new interest throughout Europe in this traditional wax process.[100] This interest may have reached as far as Japan and been one factor in stimulating a revival of Japan's own forgotten history in wax-resist textiles.

Three men—Tsuruichi Tsurumaki, Tomonosuke Ogō and Takeo Sano—have played central parts in reviving and furthering rōketsuzome as an art form in twentieth-century Japan. Their personal stories, taken together, span the rediscovery of the ancient process of rōketsuzome and the development of the technique into a vital contemporary art.

Tsuruichi Tsurumaki

Throughout the late 1800s the Meiji government sent numerous textile workers to Europe to learn new techniques and update Japan's weaving industry. Among those visiting Germany at the turn of the century was a young man named Tsuruichi Tsurumaki (1873–1942), credited today as having been "the father of modern rōketsuzome." Tsurumaki's background was in weaving, *yūzen* and dye technology. Whereas the government's focus was on modernizing the weaving industry in Japan, Tsurumaki chose to do extensive research on the areas of his own interest— natural dyes and resist processes—publishing his outstanding early volume, *Senshoku binran* (Handbook of Dyeing) in 1907. He also did practical research in wax resist and encouraged his students at the Kyoto School of Industrial Arts and the Kyoto Dyeing Laboratory to continue this research in rōketsuzome for use in the textile industry.

It seems possible that Tsurumaki's interest in the wax-resist process was spurred by the batik revival in Europe that occurred while he was abroad, but at the same time there was a growing awareness of Japan's own heritage in the treasury of textiles in the Shōsōin. As early as 1876, the Minister of Home Affairs had appealed to the Emperor to make this valuable collection available for study:

> The textiles preserved in the chests are getting more and more dilapidated. If the day of their being taken out happens to be windy, they will easily become tiny particles and lose their shape. Should it be permitted to release about one chestful of the cloths that might serve as materials for study on textile designs, to paste their fragments into albums and to keep the albums in the Repository as well as the Home Ministry Museum and prefectural museums, it would supply valuable sources of information about old textile designs and would also help eternal conservation of the precious pieces.[101]

Eventually, in response to repeated petitions, parts of the collection were placed with the national museums in Tokyo and Kyoto, generating greater interest in the study and preservation of the Shōsōin treasures. From 1892 through 1904 textiles were checked, classified and repaired—work that was later continued by the Shōsōin section of the Nara Imperial Museum. Specific textile scholars were at last able to view and research limited pieces of the collection. Art historian Muramatsu says that it was when Tsurumaki was able to see the ancient *rōkechi* at the

Figure 18 Tsuruichi Tsurumaki. *Indo sarasa-fū obi* (Indian Sarasa-style Obi). Wax resist on silk. 384 x 32 cm./151 x 12½ in., early Taisho period. Collection of the Museum of Kyoto. Photo: Yusuke Tange.

annual airing of the collection that he became inspired to revive the textile resist process (5).

Although Tsurumaki is known as a researcher and technician rather than as an artist, he was quick to display his own personal samples of rōketsuzome at any opportunity for the purpose of encouraging others in this interesting work. He served as a judge of the first Industrial Exposition in 1914, and his experiments using wax resist with natural dyes were presented to the public there as *shin-rōkechi* ("new batik"; Figure 18). Although cracking of the wax in rōketsuzome is considered a fault by some, Tsurumaki enjoyed this unique feature of the process, and his work often included a deliberately crackled background. In later years, he left much of the dye research work to his assistant, Someto Akashi, and concentrated on his own artwork (Uemura 17).[102]

In the Tokyo area too, interest in rōketsuzome was growing. Records show that rōketsuzome was taught from 1913 at the technical high school in Tokyo's Kuramae Ward (Muramatsu 5). In 1915, Tokyo painter Sanzō Wada returned from Europe with such a strong interest in *sarasa* that he went to India that same year to conduct research. With the help of *senshoku* artist Komatarō Yamagata, he was able to produce two rōketsuzome screens in 1918 that took the established Tokyo

Figure 19 Matsugorō Hirokawa. *Senshoku byōbu* (Dyed Screen). Wax resist on cloth. 70 x 180 cm./27¹/₂ x 71 in., early Showa period.

art scene by surprise. Since he was already a well-known painter of Western-style art, his work in a craft medium caused much attention and became a catalyst for interest in rōketsuzome among artists in Tokyo (Tsuchiya 11).

Tokyo textile artists Komatarō Yamagata, Kado Sakurai and Matsugorō Hirokawa were all pioneers in rōzome's development. Hirokawa was interested in Java batik and historical Javanese patterns. Using his superb drawing skills to master the use of the Javanese *canting* tool, he created many large, vibrantly colored hangings in a linear style (Figure 19). His study of both Indian and Javanese batik can be seen in the enclosed border patterns that were typical of his rōzome of the late twenties and thirties. Hirokawa wrote art criticism and general essays and, as a leader of the early *senshoku* movement, was active in organizing various groups and symposia. His colleague Yamagata portrayed the splendors of industrialized Japan. Smoke-belching chimneys, fiery furnaces and modern cranes are surrounded by images of steamships in his vividly dyed works (Figure 20). Hirokawa, Sakurai and Yamagata all won awards for their rōketsuzome in the late twenties after the Teiten (Japan's government-sponsored national art exhibition) added a new crafts division to the existing painting, calligraphy and sculpture sections.[103]

Figure 20 Komatarō Yamagata. *Kijūki no zu* (Derrick Design). Wax resist on cloth. 409.1 x 207.4 cm./161 x 81³/₄ in., 1928. Suntory Museum.

Tomonosuke Ogō

Ogō is honored as the leader of the first wave of rōketsuzome artists. He was mentor to many of the contemporary artists and professors presently teaching dyeing at art universities. His influence is still felt throughout the textile world in Japan. Ogō was born in 1898 in the center of the Kyoto dyeing district, where his father cut stencils for commercial kimono. His father hoped he might eventually take over the business, but young Ogō had other plans. The work of designing *yūzen* patterns for kimono or painting in the traditional *nihonga* Japanese style seemed far more attractive to him than the tedious, exacting work of stencil cutting.

After elementary school he was allowed to attend a municipal training school and, at sixteen, was admitted to the arts and crafts higher school. He concentrated largely on *nihonga* throughout his student years. During the Taishō period (1912–26), artists throughout Japan were influenced by ideas and styles from the West. The image of a solitary artist working alone in a studio to produce "art" became central in the context of the romanticism of the period and was a powerful lure for people like Ogō whose interest was not in craft, but in art. Like many young artists and writers of the era, Ogō was considerably influenced by the new magazine *Shirakaba* (White Birch; launched in 1910), which featured brilliant pictures of modern Western art and introduced readers to a range of Western concepts. In his later years, Ogō often related that his love of Western art was first awakened during his years as a student when he spent days consuming *Shirakaba*. Ogō is known for his strong appreciation of *monozukuri*, or "the making of things," a concept that is associated with a romantic view of the artist working alone to create art or art objects. This contrasts directly with the Japanese traditional style of group craft production and undoubtedly is rooted in Ogō's exposure to Western art and thinking. The idea that artisans could not only be skillful, but also could use materials to express personal feelings, was new to the decorative textile arts.

Life in Kyoto was less adventurous and more traditional than the Tokyo *Shirakaba* viewpoint would suggest, though. It consisted of conservative painting (Maruyama Shijō-ha),[104] the world of tea and *yūzen*-style dyeing (Muramatsu 4). However, Ogō soon had an opportunity to be exposed to a wide array of ancient textiles when he was chosen as one of the illustrators of a ten-volume compendium of world textiles being prepared by the new Nishiki Orimono Museum.[105] Planned for use as a resource material for textile artists, the volumes were completed between 1919 and 1928 and included gouache detail paintings of textiles from Coptic Egypt, India and China, as well as from classical Japan. At age twenty-one, Ogō became the youngest of the artists selected to work on the project when he began working on the third volume in 1920. A privileged observer, Ogō sat with the ancient textiles and rendered the minute details of their line, color and form over a period of eight years, receiving an education not to be had in any art school. Without a doubt, this influenced his future work and artistic style. This textile compendium project convinced him that it was not *nihonga* but *senshoku* that he wanted to do. Yet it was still a number of years before he began to work solely with wax resist. While in his twenties, Ogō was employed as a designer by the Tatsumura Weaving Company. Company president Heizō Tatsumura was eager to study and reproduce the Shōsōin textiles that had just recently been placed on public view for the first time, and Ogō was also selected to take part in this project. As a result, Ogō had opportunity, while he was still quite young, to learn textile history by observing closely some of the finest work produced overseas as well as the best of his own culture.

Ogō first exhibited his rōketsuzome pieces in 1927 when he joined a group of *senshoku* artists showing at the Mitsukoshi department stores in Tokyo and Osaka. Readers may be surprised to learn that department stores are well established in Japan as the sites of prestigious art exhibitions. Several of the largest present-day department store chains started out during the Edo period as drapers or sellers of kimono and dry goods.[106] Over the years these stores grew and prospered, becoming natural supporters of the textile and other arts through the sponsorship of major exhibitions. Most large department stores now have exhibition spaces where rotating shows of exceptionally high quality are held. The show held at Mitsukoshi in 1927 was similar.

This marked the first exhibition held by individual *senshoku* artists (Muramatsu 4). Ogō was invited by the renowned Gekka Minakawa, who was then still building his own career. Like organizer Seika Yamashika, Minakawa hoped that this show would gain new recognition for the *senshoku* artists. Figures like Tatsumura, Kawashima and Date were well known in the field of textiles, but were in fact the directors of large textile companies and not artists in their own right. Very few *senshoku* artists, unlike people working in the fields of ceramics or lacquer, had any individual identity apart from the company for which they worked (Muramatsu 4). Artists including Minakawa and Yamashika in Kansai and Hirokawa, Sakurai and Yamagata in Tokyo were all working to change this.

At the age of thirty-four, Ogō gave up all other artwork and devoted himself solely to rōketsuzome, winning entry to the tenth Teiten exhibition in 1932. He received the highest award in 1936 and later the *tokusen* honor (lit., "special award"), which meant that he could exhibit in the yearly show for life without any further jurying. His early work showed the influence of his classical studies and was also characterized by the *sarasa* patterning, Japanese myths and images from the Shōsōin textiles, which he used in the borders of his works. As his style matured, he returned to his original purpose in working with rōzome, "not only to show my originality freely but also to incorporate my taste for *nihonga* into my work using my skill in brush painting" (Muramatsu 6).

Figure 21 Tomonosuke Ogō. *Ame* (Rain). Wax resist on silk. 170 x 185 cm./67 x 73 in., 1953. Collection of Kyoto City University of Arts.

In 1939, Ogō was honored with a solo show at the Kyoto City Art Museum. Critics suggested that many older, more established artists had been passed over for this honor, but Muramatsu asserts that "no one displayed Ogō's level of originality or consistent quality at that time" (6). In the immediate postwar years, it was Ogō who shone brightest, moving on to an unprecedented level of abstraction and clarity. His *Sangetsu byōbu* (Mountain Moon screen), with its simple lines and lyrical quality, set the standard for many evolving artists of what could be achieved in contemporary rōketsuzome (see Plate 11).

From 1949 until shortly before his death in 1966, he was an honored professor of dyeing at Kyoto City Art College, working with his colleague, well-known *katazome* artist Toshijirō Inagaki, to teach the second wave of *senshoku* artists, who are now in mid-career. It would be hard to imagine two more dissimilar artists than Inagaki and Ogō, whether in terms of their personality, teaching style or artwork. Tomonosuke Ogō was never named a living national treasure, although this honor was accorded to the more outgoing and politically minded Inagaki. Yet there is little doubt that the fine, skillful work Ogō produced over the course of his lifetime, like his views on the art, have had a tremendous impact on the growing field of textiles in Japan (Figure 21).[107]

Takeo Sano

Sano, who is today Japan's most highly respected master of rōketsuzome, helped shape the art throughout most of this century. He was born in Hyōgo in 1913 and grew up, like so many Kyoto artists, surrounded by the *yūzen* industry. Sano remembers, as a child in the early 1920s, attending an exhibition of "new rōketsu" by Tsuruichi Tsurumaki at the Kyoto Daimaru Department Store and being inspired to try his own summer project in batik. When his older brother began studying hand-drawn *tegaki-yūzen* and attending the arts and crafts school, Sano, who was then in his teens, was allowed to go to Kyoto with him. Takeo soon realized that he too wanted to create something, and entered art school. Sano was not inspired by the traditional *yūzen* designs, which seemed to him to be nothing more than the "traditional patterns of bygone days." He had seen the rōzome work of Matsugorō Hirokawa at the Teiten exhibition, and so as his graduation from art school approached he began his own research and experiments. There was no one to teach him, so he simply "went to the library, found some illustrated books and tried to create something with feeling" (1983 10). The large 180 by 250 centimeter (6 by 8 foot) screen that was his first effort took three months to complete. Surprisingly, this work was accepted in the fourteenth Teiten exhibition, and Takeo Sano was launched in a career of rōketsuzome. The year was Shōwa 8 (1933), and Sano was just twenty years old.

Tomonosuke Ogō made a point of meeting and encouraging this young man who showed so much promise. Sano tells us that:

> At the time, I did not completely understand what art and craft really were when this strange man came to me. I realized he was the great *sensei* at the art college and I was quite nervous while talking to him. He was so calm and encouraging that I was very impressed. Through his friendship, I was introduced to Gekka Minakawa and Seika Yamada and later I met Toshijirō Inagaki too.[108]

Although close to fifteen years younger than some of these men, Sano was accepted and later asked to become part of Moyurasō, a group formed to promote the exhibition of textile art with specific interest in creativity rather than only dyeing skill.[109] The group held its first exhibition at Osaka Takashimaya, with the support of Naojirō Iida, past president of the department store, and of the Tatsumura Textile Company. These retailers were interested in promoting the work of this group "for creative fashion and interior design" partly because they found traditional *katazome* and *tegaki-yūzen* too old-fashioned. Even in the war year of 1941, the work sold well to wealthy members of Osaka society, and both businessmen and artists were encouraged.

Soon, however, the severity of the Pacific War put an end to the production of art. After 1942, all supplies had to come through the government. Natural dyes were available but chemical dyes that came from Germany and Switzerland were more difficult to get. Since wax was a petroleum product, it was especially hard to find. Temples and shrines received a certain allotment for candles through the government, and some artists used the burnt-down stubs of candles left over from temple supplies as a wax source.[110] Well-known artists were allowed chemical dyes and wax according to a government ranking system. Artists whose work pleased the government were able to receive more supplies. In 1944 and 1945, everyone was obliged go to war. Inagaki went north to the port of Maizuru. However, Sano received a waiver for ill health and Ogō, at forty-seven, was able to avoid compulsory military service. Sano remembers being forced to stop outside sketching when the police reprimanded him and Ogō for drawing at the zoo. He relates that they all drew a lot of vegetables at home, "when the government let us have vegetables."

In 1946, Sano received the top prize in the postwar government-organized exhibition, which had recently been renamed the Nitten.[111] The next year Ogō, who had always been interested in building relationships and encouraging young artists, arranged a meeting between Sano and Kageo Miura, who was then an emerging artist in his early thirties. They sat together and talked of the Moyurasō group, the concept of *monozukuri* and their common desire to live by their own work. Later, Miura joined Sano, Minakawa, Yamada, Kasugai and Imanishi to form the Takumi group to promote their work through small exhibitions in the difficult postwar years. As the reputations of his seniors Ogō and Inagaki grew in the 1950s and early 1960s, Sano continued to be connected to them and the three came to be known collectively as "*Sanba-garasu*," or the three "big blackbirds" of dyeing. It was Ogō's mantle that Sano received as he followed him as a professor of wax resist at Kyoto City Art College in 1961.

Sano's work is marked by sensitivity and respect for the unique qualities of rōzome. A purist, he prefers to work only with simple materials: wax, dye and cloth, relying on his drawing ability and skillful wax manipulation to make every piece sing. Sano was among the first to perfect the half-resist process called *han-bōsen* that has added to the restrained lyricism of his superb work (see Plate 12). Now in his early eighties, he continues to exhibit in the annual Nitten exhibition and small solo shows and to work on a variety of writing projects that trace the history of rōketsuzome for younger generations.

In the 1950s new groups were formed, among them the Modern Art Association. Seigō Hirokawa, the son of Matsugorō Hirokawa and now a professor emeritus of Tokyo Liberal Arts University, was a leader among the Tokyo textile artists

Figure 22 Seigō Hirokawa. "GO! GO!" Wax resist. 145.5 x 97 cm./ 57¼ x 38¼ in., 1967.

Figure 23 Gekka Minakawa. *Iso no nami* (Seashore Wave). Wax resist. 160 x 94 cm./63 x 37 in., 1986 (completed when the artist was 93 years old, one year before his death).

of this group. His work in Abstract Expressionism and urban lifestyle, using rōketsuzome and a distinctive dyed line, is shown regularly in the Nitten (see Plate 13 and also Figure 22). Others who work in a contemporary style include Tōichi Motono, former faculty member of Osaka Art University, and Yasuhiko Tanaka of Kyoto; both these artists produce strong, abstract rōketsuzome work that is consistently featured in Modern Art Association exhibitions. Motono's large paintings of bold geometric forms do not look like fabric. They have the same impact on the viewer as modern oil paintings, yet this artist insists on working with cloth and dye, which he feels are the materials that best express his ideas (see Plate 14). Yasuhiko Tanaka's unusual abstract work incorporates a textural appearance achieved by his unique application of wax with various cloth-wrapped rollers and wax stamps (see Plate 15).

A number of other important rōketsuzome artists have made an impact on the field through their unique work, innovative techniques and teaching. Gekka Minakawa (Figure 23) was an extremely prolific artist who worked until his death in 1987 at the age of ninety-four. Minakawa was a friend of Ogō's from the 1930s as well as a patron of Sano's when the latter was first starting out. Minakawa worked first with paste-resist dyeing but from the 1960s concentrated on wax resist. A number of his monumental dyed silk panels can be seen each July in the form of decorative hangings on nine of the thirty-two wooden floats drawn through the streets of Kyoto in the traditional Gion Festival parade (see Plate 16

Figure 24 Gekka Minakawa. *Kujaku no zu* (Peacocks). Wax resist on silk, 333 x 170 cm./ 131 x 67 in., 1961. (Seen here decorating one of the lavish floats appearing in Kyoto's Gion Festival, held each July.) Photo: Taizō Minakawa.

and also Figure 24). Taizō Minakawa continues in the same field in which his father distinguished himself, creating giant wax-resist panels that have the visual weight of tapestry weaving. His travels around the world and his large collection of Coptic textiles have served as important sources of inspiration for his work (see Plate 17). Shōsaku Teraishi, a long-time member and currently a juror of the Nitten Association, continues to work with line and half-resist techniques even now, in his late seventies (see Plates 18 and 19). Teiji Nakai, a professor at Kyoto City University of Arts, produces rōketsuzome that not only takes as his subject natural motifs but also uses indigo and other natural dyes; the use of these materials is quite unusual among contemporary rōzome artists (see Plate 20). Kageo Miura and Tsukio Kitano, both professors emeriti of Kyoto City University of Arts and respected artists in their own right, are featured in the personal interviews that follow. Works by many of these masters have been collected by the same forward-thinking professional with a deep concern for the future of rōzome.

Junji Ozawa, textile collector and president of the Daimatsu Company, has long been aware of the importance of dyeing to the Japanese arts. With the shift in lifestyle away from the traditional kimono, which was once the mainstay of the textile artist, Ozawa has looked to other avenues of recognition for dyeing work, not only in the realm of fashion but in that of fine art appropriate for display in public and private spaces. Together with the committee that he established, Ozawa has sponsored exhibitions at local galleries for emerging artists and has also founded and sponsored an important yearly exhibition, the Seiryūten, at the Kyoto Municipal Museum. This show features large panel works by thirty artists selected annually who work with resist-dyed fabric. Every year since 1990, a number of these contemporary works have been purchased for permanent display in a proposed Museum of Dyed Textiles. It is hoped that with private sponsorship and the necessary governmental support, the traditional arts of resist dyeing that were revived this century will not once again disappear.

INTERVIEWS

Innovation

Purists in the field of Japanese textiles feel that wax, dye and cloth are all necessary to the definition of rōzome, but others are more flexible in their thinking, allowing for new interpretations, materials and technology. The following four artists set the stage for modern rōzome. It happens that two of the artists regularly producing the most innovative work are masters, now in their seventies, who have served as teachers of the second and third wave of artists. Despite our assumptions about age going hand-in-hand with conservative viewpoints, these artists delight in challenging any narrow definitions of wax resist. Kageo Miura works not only with dyes, but also with pigments to achieve his characteristic and unique opacity. Tsukio Kitano often paints wax on paper, instead of on cloth, and then pours on the dye and pigments, for a very individual approach. The younger Kohrow Kawata "stains" his paintings with a combination of dye, paste and wax as he explores the possibilities of these two divergent resist materials. Tadayoshi Yamamoto chooses to screen his resists onto the fabric using photographic images with his own synthetic cold wax compounds. Wax, dye, cloth. These innovative artists neatly sidestep any absolutes, identifying themselves as rōzome artists and yet constantly pushing against the edges of the definition.

Figure 25 Kohrow Kawata's tatami-floored studio is in a former kimono factory near the old Nishijin textile area of Kyoto.

Kageo Miura

Regal celery and floating purple cauliflower glow eerily in the night while orange peppers fly toward a moon made of cabbage. Willow leaves form a rhythmic chorus line, kicking their limbs like a row of Rockettes. Shapes in surreal colors glow from the silk, accompanied by a mysterious code that runs along the edge of the painting or screen. The creator of this unusual work, a smiling, white-haired, nature-loving gentleman, sits in his sunlit studio, high above a village in southern Kyoto, explaining his work and life.

Even at the age of seventy-nine, Kageo Miura sparkles with a buoyant and youthful spirit. Unassuming in manner, he is an appreciator of the classics and of Zen philosophy. Born into a famous Kyoto *hyōgu* family of scroll and screen mounters, he was trained from an early age in traditional aesthetics, through the restoration work of his seventh-generation craftsman's family. When Miura was born in 1916, his father was in Boston doing screen restoration at the Museum of Fine Arts. It was presumed for a time that the younger Miura would carry on the family tradition, but many of his family's plans changed with World War II and Miura's father's early death.

In the late 1940s, honored textile artist and teacher Tomonosuke Ogō was actively working to encourage and introduce younger rōketsuzome artists. Even before the war Ogō had begun to generate a sense of pride among artists by promoting the concept of *monozukuri*. This term literally means "the making of things," but is rich with connotations of artisanship, suggesting a pride and joy in the production of a work of art. Ogō's romantic and idealistic talk about the life of an artist could well have been the impetus that influenced Miura to leave his steady job as a designer at Marubeni Trading Company and dedicate himself to a career in rōketsuzome art.

Wax resist has always attracted free thinkers and those who yearn for the life of a solitary artist working in a private studio. Rōzome—unlike other forms of dyeing traditionally tied to the production of kimono by teams of workers—can be done by one artist working alone. However, it was not easy for Miura to pursue his love for this art form. In postwar Japan few artists were experienced in working with it. Materials were scarce, and no safe way to remove wax was readily available. Such technical problems made the production in wax resist of kimono, which had always been the lifeblood of Japanese textile artists, very impractical. Times were extremely hard and yet artists continued to work and government-sanctioned exhibitions were held, even as stories persisted of destitution so great that people were selling their old kimono for food. To support himself and his young family, Miura produced large pieces for exhibition, as well as many small pieces that sold more quickly. Miura formulated ways of working with the materials available, such as candle stubs left over from the frequent power blackouts, and relied on indigisol (vat) dyes and repeated hot soapings for wax removal. His persistence was rewarded in 1947 when his work was accepted for the first time in the prestigious Nitten, or All Japan Art Exhibition. Today, as a professor emeritus of Kyoto City University of Arts and one of the Nitten councilors, he continues to exhibit with this group, encouraging younger artists as his teacher and mentor Ogō had fifty years before.

Miura is famous for the innovative exploration of soft natural forms (flowers, vegetables and roots), but his early work of the 1950s featured strong, bold lines, contrasting colors and an elegant simplicity. A folding screen from 1954 titled *Canal* explores in a simple abstract line and tones of black, gray and green the canal lock system, while also incorporating a human figure. In 1959 he won the top award at the Nitten exhibition with *Oboro* (Haze), a superbly drawn abstraction of a bellowing cow and bull, dyed in subtle shades of gray and blue but characterized by a bold, dynamic line.

As he sought his own individual style, his work of the 1960s suggests an interest in new materials, abstraction and bright color. His novel dyeing of hessian or burlap cloth in bright hues, cut and reassembled as inlaid paintings, occasionally calls to mind the color-field paintings of the American Expressionists. Miura's mature work has found perhaps its finest expression from this base of abstraction, color studies and the exploration of the qualities of rōketsuzome.

His active family of three daughters and four grandchildren has also influenced his art. In particular, his middle daughter's studies in *nihonga* (Japanese-style painting) opened a new door onto color and unusual materials. When Miura realized, in the early 1980s, that the traditional *nihonga* ground pigments could be laid on top of one another and thinned to create a shaded blush, he began to experiment with them in his rōketsuzome work. This, together with Miura's outstanding design sense and playful choices of subject matter, has resulted in a distinctive style wholly his own.

Miura's work has always been firmly based in drawing and sketching. Old photographs show a youthful Miura in beret off touring Japan to sketch with his elderly mentor, Tomonosuke Ogō. Miura's orderly work habits are illustrated by his sketchbooks of bamboo shoots. A voluminous address book of alphabetized vegetable names gives him a color-coded reference number for each subject among the more than fifty sketchbooks on the shelves lining his studio. Volume forty-five is filled with sketch after glorious sketch of bamboo in all its forms and at every stage of its growth cycle. Color notations or watercolor washes are added for future reference. Notes on the pages remind him of the day specific shoots were sketched and the outdoor market or field from which they came. Some sketches feature produce from local farmers' markets, while others may show vegetables picked up during trips to mountain villages or coastal peninsulas. Certain sketches date back as much as fifty years, to trips he took with Ogō.

Miura is well known for his outstanding use of color and space. He does not feel the need to be true to original color, and he uses dyes and pigments to express the objects' essence or perceived energy. His response to objects, he says, takes the form of color. One obvious influence on Miura's artistic sense are the turn-of-the-century Fauves, who sought to detach color from any descriptive function and use it expressively and structurally. Miura's studies of Korean temple painting and Indian mandalas have also influenced his color sense.

Miura admires beauty and finds it in places that we may not think to look. Miura's vegetables and roots transform our thinking about humble plant life. His willow leaves dance across the paintings like chorus girls, green onions and celery stalks become floating clouds, and mushrooms reach down with elongated arms from heaven while peonies raise their petals in praise. The paintings, screens and kimono surprise and amuse us, as does their complex but playful creator.

To a Western eye, the most disconcerting thing about a Miura painting or screen may well be the composition. Objects appear to fly out of the picture frame. In some works there is virtually nothing in the center; all motifs hug the edge. When Miura does his full-scale sketches on brown paper tacked to the wall of his studio, he slips a piece of scrap paper behind to keep the lines from running over the edge onto the wall. Western art training may encourage us to complete a composition within the space, but Asian sensibilities are at work here. Miura is keenly aware of eye movement, rhythm and tension, and wants his work to broaden an image, expand it and move outward with it. He says that the viewer's eye will automatically complete an unfinished object in the same way that a Zen ink-painted half-circle compels a viewer to complete that image.

Technology and an international flavor have been taking on new importance in Miura's work lately. Miura is not an English speaker, yet rainbow-hued titles in English or Japanese words written in the Latin alphabet appear at the borders of some works. Cryptic codes or symbols hover like strips of computer icons at the edges of others. Miró-like lines work their way in, and circles, triangles, hexagons and other geometric symbols recall American Indian hieroglyphs for rain or sun. An intuitive artist, Miura simply says that these shapes were needed at the edge to complete the composition; *this* shape, *this* color, not any other. The shapes speak of technology rather than nature; of symbols and not botanical form. The contrast between these elements is what now intrigues Miura.

Kageo Miura's work is shown in Plates 21 and 22 and on the front cover.

The color quality and glowing opacity of Kageo Miura's work come from a unique combination of materials and techniques. While *ganryō,* or pigments, are sometimes used with stencil dyeing, notably in the *bingata* textiles of Okinawa, a special combination of pigment and wax-resist and the extensive use of *ganryō* are unique to Miura's work.

For both his large folding screens and his smaller panels, Miura chooses a thin, slubbed raw silk, covering it entirely with a dark natural dye, often *katekyu* from the Asian acacia for black and brown shades or *shibuki* from the wax myrtle for ochre and mustards. He then applies a mordant (such as alum, iron or chrome) and dries and heat-sets his colors. Next he transfers his design to the dark background and applies wax to the areas where he wants to retain the original color. He then applies *ganryō*, which are opaque, water-soluble pigments bound to fiber by a soybean solution or by *nikawa* (for information on binders, see also Nakano and Stephan). He uses a variety of colors such as bright blue azurite (*gunjō*), oyster shell white (*gofun*), Indian red (*bengara*), King's yellow (*sekiō*) and verdigris green (*rokushō*). These pigments are readily available in Japan at art supply stores since they are regularly used in *nihonga*. Pigments come in powdered, granular and stick forms. Granular pigments need to be ground to a finer consistency with a porcelain mortar and pestle and then mixed with binder before applying (see Appendix). To build up color, Miura applies two or three layers of *ganryō*, letting each coat dry between applications. Later, he removes the wax and does some touching up.

Miura was first attracted to the use of *ganryō* because its properties are so different from those of dye; he likes its opacity and the fact that one color can be laid down next to another without bleeding. He continues to produce obi and kimono with acid dyes, using *ganryō* only in his wall art.

Tsukio Kitano

He never planned to work with cloth, dye or wax resist. When he was a student, he accepted the idea that textile art was merely decorative and somehow inferior compared to oil painting, the domain of real artists. So Kitano trained in high school and later at the city art college as a painter, using oils and the pigments of Japanese traditional *nihonga* painting. Then one day, in 1946, he saw a screen that was to alter the course of his life. It was a simple blue-gray paper screen of a moon, mountain and river by Tomonosuke Ogō (see Plate 11). Ogō was then a well-known *rōketsuzome* artist, but young Kitano saw this work not simply as an example of "dyed art" but "fine art," worthy of a place in any museum. Kitano immediately changed his mind about wax dyeing and began an odyssey of exploration that continues today.

Now, at seventy, Kitano continues to explore new techniques and materials while resisting any preconceived ideas about art and craft.

> Should you really be speaking to me? I don't do kimono. Some people would say I don't even belong in a book on rōketsuzome because I like using paper more than cloth. Ogō-*sensei* always *did* warn me that if I started working on paper I might never get back to cloth. However, wax resist is important to me. It is more tedious and has more restrictions than oil or pigment painting, but you can't get that line quality by applying a brush directly to paper. That line comes from a resist process.

Kitano was in the middle of his training as a painter when the Pacific War intensified and he was called away to draw designs for munitions and aircraft engines. In 1945 he was able to graduate, and it was soon afterward that he encountered Ogō's *Sangetsu* screen that was to be so influential on his career. He joined one of the many art groups that developed in the late 1940s and 1950s. These groups met to encourage younger artists, share techniques, critique one another's work and, most importantly, promote participation in the government-sponsored Nitten. All were influenced by Ogō's dynamism, free thinking and shift in emphasis from craft kimono to the expressive world of art. Kitano explains that, "He used craft techniques to create 'fine art.'"

Kitano began his career working with natural dyes on cotton and silk but later added chemical (Procion) dyes. His early subjects were birds, animals and other natural forms. In 1961, his expertise was recognized when he won the coveted *tokusen*, the Nitten's highest award. Exhibition rules specify that winners of this award can enter their work in all future Nitten competitions without ever again undergoing jurying. This meant that Kitano was free from that point to work with the materials and themes that most interested him.

Many of the pieces he did in the 1950s and 1960s reflected the abstract work being done abroad in painting. Publications and exhibition catalogs on the Abstract Expressionist movement in the United States and Europe spawned small study groups of young artists like him, who were eager to see and discuss the new work. In the early 1970s he did a dynamic series in indigo-dyed cloth that explored abstract shapes and at the same time celebrated the unique qualities of fabric. In this series, somber areas of blue and brown are abruptly cut or defined by coarse rows of black cotton stitches. The edges are frayed and some stitches are left hanging loose, as if to emphasize that the work is done on cloth.

The 1970s were also a time of developing themes of special interest to Kitano. Though not a Christian himself, he was touched by the story of the Japanese Christians who worshipped underground for three centuries in response to severe persecution during the seventeenth century. His interest in this theme developed into an arresting series of paintings of figures, arms crossed or bound, that appear to float silently across the picture plane (Plate 23). "It seems my best work comes when I have a theme that fires my continued interest over a period of time and that sustains a series." This is also true of Kitano's series of hands from the 1970s, which followed a serious injury to his own hand. This group features hands crossed, locked around a wrist or clutching at flowers. His paintings of large, entwined fingers hovering over subterranean Madonnas can be viewed simply as interesting spatial and color compositions or more symbolically as statements on suffering, persecution and discrimination.

Currently a professor at Ōtemae College and professor emeritus of Kyoto City University of Arts, Kitano continues to exhibit the kind of energy and artistic curiosity one would expect from a much younger man. While some artists would be happy to repeat their own successes, Kitano continues to branch out into different techniques and themes. His paintings of nudes in the 1980s were called erotic and provocative by local art writers (Plate 24). His latest series combines his interest in the Christian theme with his love of music. The series was inspired by Debussy's tenth Prelude for Piano ("Sunken Temple") and shows churches submerged in water. This intriguing series is just his latest response to Ogō's challenge to create fine art.

It was Ogō's works on paper that first inspired Kitano to become a rōketsuzome artist, and indeed Kitano has returned to paper many times, doing extensive research on support papers and pigments. In the past he has worked with linen paper, but since 1961 he has been using *gasenshi*, a paper originally produced in China especially for work by ink painters.

The process he developed is unique. First he covers the border of the paper with a layer of wax to keep it from warping too much when wet. Next he uses wax to mask the areas he wants to keep white, and then sprays the entire surface with water. At this point he has finished preparing the surface and begins to paint and to pour *sumi* ink and pigments across the paper. The pigments or *ganryō* used in traditional Japanese *nihonga* painting are diluted with *nikawa*, a natural binder made from animal byproducts. To create unevenness or a special pattern he places scrap paper underneath the *gasenshi* to control the pooling of the pigments. Ogō once suggested that he place wool blankets underneath to soak up excess water moisture and indeed Kitano has found that wool is the best base for drawing water from a piece while creating interesting patterns. Once the base layer of color has dried, he applies more wax and pigment to refine and sharpen his image. Kitano removes the wax with solvents and relies on *hyōguya*, or professional screen makers, to smooth the finished painting during the process of mounting.

Tadayoshi Yamamoto

Very few artists have done the kind of traditional apprenticeship that Tadayoshi Yamamoto has. At the age of sixteen, Yamamoto left school in Hyōgo Prefecture and went to Kyoto to study *nihonga* and oil painting. In order to support himself, Yamamoto decided to look for art-related jobs. The one he found was as an apprentice to a kimono dyer.

Apprenticeship has a very long history in Japan. Since the reign of Emperor Ōjin (270–310), dyers and weavers who immigrated from Korea and China were often asked to teach their skills throughout the country, sharing their expertise and furthering knowledge of the textile arts. At the height of the Nara period (710–794) an official Office of Dyeing, Weaving and Sewing Work provided for the needs of temples and the court. By the twelfth century, the guilds had become powerful enough to operate independently of imperial patronage and to function like many of the European craft guilds of medieval times. One important element in the guild system was the traditional apprenticeship, set up to encourage the continuation of technique and skills.

In Japan, the young apprentice, or *deshi*, was taken into the workshop as a student, trained in the craft and taught to assist the master. *Deshi* worked long hours for little money. After ten years, an apprentice was usually considered skilled enough to leave the master. The former *deshi* would then traditionally set up his own shop, with the former master transferring some of his longest-standing customers to the new enterprise, to help ensure its success and to express his thanks for years of service.

Many of the second-generation of rōketsuzome artists received, first, an art education at university and, later, some hands-on experience at a kimono company. Yamamoto, however, came to the textile arts through the time-honored apprenticeship system. The industrious, gregarious artist is somewhat proud of this element in his background.

> Although I have no art university training, and was a high school dropout at sixteen, I have had as thorough a *senshoku* education as any of my contemporaries. For ten years I did all aspects of Japanese traditional dyeing and in my limited free time took lessons in painting. Soon I learned it was dyeing that I most wanted to do. I had my work accepted in the Nitten exhibition in Tokyo when I was twenty. I had some success early, but after ten years I was not satisfied with the direction of my work. I wanted to explore new techniques. When I turned thirty I left Japan with my wife and traveled to Paris through Russia, Austria and Czechoslovakia. This was an exciting education.

In Paris from 1968 through 1969, Yamamoto studied copper etching and silk-screen techniques at the William Hayter studio, "Atelier 17." There he was encouraged to try many new techniques. While in Europe, Yamamoto learned that the art of silk-screen production, or serigraphy, was actually an outgrowth of Japanese *katazome* picked up by the Germans during visits to Japan in the Meiji period (1868–1912). But while stencils wear out in time, though, screens are much stronger, and Yamamoto quickly saw their possible application to textiles. After traveling through more than fourteen countries, the adventurous Yamamoto returned to Japan, ready to try out the innovations he had learned on his own kimono work.

Working with photographic serigraphy and the "split-font" technique, which uses a variety of colors on one screen, Yamamoto screened thickened dyes on silk. He was encouraged to find a way to screen a resist onto fabric and soon developed his own distinctive dyeing style. Yamamoto's screens were very much like the paper stencils used for centuries by his countrymen, but for six years, his work was not accepted into the crafts section of the Nitten competition: this section accepts only works produced by hand, and his pieces were not thought to meet this requirement. However, Yamamoto's innovative blend of screen print, wax stencil and traditional rōketsuzome was eventually recognized and his work has now twice won the highest award, the coveted *tokusen*.

Yamamoto has continued to search for new, improved techniques. He uses a variety of new resist mediums, such as *ekirō*, *dakku* and dammar resin, to make his work easier (see Advanced Wax-Resist Techniques, page 174). His folding screens and kimono all take their themes from nature, which creates a striking contrast with the high-tech methods he favors. He produces his photographic screens from pictures of birds in flight, winter trees and mountain horizons shot on trips to the northernmost island of Hokkaido as well as at local temples. Yamamoto has also done some exceptional work with *rō-shibori* and in 1985 exhibited a series of four $2^1/_2$ meter (8 foot) standing screens that used this technique to depict the changing seasons.

A well-known artist, Yamamoto is also a respected businessman and owner of his own dyeing company, where he employs ten workers producing thirty to forty kimono each month in addition to various interior textiles and fashion accessories. Although he came from the traditional craft apprentice system, he has chosen not to continue with tradition but to use every innovative process available to produce finer work. His efforts are now being rewarded. In the future Yamamoto can be expected to continue to combine modern technology and age-old techniques to produce work that goes well beyond any narrow definition of textile art.

Tadayoshi Yamamoto's work is shown in Plate 25 and on the back cover.

Kohrow Kawata

Lone, deserted buildings on a winter beach, a rusted oil tank in an almost-white snow field, craggy rocks in a strange, moonlight sea. Kohrow Kawata's dyed panels have a bleak solitude about them, yet the viewer's interest is awakened by their unique and unconventional use of dye and cloth. The fabric looks "distressed," faintly stained with puddled dye. In a recent exhibition of smaller pieces, vulnerable flower shapes floated on these stained backgrounds, showing a delicate and sensitive touch. The carefully shaded rock and building shapes Kawata often uses easily transform into abstract shapes, and at times resemble the giant stained canvases of the American Abstract Expressionists. "I use nature as a means of working with form, but it's really color and the absence of color that fascinate me."

In the 1980s, Kawata's work involved the exploration of white—the white of a beach in winter, or that of a barren field of snow. At first a viewer sees only the absence of color, but upon closer inspection the subtleties of exquisitely dyed cloth, with its delicate shadings, become evident. The color is applied in thin layers, staining the fabric rather than dyeing it in the usual way.

> Since I developed my work process from my own experiments, it is far from either traditional wax-resist or paste-resist in technique. Since wax is petroleum- or oil-based and paste is a water-based resist, I can work both of them into the fabric, and they repel each other while creating a barrier for the dye. I like working with the crude and biting "acid" dyes on rough, textured linen and silk. These dyes are a contrast to the responsive and pliable "direct" dyes that are especially good on flax or cotton. Lately the color of lead, a flinty blue-gray, attracts me. It's the dark gray of the sky next to the northern sea of Hokkaido.

As Kawata relates, he was never trained as a dyer, but he learned most of what he knows through firsthand experience and years of experimentation. "It was only after graduating from the oil painting department of the city art college that I developed an interest in dyeing and textiles." When he was a student, Jackson Pollock and Jean Dubuffet influenced his painting. Curiosity about the early history of Buddhism and the origins of Japanese culture led Kawata to explore more traditional artistic processes. He received encouragement from rōketsuzome artist Kageo Miura, and a generous gift of studio space from a group of Nishijin businessmen. "In the sixties, things were not as commercial and competitive as they are today. The men of the Nishijin weaving district who helped me were not just kindhearted people, but enterprising businessmen. With an eye to the future of Kyoto textiles, businessmen sometimes gave young promising artists some assistance without expecting anything back right away." This support gave Kawata a chance to explore the *senshoku* medium and develop his own distinctive approach to dyed fabric with a minimum of financial worries.

Life was not always so kind to Kawata, which seems evident from his deeply reserved manner. His childhood memories are indelibly marked by the war and the hardships that followed it.

> I was born in 1941, and my mother and sister escaped to Nara with me as a small child. The firebombs had destroyed our Osaka house. Even after the war, we shared living quarters with other displaced people, since we had no home to return to. During that time, my sister died. I was told that it was from pneumonia, but now I believe her early death was from malnutrition, which we all had, and from poor medical attention. I feel that these early experiences may still have some deep emotional effect on my life and work.

Kohrow Kawata teaches part-time at two universities and produces a limited number of kimono each year in his traditional warehouse studio in the northwest area of Kyoto (Figure 25). In addition to teaching and kimono production, he is an active exhibitor, holding solo shows in New York City, Kyoto and Tokyo. He has also taken part in numerous group shows at the Itami City Craft Center, and the Museum of Kyoto and in Australia. One reviewer of a 1994 Kyoto solo show praised his latest work for the "mysterious translucency found in all of his abstract expressions" and said that "the strength was there. His artwork has gone beyond the narrow concept of *senshoku* and has the freedom often seen in paintings." In the past, Kawata was a regular exhibitor in the national Nitten and regional Kyōten exhibitions, but recently, as a protest against what he calls the overly traditional direction of the Nitten's management, he elected to stop participating in that show. This has made his life much more difficult, since participation in the Nitten is a prerequisite for entrance to many other prestigious exhibitions. Kawata is now looking for other avenues for bringing his sophisticated and subdued work to the public.

Kohrow Kawata's work is shown in Plate 26.

Figure 26 A bright, sunlit studio provides a clean workspace
for Shigeki Fukumoto to prepare his dyed screens.

Technique

Creating art with wax and dye poses many technical challenges. Wax that is too hot drips and oozes, allowing for little control, while cold wax sits quietly on the surface, not penetrating the fabric and not resisting the dye. Dyes can be full of energy and glowing color in the hands of a master and yet quickly become muddied and disappointing when used by a novice. It takes ten or twenty years to become truly expert in handling these materials, and longer to exhibit the control seen here. Many artists combine a variety of techniques to produce their more complex pieces. Shigeki Fukumoto and Shoukoh Kobayashi both work with the *fubuki* technique, spraying hot wax droplets onto cloth for a stippling effect. Fukumoto adds stencils to the *fubuki* process to mask out selected areas and create stunning screens that shimmer like optical illusions. Kobayashi starts with a black linear grid and *fubuki*, then adds a form of *bokashi* shading adapted to his own powerful style. Mitsuo Takaya has mastered the difficult *han-bōsen*, or half-resist, technique, using hot wax brushed onto the fabric to produce a shaded application. His control is immediately apparent to anyone who has attempted this technique. The narrative imagery of Yuki Katō's arresting panels is enhanced by her skillful use of stenciled resists to produce patterning and architectural detail.

Shigeki Fukumoto

Radiant color glows from Shigeki Fukumoto's abstract compositions. Diagonal stripes dyed in pastels shimmer across the cloth like sun over a chrome surface. The patterned designs cascade across the panels dyed to look like layers and folds. They remind us at first of silken bolts of cloth for modern kimono, but at the same time there is something quite polished and sharp about them. Recent work, involving multidimensional shapes wrapped with glowing colored cloth, echoes the Japanese folding screen while utilizing the natural play of light and shadow. Fukumoto's technical expertise and familiarity with the strengths and limitations of his materials have produced some extraordinary work.

> For the dyer, the art of dyeing is a sparring match with fabric and dye—two very tough opponents indeed. In the process of dyeing, the dye asserts the full force of its personality—as if it were alive and had a will of its own. In so doing, it imposes certain technical limitations upon the dyer. A dyer, there-fore, has to decide how he wants to deal with the selfish demands of his materials: kill them or let them live? Among the many advanced dyeing tech-niques in use today, most aim at defeating the physical properties of fabric and dye, subjugating them to the dyer's demands. I prefer to let them live.

Since his first acceptance in the Lausanne Biennial (1987) and the Lódz, Poland, Triennial of 1992, and his continued participation in the France-Japon exhibitions in Paris (1984–92), where he was a six-time award winner, Fukumoto has become one of the best known of the younger Japanese rōketsuzome artists. Not only a consummate artist but also a prolific writer, Fukumoto is the author of three books on the art of Oceania and a regular contributor to numerous maga-zines.

Fukumoto grew up in the home of a kimono dyer, the middle child between two sisters. While he was majoring in oil painting at the city art college, his father became ill and Shigeki was required to learn the rōketsuzome dyeing process and take over production of the line of kimono until his father's recovery two years later. Though he was still a student at the time, his work sold well enough to pro-vide income for the family and to finance his first trip abroad. Amid the surging economy of the early 1970s, Fukumoto found himself able to sell almost every kimono he produced. This early success decided his choice of rōketsuzome art as a career. His background in painting and woodblock printing gives him a "fine arts" orientation toward his work with dye and fabric. "I work with wax because it is considered difficult and I enjoy using it to its best advantage . . . I feel that the wax, color and fabric help magnify my abilities."

Fukumoto's home and studio lie beside a running brook in the heart of the busy city of Kyoto. The sound of moving water permeates his work space (Figure 26). All through the house, dark, primitive artifacts are placed next to the artist's own polished, glowing pieces. The contrast could not be more arresting, and many visitors ask about the connection. While a student at Kyoto University of Fine Arts, Fukumoto had opportunity to participate in a study trip to New Guinea. This trip had a lasting impact on his thinking and his work. He says he was surprised to learn that tribal art was so powerful and alive. He describes the artwork he saw as being full of "the smell of the soil." While his fellow artists went off to search for identity in Paris or New York, he was attracted to Oceania. Over the next ten years, all his extra money from kimono production went into traveling in Southeast Asia and the publishing of three books in Japanese on Melanesian art, tapa cloth and the costumes of Oceania. The dark, earthy tones of his tribal art collection form a strong contrast to the clear, polished refinement of his new work, yet both kinds of work display a quiet power that accords well with the artist's own vitality.

Fukumoto is very interested in language, the meaning of words and semantics. In an article called "Japan and the Art of Dyeing," he objects strongly to the American use of the word "surface design" to describe his art.

> I am a *some* (lit., "dye") artist, but I have trouble defining myself when asked in English what kind of artist I am . . . If I call myself a "dyeing artist" I'm in danger of being mistaken for a "dying artist" . . . What about "surface designer," you may think, but in fact this too has its problems because in Japan we use the word *some* precisely to designate objects which are *not* surface design. Our word for dyeing refers to designs that do not restrict themselves to the surface . . . but actually sink into the fabric. Dyeing, or *senshoku*, thus in fact has the exact opposite meaning of "surface design" . . . [This makes] the very idea of referring to *senshoku* as "surface design" absurd (13).

The themes of Fukumoto's work have changed every year or so, but are united by his characteristic sharp edge and the *bokashi* (shaded dyeing) technique that produces his distinctive colors. Traditional Japanese concepts of layering, wrapping, and concealment, as well as motifs of water, reflection and rainbows, have all been featured prominently in his work of the past. Commissions from hotels and other public spaces have recently pushed the scale of his screens and panels to sizes as large as 6 by 3.5 meters (20 by 10 feet), forcing him to build a new studio. But more than scale, it is multiple layers of color, changing patterns and dramatic control of dye that sets the work of Shigeki Fukumoto apart from that of his contemporaries.

Shigeki Fukumoto's work is shown in Plate 27.

Fukumoto works with a variety of dye and wax application techniques to produce his distinctive pieces. All his work is done using fiber-reactive dyes on Turfan cotton, a lustrous long-fiber cotton produced along the old Silk Road in western China. Multiple layers of dye and wax give the depth of subtle color seen in his work. He uses the *bokashi* wet shaded dyeing technique to achieve the glow that is his trademark. Fukumoto is a master at controlling dye and the shade of color, which is vital to this technique. He works with numerous hand-cut stencils, often layering some on top of others to form optical effects. One tool he favors is the *shike-bake*, a long-bristled brush. He first soaks this brush in hot wax and then taps it with a stick, sprinkling dots of wax over the stencil-covered cloth in the areas he does not want the next layer of dye to penetrate (for a discussion of the *fubuki* technique, see page 179). Finer wax dots require different brushes. Fukumoto also creates delicate patterns with a cloth-covered stamp soaked in wax and pressed through stencils onto the fabric surface.

Shoukoh Kobayashi

Shoukoh Kobayashi's surreal work brings many things to mind: the giant sand dunes of Tottori in western Japan, the raked pebbles of Kyoto's Zen temples, rhythmic seashore patterns. Even on the train to Kobayashi's house and studio in suburban Kyoto, the scenery outside the window looks like beautiful dyed panels. Row upon row of deep green tea bushes flourish beside the tracks. The continuous pattern is broken only by black frost covers, pushed back to allow the tea plants to catch the dwindling winter light. This scene is straight out of a Kobayashi painting and also typical of Uji, where tea has been "master" for four hundred years.

A short car ride takes us to a part of town that the artist jokingly calls "Kobayashi *mura*" ("Kobayashi village") since so many of his relatives live clustered there. Three artist brothers have built new homes and studios in what was formerly a tea field adjoining their parents' home. Entering Shoukoh's clean, traditional-style home, those tea rows seem to have been revived in the abstract dyed panels that surround us. Kobayashi is drawn to minimal landscapes, but the titles of his latest works, like *Echo, Rhyme of the Wind* and *Wind Direction*, show an interest in motifs beyond the realm of landscape, into the unfamiliar province of things not visible (see Plates 28–29). "How can you show sound waves, the movement of wind or electrical waves bouncing off distant satellites? This intrigues me, and in my newest work, I was inspired to paint things that cannot be seen but that do exist in a nonvisual form." In 360 centimeter-long (12 foot) folding screens on the theme of sound, or miniature tea ceremony screens that stand only 51 centimeters (20 inches) tall, the same luminous, awe-inspiring quality is there.

Born in 1955 to a family of metalworkers, Kobayashi chose textiles as a way to assert his individuality. Since his oldest brother was a sculptor, his father a renowned metalworker and his second brother a potter, he was left only the fields of lacquerwork or textiles to explore if he wanted to be different. Kobayashi was a tall and athletic figure and even won a sports scholarship to university, but chose the path of the artist.

It was through his studies in textile history, and specifically the examples of seventh-century *rōkechi* work of the Shōsōin repository, that he became interested in exploring the design possibilities of wax resist. A few years after graduating from Osaka University of Arts, Kobayashi apprenticed himself to a Kyoto kimono dyer, hoping to polish his technical skills and find his own artistic "voice." After five years of tedious, repetitive production dyeing, he had gained skill in a great many techniques, including *bokashi* (shading) and the careful color matching needed for the kimono industry. To this day Kobayashi continues to dye kimono and obi in his own distinctive style, but only for two or three special customers each year.

One of the first things that appealed to Kobayashi about rōketsuzome was the dynamic, hard-edged line it produces. In his early work he often used cactus and flower motifs, which emphasized his special interest in line and pattern. It was not until he had added the wax stippling *fubuki* technique that he was able to obtain the texture and depth of color that he was looking for. Kobayashi explains that *fubuki* (meaning "blizzard") is produced by dipping a long-bristled brush into unusually hot wax and tapping it across a dowel to produce the characteristic splattering of fine wax dots over the fabric. Six to ten layers of dye and wax dots placed on the fabric's surface then produce a kind of pointillistic color and texture not available with any other technique. In Kobayashi's pieces, dark black stripes contrast with the smooth, glowing *bokashi* shading for a luminous effect reminiscent of shell cut into black lacquer.

In addition to his work as an instructor of textile design and art at Kyoto Seika University and Kyoto University of Education, Kobayashi still finds time for days of concentrated studio work in the two-room atelier behind his home. Once his day begins, he works long hours with lengths of satin-faced silk tacked to large wooden frames, rarely emerging from his studio. He applies acid dyes to the back of the fabric and blends them into the front. The dark lines come first, with colored areas and *fubuki* added later. When the scale of the work extends to more than 13 feet (4 meters), he calls to his wife to come from the main house to help him turn the huge frames.

In recent years, Kobayashi has received numerous awards and invitations. His work was included in the fifteenth Lausanne Biennial in Switzerland and the third Kyoto International Textile Competition. Not content with the usual two-dimensional presentation of Japanese screens, Kobayashi sometimes folds his work back, surrounding the viewer in a surreal "landscape." His Lausanne Biennial screen bent back on paper hinges to form a curved "wall" that diminished at either end. *Kyō/Echo*, an award-winning piece at the 1992 Kyoto Crafts Biennial, was designed to be exhibited horizontally and folded back, to create a half-drum–shaped projection emanating from the wall with a marvelously luminous moonscape "skin" (see Plate 29).

A warm and friendly young artist, Kobayashi speaks freely of his admiration for his fellow fiber artists in Kyoto and credits his father as a primary influence. The clean lines of the traditional Japanese house are an elegant backdrop for Kobayashi's powerful abstract work. Throughout his own home, arrangements of textile screens, patterned pottery sculpture and inlaid metal boxes honor the talented family into which he was born.

Mitsuo Takaya

A solitary island sits in the middle of a rich turquoise sea, surrounded by configurations of stars that have been used for centuries by sailors for navigation. The island is haloed in glowing light. Though isolated, it is not alone, because the sky above is etched everywhere with animal patterns (see Plate 30). In another view, the island sits in a black, stormy sea. Rolling thunderheads have gathered above and are outlined in an ominous electric orange line. But a shaft of white light breaks through a small rift in the clouds, producing a calm sphere of blue just in front of the island.

The recent work of Kyoto artist Mitsuo Takaya is rich with symbolism. When considered as part of a body of work created over a lifetime, the current series stands as a significant point of transition and a maturing of both technique and concept.

Natural wonder has been a theme of Takaya's for more than twenty years. In the 1970s, his white bird forms were often contrasted against stark brown landscapes. These shapes evolved naturally into the tree and branch forms that were his main themes over the next decade. In one work from this period, a distant view of bare trees lies on top of large, detailed branch forms that appear to reach off the picture frame in supplication.

Experiments in the difficult wax-application technique known as *han-bōsen* (see Advanced Wax-Resist Techniques, page 176 and Plate 31) and a sensitive use of space and surface mark Takaya's work of the late eighties using mountain and cloud forms. His present sea/island series seems the culmination of the drama and movement that has always been a trademark of his compositions. Whether the subject was the sea or a mountain, turbulence and energy tended to move across every screen. In Takaya's work in the past, clouds burst, snowstorms erupted and mountains appeared volcanic.

This turbulent art can seem at odds with its quiet creator, a thin man who smiles readily and who just passed his fiftieth birthday. Takaya's experiences of hardship emerge gradually in conversation:

> My father was a kimono salesman. I was the third of four boys, born during the war, and my only early memories are of there not being enough. I only remember being hungry, always hungry, every day. It's hard to imagine in these days of plenty.

During the war years, the second and fourth boys were evacuated to the country while the oldest son and Mitsuo stayed in the city. This was a calculated decision meant to ensure that at least some of the children would survive the firebombing and be able to carry on the family line. In fact, all lived, the eldest becoming a doctor and the next a pharmacist. The youngest son took over the failing kimono business, which left Mitsuo free to become an artist and university professor.

> All my life I had only wanted to be an artist. In elementary and junior high school I was a member of the art club. I was most fortunate to be accepted at Kyoto City Art College just at the change of generations. Men like Ogō and Inagaki were just retiring and the younger men, Sano, Miura, Teraishi and Kitano, were having a profound influence on students. I was lucky to learn from both waves of dyeing teachers. Sketching in the botanical garden and drinking tea in Uji with Ogō-*sensei* I remember well, but I can't recall my academics, particularly. We weren't taught techniques so much as attitude. I didn't know what the teachers were doing at the time, but later I realized it was life lessons they were teaching: how to be a person. That kind of instruction stays with you for a lifetime. It was after graduation, when I became serious about my work, that Sano-*sensei*, who'd been my teacher earlier, took me aside and taught me some specialized techniques and encouraged me.

Watching Takaya at work critiquing the dyed pieces produced by his textile students, it quickly becomes apparent how well he took in the lessons of his masters. Offering constructive criticism and suggestions for future directions, Takaya encourages his students to experiment and develop, much the way his own teachers had some thirty years before.

Life in Japan has changed, however. One area, the production of kimono, is no longer an important part of his students' education. Takaya reminisces about the family kimono business, which folded after his father's death:

> We had hoped to keep the business going, but with the declining economy and the shift to a more Westernized lifestyle, the kimono business was hurt badly. Kimono is now *haregi*, just for Sunday wear. Small *toiya* shops like my father's can't survive nowadays. Still, the kimono business does go on. Well-known artists are able to sell every kimono they produce to some wholesaler, but the return is not so good, and most of us are busy with exhibitions and teaching. I produce kimono twice a year for a wholesaler. In the usual system, kimono go through a great many hands and are marked up five times before ever reaching the customers.

Takaya's work has brought him high praise, and he has regularly won awards in the Kyōten and Shin-kōgeiten exhibitions over the years 1980 to 1991. He is now searching for new ways to exhibit his work. He has decided to withdraw from the traditional Japanese exhibition route, with its many restrictions. This is a serious move. But it is a decision Takaya came to only after a good deal of thought, one starry night when he was alone in the mountains. Since then, his work has taken on a new, unmistakably peaceful quality.

Some rōketsuzome artists are masters of dye application, playing with the shading of color in the manner of accomplished watercolorists. However, the recent work of Mitsuo Takaya is an example of a special shading technique done with wax and pioneered by Takeo Sano, called *han-bōsen* (see page 176). While shading can be achieved with controlled layers of diluted dye, an alternative method is to regulate the thickness of the wax so that dye is allowed to penetrate the surface. This process requires both control and skill, along with an intimate knowledge of the properties of wax and penetration. Working with a mixture of paraffin and *mokurō* wax at a high temperature, Takaya applies the first layer of wax on the reverse side of the fabric. Quickly, before the original coating has hardened, a second layer is applied with a "loaded" brush. Takaya blends this away from the original with a tilted brushing motion, skillfully leaving a varied thick and thin wax application. Lightly waxed areas will accept dye on the front of the fabric, while those more heavily waxed will repel it. Speed is essential since wax can harden in less than twenty seconds, depending upon room conditions. Before applying dye, Takaya "roughs up" the wax surface that has penetrated to the front, using a coarse-bristled brush. Scratching through some of the thinner areas of wax allows varying amounts of dye to penetrate the fabric. Takaya also mixes a small amount of *rōto-yu* (oil) with the dye before brushing it on, to aid in penetration. The results are a startling and unexpected shaded quality.

Yuki Katō

Twin sisters in identical dresses ascend red-carpeted stairs and can be seen at the same time rounding the first, second and third floors; in the left-hand section of the triptych they are glimpsed in a monotone, gray-tiled bath. In the center panel, a nude woman peers out a window as water from an overflowing tub cascades out the door and down marble stairs. In the final section, a smiling woman tiptoes up the staircase late at night while a partly hidden figure waits in an upstairs doorway (see Plate 45).

Ten identical, somber women sit around a long table in a narrow, high-ceilinged room, sharing a meager birthday cake. The sense of foreboding is increased by a strange, ornamented light fixture that casts long shadows down the narrow room. At the far end, a tiny Alice-in-Wonderland door provides the only possible means of escape.

The symbolic sisters of Yuki Katō's work share with us a disturbing narrative of what Katō calls "female rites of passage, with all that fear, jealousy, competition and distress." The Katō interiors, with their tilted ceilings, long shadows and florid wallpaper and carpets, all suggest the kind of fun-house world that is familiar to us from nightmares. Yuki Katō's complex wax resist has been called "psychological narrative art." It elicits a variety of responses from viewers.

> Men rarely comment on my work. At most, they may say that it's curious or interesting. Meanwhile, women get very emotional about it and tell me it's frightening or scary. I guess they really see themselves in these rooms or situations and react. Some may call this a fantasy world, but it's real to me. It's the way I see life.

The quiet, guarded creator of this surprising work in rōketsuzome lives and works in a studio high above Lake Biwa on the outskirts of Kyoto. Her home is full of mementos of her numerous trips through Asia. The lilting music and incense are from China, while the bamboo birdcage collection is from Hong Kong and the lacquer from Vietnam; there are also jade miniatures from Taiwan and statues that were found in Cambodia. Once a year Katō travels alone to other Asian countries, absorbing the colors and textures of places that, in ancient days, influenced her own culture. For the most part she simply watches and takes notes. Occasionally she sketches, but it is mainly the people and relationships she is interested in, rather than the landscape.

> When I was young I was quite interested in Freud, and I do still enjoy psychology and analysis, though not in an academic way. I am always studying relationships and thinking about what is going on. This feeds my work. But

movies are also important. Lately Chinese movies have especially influenced me. I think of my art as movie frames, with each of my paintings being one frame of an ongoing story. Some screens are time sequences, showing the events of an entire evening. In most of the work, I try to put everything into the small space using multiple angles. I try to create mystery and mood, and tell a story the way I see it.

The elder of two sisters, Yuki Katō was born on the northern coast of Japan, in Fukui. She was shy as a child but was fortunate in having an art teacher who recognized her talent and encouraged her. This teacher told her that although life was difficult for women in the arts at that time, there would be a place for them in the field when she was grown. Katō began her college studies in printmaking and graduated in 1975. From 1974 to 1989 she exhibited her prints, winning numerous awards; in the late seventies, however, she became interested in textiles and learned to work with dyes at a Kyoto kimono company. After five years with the company she began doing free-lance work and now supports herself as a colorist, dyeing the detail work for brilliant *yūzen* kimono.

Detail and pattern are a vital part of Katō's work. Architectural detail has fascinated her for years, and she often works with architectural photo books as references for her dyed screens. She adds details such as wallpaper and carpet patterns to her paintings with the specialized resist medium *dakku* and stencils. Light and shadow, multiple viewpoints and a Cubist perspective all contribute to Yuki Katō's fascinating paintings.

Katō does her work on silk fabric using acid dyes. Occasionally she adds natural dyes as well, for their *shibui* (quiet, tasteful) quality. "A final coating of natural dye will often tone down the acid dyes and give me the somber mood I'm looking for." She does not do preliminary sketches but prefers to work on paper the size of her final screen, transferring the idea to her fabric with an *aobana* pen. She works first with the foreground, blocking in shapes and reserving the areas for figures with wax. The wallpaper, carpet and tile patterns that Katō creates are done with a cold resist called *dakku*, a polymer resin (see Advanced Wax-Resist Techniques, page 187). *Dakku* acts as a resist, and can either be applied with a stencil or painted on by hand. Yuki usually mixes dye directly with the *dakku* paste and applies the mixture to the front of the fabric with a brush. She is able to do elaborate patterns this way with freehand drawing, relying occasionally on stencils. Katō first applies her intricate designs in resist, then carefully brushes a background color onto the reverse side of the fabric. *Dakku* is not a strong resist, so it is necessary to apply dye only to the reverse. After the fabric has dried, it is steamed in order to set the dyes and the resist medium.

Figure 27 Keijin Ihaya prepares one section
of a two-panel screen in his city studio.

Tradition

Landscape and lifestyle are changing rapidly in postwar Japan, and yet links to tradition remain strong. Ironically enough, even though the Japanese wax-resist process was only rediscovered this century, tradition often plays a role in bringing artists to the world of rōzome. Quite a few wax-resist artists were born to a life in the textile arts. Yusuke Tange, for instance, was raised in a family of kimono wholesalers. Trained since childhood in the aesthetics of this traditional form of dress, he himself grew up to become a designer of the product that his family had marketed for generations. Some artists emerge from other traditions. Yoshito Tanino's father was a fisherman who worked the northern coastline, and memories of pulling in nets under moonlight continue to fuel the artwork that Yoshito is doing now, some thirty years later. Midori Abe grew up in a house that spilled over with her father's oil paintings and artist friends. She lives at home with her parents, as is common among Japanese women who remain single, and has taken over her father's studio, although her work is in a different medium. In a country that has long required married couples to use the same last name, a custom arose in which promising young men married into a woman's family as "adopted sons," carrying on the family name and business. Katsuji Yamade is one who has observed this old custom, agreeing to help maintain the artistic lineage of his wife's father, another well-known wax-resist artist. Katsuji's style, however, is contemporary and entirely his own. Concern about the destruction of the Japanese landscape is an important source of images for his work. Keijin Ihaya often treats this same theme, holding up a mirror of age-old rice fields to the encroaching urban sprawl. These are thoroughly modern rōzome artists whose exciting new textile art owes a debt of gratitude to tradition.

Yusuke Tange

Yusuke Tange is a Kyoto man through and through, very much the product of an ancient city immersed in textiles. Five centuries ago, the Nishijin weaving district was established in the northwestern sector of the city as the center of Japan's silk-weaving industry, and the area has grown and prospered ever since. Even through Japan's recent economic downturn it supported over twenty thousand working looms spread throughout the district in vast factories and humble home studios.

South of the Imperial Palace is a less well-known, though historic, textile-producing area known as the Muromachi district. It is here that the vast majority of Kyoto's exquisitely dyed kimono are produced. Along the area's east and west borders flow the Hori and Kamo rivers, once well known as sources for the clean, unspoiled water essential to the production of dyed kimono.

Long strips of colored cloth were rinsed daily in these moving waters and colorful kimono lengths were dried along the riverbanks and under the bridges until after World War II. Visitors to the city were told that Kyoto's level of prosperity could be judged by how red the river was—red, that is, with excess dyestuffs from the newly rinsed kimono carried downstream. Now the river is too polluted for the fine silks of Kyoto, and all such rinsing takes place in very long, white-tiled troughs inside the district's many textile processing plants.

Yusuke Tange, textile designer and dyer at the Tange Shin Company, grew up in the Muromachi kimono world. His family has worked for four generations as *toiya*, or kimono wholesalers. Usually such dealers do not design kimono themselves. Instead they bring their acute sense of color and aesthetics, as well as their vast knowledge of dyeing techniques, to the business of commissioning designers and craftsmen. Their personal relationships with artisans and the workers in the processing plants of Muromachi, who together produce commercial kimono, are vital to their livelihood. *Toiya* are the master coordinators of the ten to fifteen possible steps that result in the final product sold wholesale to kimono shops throughout Japan.

Tange grew up in the kimono business. He remembers, as a small child, riding in the bicycle basket as his father made his rounds through the streets of Muromachi, picking up or dropping off rolls of kimono fabric at various processing plants.

> Stops included the *hikizomeya-san*, the background dye painter, the *itomeya-san*, outliner of designs in paste or the *kihatsuya-san*, the worker who removed the wax and steam-set the kimono lengths. I learned the business when I was quite young. At home, I played with my brother and sister among the rolls of kimono fabric. Like typical children, we often got into trouble for using the

large company *soroban* (abacus) as a skateboard or taking dyed *furoshiki* (wrapping cloths) and bamboo rulers to use as Zorro capes and swords.

Yusuke Tange is unusual for someone from a *toiya* family because he has also been trained as an artist/designer. As an independent young man he received a university education but chose to apprentice himself to a rōketsuzome kimono artist at the same time. Every day in addition to his regular university classes, he put in five or six hours at his teacher's dye studio, learning the various techniques needed to design and dye kimono. He studied dye techniques seven days a week throughout the year, and full-time during school holidays. After a total of seven years he began working for himself, designing and producing his own line of rōketsuzome kimono and, later, hiring his own assistants. In 1982, when his production dye studio included seven employees, he was invited to join forces with his family's company, which was then headed by his older brother.

Yusuke Tange's designs come from a lifetime steeped in Muromachi kimono and a love of nature. In the company he produces seasonal designs in a multitude of color variations for the wholesale market to be executed by his workers or various specialty houses. He considers this his commercial work, different from his one-of-a-kind art kimono for exhibitions or special commissions.

Tange's work was first chosen for the Nitten exhibition in 1976; this was followed by a solo show in Kyoto the next year. As a young artist he was selected to demonstrate rōzome for the 1978 World Craft Conference, which was held in Japan. In 1977 he also helped to form Mikumo, a textile group organized to provide a different venue for the experimental work of young *senshoku* artists, to augment the usual, more conservative competitions. Tange has exhibited in the United States as well as in Sydney, Australia, where he led a one-week workshop on the rōketsuzome process.

Tange's work has continued to change through the years, though his outstanding design and dyeing skills have always been a hallmark. His early rōketsuzome work was decidedly modern and used abstract geometric shapes sometimes combined with exquisitely shaded natural forms. In the late seventies he became more interested in materials and produced a number of brilliant, rainbow-hued thread and Plexiglas sculptures. Lately, however, his work has gone back to a concentration on surface design. His exhibition pieces are usually large dyed folding screens, sometimes shown together as walls about 8 meters (25 feet) long, framed single panels or multiple segments of floral or natural forms. Tange's dynamic sense of design and space, along with his precise technical skill in both drawing and dye application, have won him honors as well as juror status at the Shin-kōgeiten (New Craft Association) annual exhibition.

Tange's three roles of businessman, artist and kimono designer are combined in the new modern building erected in 1991 on the site of his first dye studio. The first and second floors house company offices and the dyeing studio, while the third floor, with its panoramic view of the tiled roofs of Muromachi, provides space for Tange's private studio and living quarters for his family.

Yusuke Tange's work is shown in Plate 34.

Yoshito Tanino

Many of the artists who work with the rōketsuzome process were raised by parents who were involved somehow in the field of art. Some worked in metals or clay; others were screen or scroll mounters, and still others were kimono wholesalers. The children grew up surrounded by the world of art, influenced from a young age by constant contact with the aesthetics and materials that were simply a part of their family's business.

But one father was a fisherman and raised his children on the rugged coast of the Japan Sea. Yoshito Tanino is surprised that anyone would be interested in his early years, but his lyrical, flowing designs seem to be a part of the sea of his childhood.

> I remember my father waking the older children at three in the morning, to help him bring in the nets. We lived just thirty meters from the sea and when the catch needed to be hauled in, we were there to help. I was only eleven or twelve and thought it was quite a hardship to get out of my warm bed in the middle of the night, but I did enjoy working with my brothers and sisters in the dark. One of my most vivid memories is of seeing my father, at early dawn, suddenly stop his work, put his hands together and bow toward the sun just as it peeked over the horizon at sunrise. That was a sacred moment for my father.

Artists learn many things from parents. Perseverance, family unity and reverence are strong gifts to carry into adulthood.

Yoshito Tanino left his coastal hometown after junior high school to find his own way in the city. He was hired by a *yūzen* kimono company that generously agreed to send him to the city's dyeing and weaving school for three years of further training. It was a good practical education in dyes, chemistry and mathematics, but it offered little design training. Further study on his own with a well-known oil painter helped Tanino develop his talents. But during one cold winter night of concentrated work, Tanino had a frightening accident with paint fumes after working for hours in an unventilated room. He awoke the next morning to find himself unable to talk or move. From that time, Yoshito could no longer work with oil paint without becoming ill, and his teacher advised him to do creative work only with dye and fabric.

The next year, when Tanino was twenty-four, he was accepted for the first time into the national Nitten exhibition, with a piece called *Night Festival*. Working in his friend's studio after hours, with no heat source for melting wax, he was pushed to devise his own resist medium for his work. Watching traditional Japanese candle makers work with rolled sheets of wax, he realized that wax does not have to be hot in order to work as a resist. The innovative screen the young Tanino completed was more strongly related to his painting studies than to the dyed work of the craft division, and it was received as a bright new vision.

Tanino continues to experiment with resists, using blends of pine resin, non-flammable organic solvents and traditional paraffin to get unusual resist qualities not seen in other artists' work. He prefers to leave the details of the process that creates fascinating and subtle weblike patterns a mystery. Tanino does tell us that in addition to brushing on hot wax, he works with his special wax product, rolling it on or sometimes applying it through paper stencils.

At first Tanino was attracted to the theme of festival and did a series of vibrant abstract screens; however, he is now best known for his powerful work with images inspired by the sea. A recent screen on that theme, *Symphony: Wave and Light*, took first prize in the 1993 Nitten:

> The Japan Sea has so many faces: the winter sea is so different from the sea in the spring. The color and feeling of the sea are clearly different under a full moon or at sunrise. When I feel like sketching, I first go and sit by the sea. After a while, my inspiration comes like a message passed between me and the sea. Later, in my studio, I struggle to express the power and movement I remember. Living so close to the ocean for so many years, it has had a strong influence on me. When I don't see it for a long time I feel a kind of yearning.

Tanino now lives outside a temple in Kyoto's romantic Sagano area, with its famous maple trees and strolling lovers, many miles from his childhood home. His ties to his hometown include regular exhibitions at the local museum and commissions from the prefectural government as well as from local companies and shops. His father has since passed away and his brothers and sisters are now living in various parts of the country, but Tanino still has vivid memories and makes regular pilgrimages to the sea.

Yoshito Tanino's work is shown in Plates 35 and 36.

Katsuji Yamade

In ancient China, artists traditionally selected eight places famous for natural wonder and immortalized them in a set of *sumi-e* ink paintings or on picture scrolls. The paintings were often connected to poetic or seasonal references—the ringing of the evening bells, rain on a summer night or the autumn moon. During the Muromachi period (1333–1573) the Japanese also adopted this custom. Eight picturesque areas in the mountains surrounding Lake Biwa near Kyoto were designated the *Ōmi Hakkei,* or the eight beautiful views of Ōmi.

When young artist Katsuji Yamade went to sketch the "Eight Views of Ōmi" in preparation for a series of dyed screens, he was dismayed to find that three of the original eight locales no longer existed. The pine forest of Awazu had vanished, landfill had eliminated the sailboat view of Mount Hiei at sunset, and the quaint Seto bridge had been replaced by a modern structure where bullet trains flash by at ten-minute intervals.

Faced with the destruction of the environment and the rapid deterioration of the city itself, Yamade began to question Japan's historic love of nature. Completing this series was his way of preserving and celebrating the traditional beauty of rural Kyoto. Yamade had to use ancient paintings for reference, as well as on-site sketches. He also relied on his own vivid imagination to recreate the ancient *Ōmi Hakkei* in a unique and exciting manner.

Trained as an oil painter at the Kyoto City University of Arts, Yamade knew that traditionally the eight views were only reproduced as "fine art" in paint or ink, but he chose to recreate them in rōketsuzome.

> Rōketsu suits my personality. In oil painting you can be persistent, you can repaint again and again, even scraping off the paint if you don't like it. You can search for the effect you want. But in rōketsu you have just one chance. You make a plan at the beginning and then you follow it. There are very few opportunities to correct mistakes or to change your mind. There's a certain clarity there. It's a bit like comparing chowder to a clear Japanese soup, we sometimes say. Yes, rōketsu suits me.

Yamade was first introduced to wax-resist dyeing by Kageo Miura, a professor at his university, during a week-long introduction to dyeing for the college's fine arts students. Following his graduation in 1967 he taught for a few years before meeting renowned rōketsuzome kimono artist Moriji Yamade. Katsuji was impressed by Yamade's work and started doing rōketsuzome himself the next year.

In 1971, the young artist married Yamade's eldest daughter, who was also an art student. In marrying Sekiko, he agreed to become an adopted son and take on the family name of Yamade. Katsuji's parents in Gifu objected at first to what they feared would be the loss of their youngest son. Katsuji insisted that he was not making any essential change but only taking a new name. Some adopted sons feel the burden and responsibility of all that comes with a name and try to compensate by cutting off nearly all contact with their birth family, but Katsuji says he feels that, on the contrary, he has grown closer to his own parents.

Katsuji joins Moriji Yamade every year in a large show at which he exhibits twenty to thirty of his own kimono and obi for sale. He participates in two other kimono shows, for which he also creates fifteen to twenty pieces annually, and exhibits in the national Nitten and three regional shows. In addition, he teaches full-time at the city arts and crafts high school. Yamade is able to meet this staggering schedule with the help of his talented wife, Sekiko, who works at his side in the studio. Given this dedicated support, it is no wonder that Katsuji has been able to produce such consistently outstanding work.

Katsuji Yamade's work is shown in Plate 37.

Keijin Ihaya

Flooded rice paddies reflect the Japanese suburban landscape in bright, sunny hues. A monochrome bank of apartment buildings surrounds a courtyard that is beginning to fill up with snow. A small, forlorn man peers out at the viewer with the eyes of an ancient. The images seem direct and straightforward, but much more lies behind them: travels, impressions, childhood memories and even a beloved teacher's philosophy of life have all contributed to Keijin Ihaya's vision.

Ihaya says his work has no unifying theme, that he simply creates his panels from what attracts him. Forty days in England felt cold and inhospitable, whereas a trip to India overwhelmed him with an impression of a vitality and life force he had not witnessed since he was a small child in postwar Japan. Riding the trains in India, he suddenly remembered his childhood when trains were jam-packed with people streaming out of the city, all carrying goods on their backs, hoping to sell them in the countryside for some vegetables or a little rice to survive. After returning from India, Ihaya did the panel entitled *Man*. For the artist, this is not simply a realistic painting about an old Indian squatting in the dust, but a symbol of survival. "This man *is* life. He is that desire to go on living that I encountered so strongly in India."

A large folding screen created after his experience in England has a very different feeling. His summer in Britain felt so cold and alienating that the work developed into an imaginary courtyard in a blizzard, encircled by tilting apartment blocks in gray and brown. "Even though the work was conceived in summer, the land felt so cold and distant that I chose to use snow to convey this frozen feeling."

Keijin Ihaya lives on Mount Hiei, in a new residential development high above the busy city of Kyoto. He lives in a quiet, unspoiled area, but complains that most modern suburban homes could be found anywhere in the world and lack any distinctive Japanese quality. "One day, on the way home, I saw these modern, sterile tract houses reflected in the rice field and decided to work with that image. *June* is what I came up with" (see Plate 38). The 3 meter (10 foot) screen is done in the blue, orange and greens of a summer day just before a rain. A bird's-eye view shows a jumble of buildings with their wildly varied roofs, crammed onto a narrow peninsula of land that runs between spacious rice fields. All this is edged in bright green growth of summer, and the watery blue fields reflect clouds, birds as well as the contours of the little tract houses. The technique is clear and direct, adding to the immediacy of the image.

Ihaya is aware that many artists enjoy using the numerous refined techniques associated with rōketsuzome but he likes to work in a simple way, letting his unusual design and perspective carry his message. Much of his philosophy on art came from his schooling at Kyoto City University of Arts, where he now teaches. In the mid-1960s, when Ihaya was a student, *katazome* (stencil dyeing) was his focus. Toshijirō Inagaki, who would later be named a living national treasure, had a strong impact on his *katazome* students. Ihaya also fondly remembers his rōketsu-zome teacher, the illustrious Tomonosuke Ogō.

> Ogō-*sensei* was an old man in the 1960s, nearing the end of his life. He showed us the basic rōketsu technique by sharing samples of the various steps. After that he left us alone. He was so big at that time, so highly esteemed that we felt distant from him. Mostly we learned a philosophy of life and an appreciation of the world from him. I was also fortunate to be there when Takeo Sano arrived. Sano was young and vital and taught us more concrete techniques, carefully explaining what we needed to know. At the same time, well-known *katazome* artist Toshijirō Inagaki was also teaching at Geidai. Ogō was a lover of nature and illustrated philosophical points for his students with reference to objects, like the life of a flower or the movement of a bird. Inagaki was a "people person" and active in the politics of the art world. They were very different people with unique personalities as well as unique art styles. During my years at school I concentrated on *katazome*, but after I graduated I realized I didn't have the kind of studio space necessary for stencil dyeing, so I shifted to rōketsu.

It is ironic that space considerations brought Ihaya to work with rōketsuzome, since he now has one of the largest and most luxurious studios we have seen (Figure 27). Twelve years ago he took over the family home just north of the Imperial

Palace grounds, and he has now redesigned this into a beautiful, two-story studio with 5 meter- (18 foot-) high ceilings equipped with skylights. Such space is a true luxury in densely populated Japan, where many families of four live in about 60 square meters (200 square feet) of space, and the smiling Ihaya appreciates his good fortune. In this ideal space, he prepares the full-scale drawings he uses for his large paintings, reworking them many times over to achieve precisely the effect he wants. He renders these drawings in color before finally transferring the designs to fabric. For many years he did his work with silk and acid dyes; he now prefers the colors of fiber-reactive dyes and works primarily with cotton.

The commanding voice of this small, compact artist resonates conviction when he says that there should be no distinction between craft and art. The only real difference, he suggests, is in the intention of the person producing a work. Craft materials may be more difficult to master, he feels, but going beyond the manipulation of materials or use of technique is essential to the production of art. "Of course, technique can help. Limitations of materials can be difficult but can also give you freedom. Ogō and Sano-*sensei* taught us that dye and cloth were just materials, and we must use them to express our own feelings and our own unique style. Maybe these were not their exact words, but they felt strongly that the rōketsu process could be used for work in the fine arts."

Ihaya received recognition for the years he spent developing his concepts and technique when he was awarded the highest honor, the *tokusen* prize, for his latest work, *Waterfall* in the annual Nitten competition.

Midori Abe

Midori Abe grew up around the smell of turpentine, since her father was a graduate of Kyoto City Art College and an active painter. Through her father she met many of the well-known *senshoku* artists when she was still a young child. Abe was able to visit the studio of a neighbor who was a celebrated kimono artist and see kimono being produced there. However, during her formative years, it was classical music and piano that attracted her most; it was only when she was in high school that she realized that her dream of becoming a concert pianist was not realistic, and returned to her roots in art. Abe was talented enough to be accepted at her father's alma mater, where she chose textiles rather than oil painting as her major.

> There are a number of reasons for my involvement with textiles and rōketsu-zome. First, I had early exposure to my father's friends who produced kimono, and kimono is something I have always loved. My grandmother

lived in the Nishijin weaving area of Kyoto and throughout my childhood she sewed new kimono for me at festival time. Secondly, I am attracted to the translucency possible when working with dyes and wax on cloth. I like working with designs where I can create a veil of color, one over another. Finally, I have always enjoyed the many kinds of cloth available. In *nihonga* painting the base is paper, whereas oil paintings are done on canvas. With *senshoku*, I have the flexibility of using silk or linen or even burlap, and those different grounds can give a completely different look to the same design. I find this exciting and appealing.

Born in 1958, Abe is well known for large screens on motifs of flowers and plant life. She has been working with this theme since college and finds that it suits her style of expression well. Abe's hobby is horticulture, and she enjoys the entire cycle of plant life, from seed germination to glorious blossom and mysterious deterioration. She begins her work by simply observing, taking an image in and making it a part of herself, and only later produces it as something directly expressive of her own feelings. Her 1991 folding screen *"Natsubi"* (Days of Summer; see Plate 39) signaled a shift toward greater abstraction and freer interpretation, although she continued to use floral images as her inspiration. Lately the artist's work has also broken away from the standard square frame; she has begun experimenting with wave-shaped screens and at times presents these folded back in unusual ways.

Abe currently teaches at Seian College of Art and Design, but she enjoys working with students of all ages. In past years the industrious young artist has taught six days a week at five different venues—one university, two junior colleges, a private high school and a cultural center—and has still found time to do regular sketching and a number of group shows each year. This often meant working into the night, on Sundays and on vacations, but her efforts have not gone unrecognized; she received awards every year from 1988 to 1993 in the Shin-kōgeiten and in the Kyōten exhibition in 1987, 1992 and 1993, as well as the Outstanding Award of the 1990 Kyoto Craft Biennial. As a result, the Kyoto prefectural government cited her as a leading young artist in 1992. That year, the city's Cultural Encouragement Prize allowed her to travel for two months in Europe, absorbing the museum collections and doing some mountain climbing in the Alps.

Abe speaks excitedly about the new studio that is being built for her across from the family home in the Kyoto suburb of Nishimuko. Since she has completely taken over her father's home studio, he thought it was time to increase their working space. Midori says she must share the new studio with her recently retired father, but then, she has never really minded the smell of turpentine.

Figure 28 The largest room in Chie Ōtani's house doubles as a home studio and living quarters.

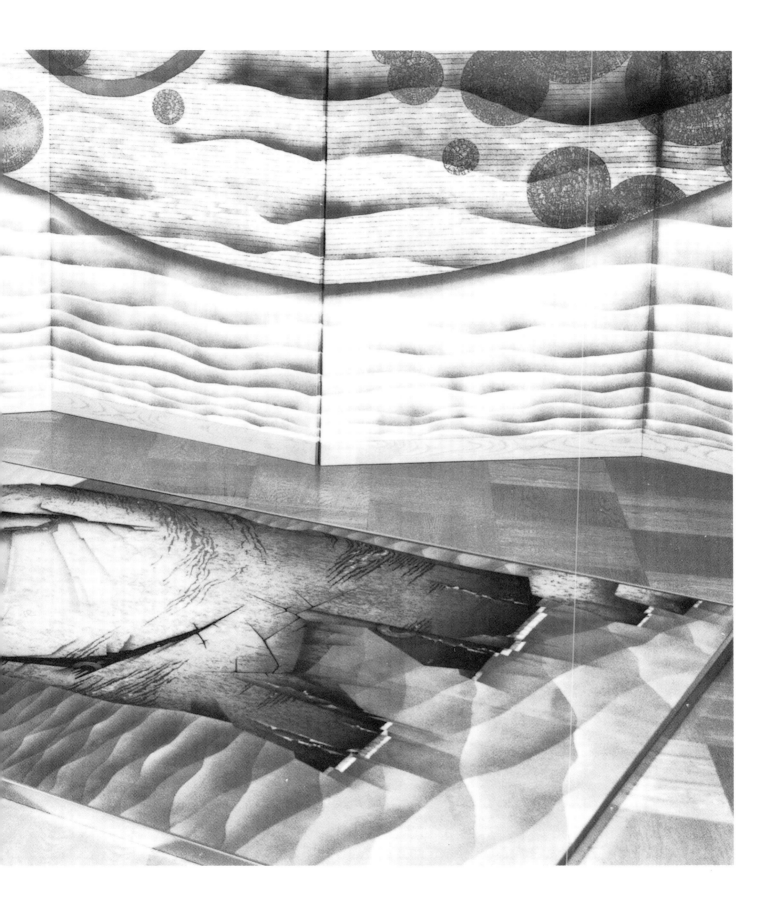

Style

Mature artists in any medium develop an unmistakable style and distinctive images. Rōzome artists are limited to some extent by their materials, but their artistic styles are diverse and exuberant. They work on fabric in a country where fabric arts have been dominated for hundreds of years by the production of kimono. Traditional images of seasonal flowers and grasses and of auspicious symbols connected with various stages of life and seasons of the year are part of every Japanese artist's repertoire, especially those who work with textiles as their ground material. But recently many rōzome artists, particularly those with an education in the fine arts, have begun to create styles and use imagery never seen on silk kimono. Yukiko Komori's bold, graphic abstractions taken from human anatomy have become her signature. Yasuko Iyanaga's liquid geometrics are also done in an abstract style but present an ethereal realm. In a land of mountains and temples, Naomaru Ōkubo's work could become trite if it were not for his special vision. Careful to stay away from what he calls "flashy techniques," he presents his work in a simple, clear style marked by a perspective that is often surprising. Chie Ōtani explores symbols and their meanings and has made an interesting development over the past twenty years from a surreal litany to a more mature personal vocabulary.

Yukiko Komori

The curve of a hip or buttock, a graceful fold of skin at a waist. These add surprising softness to the bold abstract shapes in her work. Squares and triangles break the space into geometrics, while details added with shading enhance the segmented units. The white of the fabric resonates with stark accents of black and primary red and blue. Yukiko Komori's work is powerful and modern and comes from another strain of rōketsuzome tradition, inspired more by the painting of the West than by the silks of Japan.

Komori is an only child who lives with her parents in a small house near Kyoto. Now in mid-career, she says that her parents have given up on her and presume she will never marry, since art is her overriding passion.

> Ever since I was a child I liked drawing pictures, and I first started doing oil paintings in junior high school. In high school I saw a lot of great paintings by professional artists but grew frustrated when I realized how poor mine were in comparison. Through the encouragement of an art teacher, I tried working just with design and pattern and was so intrigued that I joined the textile design department at college.

The classes in design and dyeing seemed to suit her talents, but she soon also discovered drawing classes that worked with the nude body. Wanting more time to sketch in these life-drawing classes, the young Komori slipped into additional classes whenever time permitted. It was not until after graduation, however, that she began to think of combining figure work with dye and fabric. Komori had always perceived the nude through Western painting. It was the work of Matisse, Degas and Picasso that inspired her to try this in the craft medium in which she had been trained.

> At first I was interested in the shape of women, the beauty of a curved line and the way it could be used symbolically. I chose to work with rōketsu as the easiest way to express this flowing line. Because I use repeated shapes in my work, I am often asked why I don't work with *katazome* stencil dyeing, but to me the more sensitive wax line is essential. Rōketsuzome, and the shading techniques that it makes possible, bring out the skin's soft feeling and the depth of color I want.

Like many artists in Japan who must work in small spaces, she creates her larger works in modular units. These modules can then be combined and juxtaposed in dynamic ways to produce paintings up to about 2.5 meters (8 feet) long. Komori originally took the female body as her theme, but her recent work has been more abstract and symbolic. Komori says, however, that she continues to be inspired by the movement she observes in the dance and yoga classes she has attended on and off since 1979.

Komori first received the top award at the 1980 Space Design Competition when it was held at the Tokyo Metropolitan Museum of Art, and has received the Artist Prize in the same competition in each of the past twelve years. In 1992 she had her first solo show, at the Maronie Gallery in Kyoto, and was encouraged by the impact her works had when grouped together, filling an entire gallery space. Komori relates that visitors to the exhibit were surprised to see such modern work in traditional Kyoto, created with an ancient dye process, but in a fresh, new way. **Yukiko Komori's work is shown in Plates 40 and 41.**

Yasuko Iyanaga

Yasuko Iyanaga is uncommon in a number of ways. While the majority of artists working with *senshoku* live in the western area of Kansai, she is one of the few from Tokyo. She does not participate in the traditional Nitten competition, but chooses instead to exhibit her work with the Modern Art Association, where her unique style and presentation immediately set her apart. Finally, as a woman in a world of male artists, she has had to defy the expectations of her parents and Japanese society in simply doing her work.

> Twenty years ago, women married and followed their husband's wishes, but I knew I wanted to maintain my own identity. I knew I would need to find work. I only hoped I could find a career that would interest me and not bury me in moneymaking concerns. Ever since I was a child, I've always loved to draw. A visit to a school friend whose father was a dyer introduced me to the field, which had a strong attraction for me even then. As the youngest of six children, I was given more freedom in my life choices than my siblings. However, my father was quite worried when he realized I was actually serious about a career in art. In the end, my family supported my choice and even became proud of my accomplishments.

Iyanaga's independence and good humor come through in her surprising work. The colors of sea, sun and sky blend in her diamond-shaped, 2 meter- (7 foot-) high wall-hangings. Hot, fuming yellows and magentas peel back to reveal a clouded sky of pale blue. Horizons of turquoise and sea green glow from a three-dimensional box jutting out from the wall. The hazy skies of her native Tokyo were obviously not the inspiration for this radiant work.

Gift From a Southern Island is a series of panels and three-dimensional forms that Iyanaga has been working on since her first visit to Indonesia to see an older sister fifteen years ago (see Plates 42 and 43). She was impressed by this sunny land and by its people and culture, and has returned ten or twelve times to steep herself in the dance, religion and spirit world of the Balinese. This is a world far from removed her Japanese roots.

When she started her current series in 1988, Yasuko watched wave patterns and the reflection of the sky in the sea from early morning to evening. She then internalized all of what she saw, in an effort to express her feelings with her work. The image of peeling back an exterior to reveal the "gifts" within is evident in the latest work. She has seen her line of vision rise and says she feels more preoccupied with the motif of sky following the death of her two elderly parents. Iyanaga's current mood is pensive, and she wonders what new directions her work may take next.

Working on silk with wax and occasionally using stencils and paste resist, Iyanaga has developed a grid series to give the illusion of space through dye application. She finds it difficult to judge color relationships when working with paste, and so prefers wax resist. Originally developed out of necessity, the grid series allowed her to adapt to a small studio space by using modular pieces. Often she was unable to see the impact of a piece, which might be as large as 4.5 meters (15 feet) wide, until it was assembled in a gallery for a solo show. Iyanaga recently moved into a larger studio, which will allow her much greater freedom in the methods she chooses.

Iyanaga has been teaching in a university textile department for twenty years, but she has been frustrated with the pace of her own advancement. She started as an assistant and was assigned office work and many trivial chores before being able to move up to the position of assistant lecturer. "There's some notion among the administration of universities in Japan that women are not serious or dedicated to their careers, which makes it difficult for them to receive promotions." She feels that most Japanese see women as suited only to working as assistants, supporting others. "Discrimination is real."

Iyanaga is pleased to be one of the ten textile members of the Modern Art Association, and she enjoys the equitable nature of this new association, which she sees as very different from the hierarchical structure of the more traditional exhibition groups. She has exhibited her work in the 1989 International Textile Competition in Kyoto and in numerous solo shows in Tokyo and Kyoto as well as in group shows at the Setagaya Art Museum in Tokyo and the Kyoto Municipal Museum of Art. Iyanaga's work has been included in group shows in the United States, Korea and Germany, where it has gained recognition for its unusual color and design.

Naomaru Ōkubo

Purple-fingered shadows reach down into the valleys and run up the slopes of tree-fringed mountains that are immediately recognizable as part of the Japanese landscape. Washes of bright pink highlight the spring hills of muted green, blue and mauve. Clouds in improbable shapes rise at the back of steep mountain ridges. Naomaru Ōkubo's screens are all large-scale works done in flat shapes with a stylized line that has come to serve as his signature. Since about 1992, a curious new element has entered the compositions. This is Ōkubo's own truck, which has begun to spring up as an unlikely motif in his wax-resist exhibition pieces.

In a land of identical small, white cars, the dark green four-wheel drive truck Ōkubo drives tends to stand out. He uses it to get off the road and into the hills where he does the sketches for his unusual 160 by 320 centimeter (5 by 10 foot) screens. Lately, the truck's back wheel cover and interior have themselves become curious elements in Ōkubo's dynamic landscapes. The artist enjoys this juxtaposition of lush landscape and man-made vehicle as an embodiment of the contrasts between traditional and modern life. His most recent painting, for instance, features a thousand-year-old temple gate. Just beyond the gate opening, barely visible, is the front hood of the beloved car (see Plate 44). Even his time off in the mountains with friends or visiting age-old temples doubles as a sketching trip for this committed artist.

Sketching comes naturally to Ōkubo, and he does some every day while his dyes are drying or while he works with the university students whom he teaches part-time. His distinctive style comes from years of sketching as well as his choice of specific technique. Some artists enjoy the fluidity of the dye and the shading abilities of the process called *bokashi*, but he has purposely avoided using this technique. Ōkubo says he has set himself the task of expressing his feelings as straightforwardly and honestly as possible. "I feel that good design is the backbone of good work and I want to eliminate anything that might interfere with this clarity, so I work basically with line and flat form. This has developed into a kind of hallmark, without many people analyzing what I am actually doing." The results call to mind the style of the work done by Tomonosuke Ogō some fifty years earlier. Ōkubo's work has been highly acclaimed and, in recent years, has won over ten awards in the Kyōten, Nitten, Kōfukai and Shin-kōgeiten national and local exhibitions.

Born in 1943 in the northern part of Kyoto, Ōkubo was raised in a creative home environment; his father was a well-known metalworker. Even as a young man Naomaru knew he could never hope to surpass his father's highly esteemed work in the field of metals. "My father knew I had a desire to work in art, so he approached one of his colleagues and arranged for me to study with him." Ōkubo then found himself working as a *deshi*, or apprentice, in a kimono company, an arrangement that was to continue for more than fifteen years. This was not a traditional apprenticeship, however, since the master was a friend of his father's, and young Naomaru was in the studio primarily to receive a broad fine arts education in exchange for daily studio work. The grounding that he received there not only in dyeing techniques, but in design and sketching has served Ōkubo well in the development of a personal style.

> When I was quite young, about twenty, I was producing very abstract work. I did no sketching and took basically a simple-minded approach. I soon saw the limitations of this immature thinking. My work may now appear more realistic, but in fact the landscapes or views are interpretations seen through the filter of my own perspective. I enjoy nature and often remember a special spot I would like to incorporate into work in the future. I go to this place and do detailed drawing of various views. Later I will return to consider the overall line and the particular layout I need. Sometimes I stay overnight. It often takes three trips to get all I want, but now I would never work without my sketches.

Ōkubo also has strong views about working within the context of *kōgei*, or craft, and says that he does not believe that *senshoku* should ever be mixed with what is called fine art. Textile arts should reflect beauty and refinement, he asserts, and a connection to fine art painting could lead to the production of work that tends toward the dark or grotesque. He admires the work of Takeo Sano, Kageo Miura and Tsukio Kitano, and points out that these artists all work with modern themes and in innovative styles but are grounded in the heritage and tradition of Japanese textiles.

Ōkubo has worked hard over the years to develop his own special style and philosophy of working and says he is now just settling back to enjoy his life and art. Over the past four or five years he has gained a new contentment; at the age of fifty-two, he says, he is now producing the work he wanted to create when he first started out. The confidence, maturity and sense of play that are all evident in his latest work would indeed suggest a new ease and comfort with his own vision.

Chie Ōtani

A strange twist of fate made Chie Ōtani an artist rather than a chemist. She had graduated from high school in 1968, the year of widespread student rioting in Japan. Most of the larger universities canceled their entrance exams, forcing top students to sit exams at their second-choice universities and making the competition even stiffer in an already highly competitive system. When young Chie was not accepted to the science courses to which she had applied, her parents insisted that she begin university that year anyway, in art, the area of her secondary interest. Her parents said they did not want to see her spend another year studying for the next entrance exams, and that since it was the desire to create a new dye that had spurred her initial interest in chemistry, perhaps she had been fated to go to art school.

At the time of Ōtani's birth in 1951, her father loved music and her mother had a strong interest in dyeing and textiles. As a young child she was involved in both parents' vocations, playing with her mother's dye pots and taking music lessons from the time she was five. She regularly won children's art exhibitions and so never needed to purchase any art materials, since these were routinely given to the winners of such competitions. A remarkable young woman even in high school, she excelled in science, wrote poetry, published a small magazine with friends and composed music. At that time, Ōtani never imagined she would be an artist or a teacher, the two professions that occupy her now.

While studying for two years at the Nara Junior College of Arts, Ōtani took a part-time job in a kimono company to add to her technical background. After graduating at the age of twenty, she applied to the top three exhibitions in Japan and was immediately accepted, to the surprise of all her contemporaries. The bold and vibrantly colored painting *Poem of the Earth* was accepted in the country's most prestigious art competition, the Nitten. Ōtani was recognized immediately for her skill and unique sense of design, winning coveted awards from the age of twenty-two. She attributes this early success to her approach to exhibitions within the *kōgei*, or craft, division.

> I found many artists competing within very narrow confines. Since college I saw that many artists chose to work in just one particular style. If that is the case then any competition is only about technique or skill and has little to do with individual perspective or concepts. I have always wanted to go beyond limits of that sort. I wanted my art to compete as fine art and not be admired only for its technical skill.

Many serious women artists have had to give up the idea of combining marriage and career, but Ōtani has been fortunate in having a supportive husband. She shares her compact home with her husband, who works as a writer, and with two very pampered cats. The cats have produced a total of fifty-three kittens in eight years, and Ōtani and her husband regularly take time from their busy schedules to scour the country for prospective owners. The center of their home is a large room divided between a small living space and a spacious, high-ceilinged studio (Figure 28). Ōtani's husband enjoys preparing and serving tea in the living area for guests, as if to refute the Japanese sexist stereotype that insists that only women are capable of preparing delicious tea.

In the studio across the wide room, a blood-red sky hovers above a turbulent purple sea in a work done in 1985. The middle ground shows waves curling and breaking to create a fine mist. A surrealistic window casement of stone frames the scene, while, in the foreground, a vivid red flower lies next to a broken violin (see Plate 32). The violin strings rise above it, the way sinuous threads of steam rise from a cup.

> About ten years ago I did that painting, *I Can Hear the Voice of the Sea*. It is located somewhere between reality and a dream. The window frame gives me the chance to look out on a world beyond. I wanted to be able to see the sea again, as I had in my childhood, to be able to smell and hear it. Of course, many artists work with a language of symbols. For a number of years, I used the violin as a symbol in my work. Here it is broken, with its strings floating up into the air. The violin here is something that once made music, but that can no longer be heard. But in my memory it is easy to hear the voice of the sea. I think the sound of the ocean is part of the universe.

Ōtani has always been interested in the language of symbols and the way artists use them. This recently led her to an interest in fractals, or the mathematical shapes that have the same structure under any degree of magnification and whose images can be generated by computer. Following a trip to Nepal in 1985, she also became concerned with the concept of *ki*, or energy. Mandala circles depicting the formation of the universe and meditation hand-positions traditionally thought to encourage the flow of *ki* have since become part of her iconography (see Plate 33). Ōtani has struggled to use her personal symbols to portray an image of the gathering *ki* or energy that surrounds us, wanting to show this energy concentration in dye on fabric.

Ōtani produces from twenty-five to thirty pieces of work a year. She has always been attracted by the *han-bōsen*, or half-resist, process and continues to experiment with this technique. She usually produces three major *byōbu*, or folding screens, ten or twelve pieces of work for an annual solo show, along with a few kimono and many smaller pieces each year. She teaches three days a week, but feels that teaching is nearly the opposite of the creative process, and so finds it difficult to make the weekly transition. "Creating is similar to having a childlike mind, very self-absorbed and solitary, while teaching requires a sociable, gregarious frame of mind." Ōtani feels the obligation to share her thinking, concepts and techniques, and is happiest when she has eager students. This adventurous, contemplative artist is now herself beginning to serve as a model for a new wave of young textile artists in Japan.

MATERIALS AND PROCESS

Wax is the element that distinguishes rōzome from the other resist processes traditionally done in Japan. Other processes use paste applied with a stencil (*katazome*) and a squeeze cone (*yūzenzome*), or binding or stitching (*shibori*) as resists to repel dye and create pattern. Wax and its synthetic derivatives control the flow of dye on cloth in multiple overdyeing baths. To understand the history of this process in Japan it is necessary to look at the importation of wax from the Asian continent, beekeeping, the development of wax candles for lighting homes from about the seventeenth century, and the cultivation later of a native wax plant. All these diverse studies provide background on the history of wax, the one product so necessary to the development of rōzome in Japan.

Historical Uses of Wax in Japan

Rōketsuzome, or *rōkechi*, as it was known in ancient times, requires the use of wax. But the availability of this product in ancient Japan seems to have been very limited. It is supposed that all the *rōkechi* pieces found in the Shōsōin collection were produced with imported beeswax, presumably from China. Bees, however, do appear in the mythology of legendary Japan. The *Kujiki* (an anecdotal source document from which the *Kojiki* was written), lists both bee-repelling and snake-repelling scarves among the ten regalia given by the sun goddess Amaterasu to her descendants upon her descent from heaven (*Kojiki* 407). Presumably, such scarves were used as talismans or fetishes to prevent attacks by dreaded bees. The *Kojiki* also reports the use of bees in the ceremonies marking the initiation of mythological deities. The technique of beekeeping is thought to have been introduced to Japan by Korea around 643 when the Heir Apparent to the Paekche (Korean) throne cultivated four hives of honeybees. However, according to an account in the *Nihongi*, this particular bee colony did not multiply (184).

The existence of bees in Japan would appear to be confirmed by designs of

Figure 29 **Edo-period candle making** Below, one craftsman grinds materials in a traditional earthen bowl. Above, another forms candles by hand around a paper core attached to a wood stick for handling. Reproduction by Kazuma Mitani.

bees and other insects seen on the bronze mirrors produced in Japan and discovered among the Shōsōin treasures. The repository also contains approximately 570 actual cakes of wax twelve hundred years old, listed in the archives as *rōmitsu*, or beeswax. Strung together on cords in bundles of about twenty, these brown, doughnut-shaped cakes ranged in size from approximately nearly 15 to just over 4 centimeters (6 to 1½ inches) in diameter, and were included among the Shōmu emperor's (724–749) household objects. The 1993 catalog *Exhibition of Shōsōin Treasures* describes the cakes as a "wax ingredient separated from *sekimitsu* (crystal sugar obtained from beehives) by adding water to it." Beeswax was "taken internally as a remedy for diarrhea and pyemia (blood poisoning), and used externally as a salve." It was "used also at casting metal objects and as a resist in dyeing" (137). In the following era, honey was considered an elixir of life and sought after by wealthy Heian aristocrats, who were familiar with Chinese medical writings. The *Engishiki* of 927 tells that beekeeping had spread throughout Japan by the early Heian period; however, there is little evidence of the use of beeswax. It was not until many centuries later, during the Edo period, that books on natural history explained the process of honey extraction and encouraged beekeeping, making beeswax available to the common people (Saitō 1: 149).

The use of wax for candles was not popular in Japan until late in the seventeenth century when the wax sumac was first cultivated for this purpose (Dunn 158). Buddhism brought the use of oil lamps to Japan during the sixth century, but initially oil lamps were found only in temples. It was only later that they appeared in public buildings and private homes. The oil, derived from the rapeseed, cottonseed, camellia or perilla, was placed in a saucer with a floating wick of hemp or cotton. Later the first inferior candles were made of hardened pine resin wrapped in bamboo leaves.[112] By the Edo period, the native sumac provided wax for candles created at first with a wick of twisted paper and later with cotton and rush. The paper core was attached to a stick and the candles were turned by hand in molten wax (Figure 29). *Rōsokuya* (candle makers) still form these thin-layer candles by hand into the shape of old oil lamp stands even to this day in traditional shops.

Traditional Wax Production

Mokurō—Native Wax

The wax sumac tree also called *hazenoki* (*Rhus succedanea* L.) is native to Japan and is a member of the same species as the tree that produces lacquer (*Rhus verniciflua* L.); *hazenoki* has been cultivated since ancient times. The importance of this tree as a source of both wax and revenue was recognized by the villagers in Ehime on the island of Shikoku in 1739, according to a document written by Sasaki Genzabei Yoshiyuki. The article says that three *rō* craftsmen were brought from old Hiroshima City to teach the planting and harvesting of the *haze* tree (Uchiko 8). Since raising *haze* fruit was a lucrative side business, by 1830 the areas around the farmhouses and along the riversides were covered with fruit-producing trees.[113] The farmers jointly built a storehouse and purchased equipment needed to squeeze the fruit. By mid-Meiji, production was at its highest. Just as the domestic market began to slump, the need increased abroad for a high-quality bleached product (*hakurō*). *Hakurō* and *mokurō* production were at their height between 1902 and 1906, but following the Russo-Japanese War petroleum waxes were introduced.[114] By 1926 *haze* production ceased in many areas, yet in the 1990s twelve Japanese *rō* factories continue to produce wax for the needs of artists, traditional candle makers, cosmetics companies and the pharmaceuticals industry, as well as the new floppy disc market.

Mokurō Processing

In late fall, when the leaves have all fallen from the trees, ripe bunches of sumac fruit are cut with a sickle about a meter long.[115] The fruit is carefully put through a sieve, spread out to dry and stored. During the winter season the *haze* is pounded into a powder, sieved to remove the hard seeds, steamed and collected into hemp bags. The bag is then put into a press that squeezes the wax from this powder. The yellowish green liquid is heated and processed into *mokurō* cakes for sale in wax shops. *Mokurō* can be further processed into *hakurō*, through a combination of exposure to the air and bleaching in the sun (Inuzuka 44).

Wax for Rōketsuzome

Wax can come from many sources, including plants, animals and minerals as well as new synthetic materials. The Japanese use a wide variety of waxes, and many combinations have been formulated in efforts to create the perfect wax-resist product (Figure 30). Traditionally, beeswax was used until the refinement of the native *mokurō* during the Edo period. Since World War II, paraffin and microcrystalline have been popular among rōzome artists. All artists, however, work with some kind of blended wax. Since traditional Japanese studios are often drafty in winter and sultry during summer, many professional artists have created different

Figure 30 **Wax products available for rōzome** Clockwise from left: paraffin, microcrystalline, *hakurō*, beeswax, Japanese *mokurō* candles, carnauba, pine resin. At center: *mokurō*.

winter and summer wax formulas. Yusuke Tange, Yoshio Tanino and Tadayoshi Yamamoto have each done research into resists and produce their own personal blended wax products.

The perfect wax for rōzome is one that does not drip when the brush is carried from the wax pot to the cloth or spread excessively when applied to the fabric. It should adhere well to fabric, resist the penetration of dye and be reasonably easy to remove later. Crackle patterns are a hallmark of batik, but the majority of Japanese artists consider cracks to be flaws and so look for wax combinations flexible enough not to crack during the dye process. Some artists, however, have explored the various types of cracking patterns that can be created with each type of wax and have used this knowledge to their advantage in their work (Figure 31).

The following are some of the waxes used by Japan's contemporary rōzome artists.

■ **Paraffin wax** (a petroleum product)
This popular, translucent white wax is made from crude petroleum. It is inexpensive and readily available and has one of the lowest melting points (50°C/122°F) of all waxes used in contemporary textile resists. When applied to fabric, it cools quickly and has a hard surface. While an excellent resist against dye penetration, it is less viscous, or adhesive, than some other waxes and can flake off or break, causing unwanted cracks. Paraffin flows onto and penetrates most fabrics very well, but can be difficult to control if fine lines are desired. This is often used as a

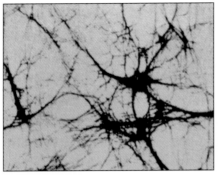

Mokurō 100%

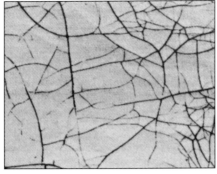

Mokurō 80% and carnauba 20%

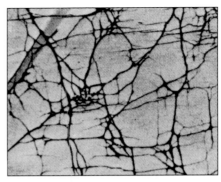

Mokurō 50% and paraffin 50%

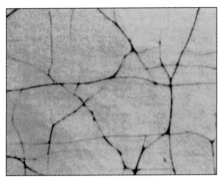

Paraffin 100%

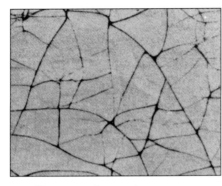

Paraffin 80% and carnauba 20%

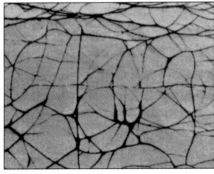

Carnauba wax 100%

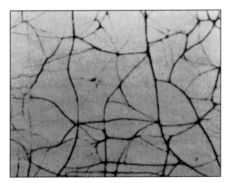

Carnauba 80% and HM wax 20%

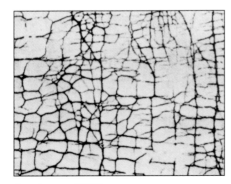

Stearin wax 100%

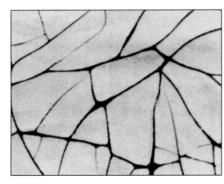

Stearin 80% and carnauba 20%

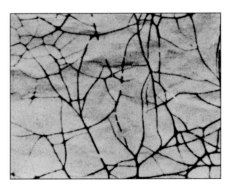

Stearin 50% and paraffin 50%

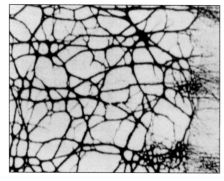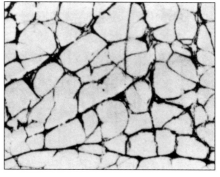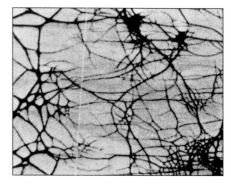

Ibota wax 100%   *Ibota* 80% and carnauba 20%   *Ibota* 50% and paraffin 50%

Figure 31 Examples of the different types of cracks produced with various wax (photographs provided by Seiichirō Takahashi).

base wax, blended with other, more flexible waxes to counteract its rapid flow and its propensity to crack when cooled. There are paraffin waxes that melt at 48°C/120°F and others that melt at 60°C/140°F. The latter are sought-after for use especially during the summer months in Japan.

■ **Beeswax** (honeycomb byproduct; *mitsurō*)
This is a yellow wax secreted by bees in making honeycombs. It has a slightly higher melting point than paraffin (58°C/ 136°F) and is flexible when solidified on fabric, but gives a good cover as a resist. It was traditionally used by the court *rōkechi* workers of ancient Japan, but because of the lack of a beekeeping industry in Japan, beeswax has always been somewhat precious and expensive. Like paraffin, it can cool very quickly and so is easily influenced by cool room temperatures. The sweet smell of *mitsurō* makes it pleasant to work with and the fumes produced by melting beeswax often seem less irritating to those who have had health problems when using petroleum-based waxes.

■ **Microcrystalline wax** (a petroleum product)
This is an amber-colored petroleum byproduct with a high melting point (75°C/167°F). Also known as "sticky wax" or "sculptor's wax," it is very flexible and even sticky after it cools on the fabric. Microwax has strong adhesive qualities and is very resistant to dye penetration. It is a good addition to paraffin-based formulas if an artist wants to avoid cracking and have a good cover. When used by itself, it is difficult to brush on and hard to remove. It seems to be particularly irritating to the respiratory system, perhaps because of the fumes it produces at the high temperatures required for it to melt. For all these reasons, microwax is usually mixed with other waxes.

■ *Mokurō* and *hakurō* wax (products of the wax, or sumac, tree; *Rhus succedanea* L.)
Mokurō, sometimes called "Japanese wax," is actually a natural plant oil in solid form obtained from the pressed fruit of a sumac, or *haze*, tree native to Japan. *Mokurō* is opaque yellow-green in color, is easy to apply to cloth and has a high viscosity.[116] The more refined variety of *hakurō*, also called *sarashirō*, is the white, sun-bleached product of the same tree and is slightly harder or less flexible on fabric. *Mokurō* and *hakurō* melt at 65°C/150°F and have a wide temperature range, making them advantageous for work during summer months. They both produce very soft, undefined cracks. They penetrate cloth well but do not resist

effectively and so are usually combined with other waxes. *Hakurō* is usually used with silk and *mokurō* with cottons, since silks are sometimes stained by the color of *mokurō* (Nakajima 27).

■ **HM wax** (synthetic wax product of Tanaka Nao Co.)
The properties of this white, synthetic wax product are similar to those of micro-crystalline wax. HM wax melts at 80°C/175°F, adheres well to cloth, has a good ability to prevent dye penetration and is soft and flexible when cool. It is an excellent choice for those who want to prevent cracks, and is also easy to remove from the fabric. Dye seldom clings to the surface of fabrics coated with HM wax, which means that it is rarely necessary to wipe off waxed areas after dyeing (Nozaki 244).

■ **Pine resin**
The fragile yellowish brown solid oil or resin that comes from the pine tree is also often blended with other waxes in Japan. Its melting point is very high (80–100°C/ 175–210°F). Pine resin is often added to other waxes to increase viscosity, but too high a ratio of this resin can make brushwork difficult (Nakajima 26). On the other hand, higher concentrations can also create delicate, weblike crackled patterns like those seen in Yoshio Tanino's work. Pine resin is an ingredient in many traditional Indonesian wax formulas, but it is now being replaced in Japan by stearin wax, which is easier to use.

The preceding waxes are regularly used by rōketsuzome artists presently living in Japan. The following, more exotic waxes are also available and are used by more experimental artists in varying amounts, in individual blended formulas.

■ **Stearin wax** (beef tallow and/or soybean oil)
A white, crystalline ester of glycerol and stearic acid is bleached and combined with hydrogen to produce this wax. The quality of this product varies, as do the solidity temperature and melting point, but 55–65°C/130–150°F is usual. It is often sold in flakes or solid blocks. Its ability to resist dye is weak and it readily comes off cloth; however, it is excellent if mixed, especially with stickier waxes that are more difficult to remove after dyeing. Stearin wax is rarely used by itself. Adding 10 percent stearin to a base wax is especially good when some soft wax cracks are desired. The result is said to resemble the veining of blue cheese (Fukumoto 3).

■ **Carnauba wax** (Brazilian wax palm; *Copernicia cerifera*)
This wax is extracted from the leaves of the carnauba palm. About five hundred grams of wax can be produced from a hundred leaves. Three different grades are

available commercially: *ichigō* (pale yellow), *nigō* and *sangō* (brown to brownish green); but it is *ichigō* that is most highly recommended for wax dyeing. The melting point of carnauba wax is very high, at 83–90°C/180–195°F; when cooled on fabric, this wax resists dye well, but it can also be fragile and very hard. Because of its fragility and lack of adhesive qualities, it is usually mixed with paraffin and stearin wax. By adding just 5 percent carnauba wax to a wax that has a low melting point, it is possible to raise the temperature by 10°C/18°F, which is an advantage in very hot weather. Raising the proportion of carnauba to 10 percent or more can produce very delicate, thin cracking effects, like shattered glass. Too much carnauba wax in a blended formula will cause the fabric to curl and the wax to peel off after cooling (Takahashi 42).

■ ***Ibota* wax** (secretion of the *ibota kaigaramushi*, or wax insect; *Ericerus pera*)
Also called Chinese insect wax; this is a white crystal animal wax. It has a very high melting point (80–83°C/176–180°F), is difficult to draw with and loses much of its adhesiveness to cloth if applied too thickly. On the other hand, thin layers can result in narrow cracks that run at right angles to one another.[117] Takahashi suggests adding some HM to *ibota* wax for an interesting effect that resembles a stonewall pattern (42). *Ibota* is usually added to wax formulas, rather than being used by itself.

Synthetic Resists

The following synthetic resists are not wax-based but are used by contemporary artists in conjunction with wax resist and by many companies involved in commercial production of kimono (Figure 32).

■ **Gum arabic** (*gomu nori*; *Acacia arabica*)
Gum arabic is ideal for producing thin lines on rōzome pieces, because gum can easily be dissolved in the same solvents that remove wax. Many Japanese artists feel that gum lines applied through a squeeze cone, as in the *yūzen* method, are easier to control than are those done with the traditional Indonesian batik *canting* tool.

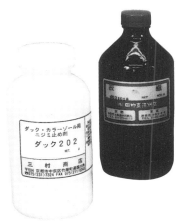

■ **Damor gum** (dammar; *damaru eki*; *Shorea*; *Balanocarpus*; *Hopea*)
This is not a wax but a gum suspended in a volatile oil; nevertheless, it is regarded as a modern substitute for wax. Found primarily in Malaysia, this plant resin is often cloudy brown, though gum of the highest quality is a clear, pale yellow. With practice it is possible to achieve the same effects as with *han-bōsen*, or the half-resist technique, using this gum rather than a hot wax.[118]

■ *Ekirō*
This is an oil-based fluorocarbon resist with an aromatic solvent, used in dyeing as a cold resist. It is widely used as a quick cold resist when dyeing color ways, or

Figure 32 Synthetic resists: *dakku* 202, *ekirō*, damor gum and *rōto-yu* (penetrating oil) used with dye for half-resist processes.

Figure 33 *Ekirō* applied to the reverse side of the fabric to create a shaded resist finish.

samples of dye color for future production. However, this cold resist can also be applied from the reverse of the fabric to create designs similar to those produced with the half-resist technique that uses hot wax (Figure 33). An *ekirō* pen has recently been developed and is being marketed by Tanaka Nao Company.

■ *Dakku* (*fusso jushi*; fluorocarbon polymer)

Dakku is a synthetic, resin-type fluorocarbon polymer developed in the 1960s for use in the Japanese textile industry.[119] It serves as both a cold resist and a color carrier, and can be applied to any fiber; its finishing requires no solvent cleaning. Three products are available, depending on the intended use and the necessary viscosity. The highly viscous Dakku 204 is used for screen printing and for *tsutsugaki*, or application through a squeeze cone. Dakku 202 is moderately sticky and can be used for freehand painting with a brush or stamping. Karāzoru T-100, a thinner *dakku*, is used to lessen the adhesive quality of 202 and 204 and to mix with dye for small detail coloring (*irosashi*). Penetration oil, which is sometimes added to dye, should never be used with any of these products or they may lose their adhesive qualities altogether. Each of these *dakku* synthetic resists may be used alone as a resist or mixed with dyes to make them color carrier resists (see Advanced Wax-Resist Techniques, page 190). *Dakku* provides a cold resist that can be removed without solvent, yet it has a number of drawbacks. Its ability as a resist is less than perfect, since it lacks the dye-repelling qualities of wax or paste. With *dakku*, dyes can only be applied to the reverse of the fabric. And, unlike wax or paste resist, once *dakku* has been applied to the fabric, no other color can be dyed in that area, since a residue of the product remains in the fabric permanently. The finished fabric is soft after washing, but overdyeing is impossible.

Health and Wax

When working with any art materials, it is important to know the properties of the products being used and to take all necessary health precautions. Little has been published for the artist concerning these issues, but awareness is on the rise around the world and some basic information is now available for those working with hot wax.

No matter what its source—mineral, plant or animal—wax is composed of similarly structured organic chemicals that liquefy at various temperatures. If overheated, the large wax molecules begin to break down and decompose. When the temperature continues to increase, decomposition releases a variety of gases, which produce that "hot wax" odor that can be smelled near heated wax pots and also as wax is being ironed out. These gases include acrolein and aldehydes such as formaldehydes and acetaldehyde, which can damage the respiratory tract (Rossol 1). People who are exposed to overheated wax in poorly ventilated rooms—even occasionally or in low doses—will develop more colds and respiratory ailments as a result of irritations of the sinus and respiratory tracts, making them unable to fight off the usual infectious organisms. This is documented by personal experience. Rossol also suggests that exposure to large amounts of these chemicals may cause bronchitis and chemical pneumonia.

Artists are advised to heat wax only to the lowest temperature at which it is possible to achieve the effects desired. Yet even thermostatically controlled wax pots do not eliminate the problem of fumes that result from overheating, since wax at the bottom next to the controls still overheats. Any level at which wax can be smelled burning is considered unhealthy. An exhaust fan is recommended for all work done with hot wax, including the stages of application and of removal of the wax with a hot iron.[120] Respiratory face masks are an additional advantage; however, none have been approved by governmental health organizations because of the range of gases involved. Masks should be used in addition to, rather than in place of, good ventilation. Personal experience has proved the value of this combination.

BASIC WAX APPLICATION AND TOOLS

Wax Brushes

Heat-resistant *rō-fude* (pointed wax brushes) and *rō-bake* (flat wax brushes) are made from sheep hair and are available in various sizes. *Rō-fude* look very much like the *sumi* brushes used for ink work but are far stronger and are not constructed with glue, since glue can melt under the conditions in which rōzome is done. A medium-sized brush with a good point is the most versatile tool for the Japanese rōzome artist.[121] A very fine brush will not hold heat very well and is best used by a skilled worker who is quite familiar with the process of wax resist. Large, flat brushes made of natural hair are good for covering background areas, but it is important to check that the wax has penetrated through to the reverse side of the fabric if your aim is a complete resist. To cover large areas, a coarser brush—for instance, a flat, stiff brush, again made of natural hair—is better than a soft one, since stiffer brushes are better able to force wax into the fabric (Figure 34). The ideal brush for general use should come to a fine point, and with varying pressure should create strokes ranging in size from fine to medium. To keep the point fine, a new brush needs to be "tempered." It is also necessary to re-form the point regularly, after using.

To prepare a new brush for use it is best to take two to three minutes to acclimate it gradually to the temperature of the wax. This can be done by immersing it, then moving it about without touching the hot metal of the pot. Remove it and reshape the point by stroking it against the edge of the pot or a wire strung across the mouth of the pot. If a new brush is simply plunged into very hot wax without care or dragged along the bottom of a heated wax pot, the bristles may curl and grow brittle, making the brush unusable (Figure 35). The bottom of an electric wax pot, or of a gas-fired or double boiler–type pot, becomes extremely hot. Any brush left lying in a heated wax pot will soon be destroyed.

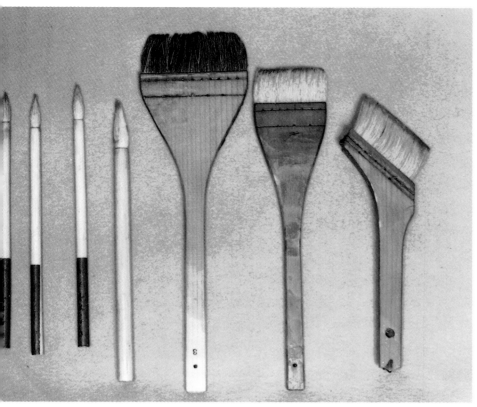

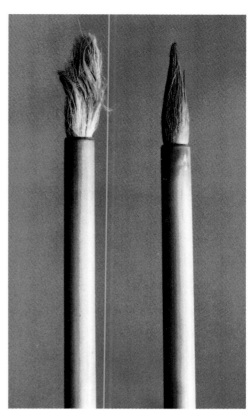

Figure 34 Brushes for use with wax; from left: the pointed *rō-fude* in four sizes, a *shike-bake* for special techniques, two styles of coarse-hair background wax brushes.

Figure 35 This photograph illustrates a wax brush with a good point and one that has become brittle and unusable from being placed in overheated wax over a long period of time.

Figure 36 Illustration showing a good penetration of wax on the left, wax that was too hot in the center, and cool wax on the right that only sits on the top surface of the fabric and has little ability to penetrate.

Wax Drawing

Wax temperature, speed of application and brush technique are all important with rōketsuzome. The brush must be regularly reheated and fresh hot wax must be used in order to penetrate most fabrics. This means returning the brush to the wax source at least every seven to ten seconds, and perhaps more often in a cool room.[122] Skilled artists are able to work with some variations in wax temperature by adapting their speed to the specific conditions without consciously thinking about it. If the brush and wax are somewhat hot, skilled artists will apply the wax line quickly, slowing down their stroke as the brush cools off, and before returning to the pot for more wax. Wax temperature is extremely important, since cold wax will not penetrate cloth and will not resist dye. Cool wax looks white when applied. Wax of the correct temperature will instantly penetrate the cloth and create a dark shape with no white edges. Conversely, wax that is too hot loses its adhesive quality and will soak through fabric too quickly, dripping and depositing lumps of wax on the reverse side. Very hot wax will not remain on the surface or resist well (Figure 36). It will be difficult to control, blurring and spreading beyond the desired line.

To apply wax, brush it on as smoothly as you can, working from the edge of the design outward. Wax cools and hardens in under twenty seconds, so to avoid breaks it is important to work in one area at a time, adding wax while that part is still warm. If the wax has cooled, soften the edge of that area by pressing your hot brush against it, melting and blending it into the next waxed area. Do not outline an entire design and then try to go back and fill in. Sharp corners should be waxed with the brush tip, and broad areas with the body of the brush.

Wax is usually brushed on twice to prevent dye penetration. In the very exacting field of kimono production, it may be applied in three layers, with the first layer being applied to the reverse, and the next two coats to the top to be very sure there is not the slightest possibility of dye penetration that could ruin the design. The second coat of wax should be drawn slightly inside the original edge, to keep it from flowing beyond the design. It should be applied with a light touch, so as not to dissolve the first wax coat. Brush lines should not be evident on the waxed surface or drops of dye may collect in those areas and create problems.

Demonstration of the Basic Steps in *Sekidashi*, or Barrier Resist

A series of photographs of the basic steps in *sekidashi* is given in Plate 55.

After the design has been prepared it should be transferred onto the fabric surface with an *aobana* pen, or onto the reverse with a light charcoal pencil. Areas that are to remain white should be covered with wax at the start. In the series of photos demonstrating this technique, the flower area was first reserved with wax. Next the artist chose to dye the background a pale ochre that would blend well with successive dye layers. The background area was given two coats of wax and then an olive green dye was brushed over the leaf area. After some parts of the leaf area had been covered with wax, a bright green dye was added. That area was then waxed, and the darkest blue-green areas of the leaf and stem pattern were applied. At this point all the wax was removed and the dyes steam-set. Next a ring of wax was painted around the white flower so that dye could be added inside that area without bleeding onto other sections. With the fabric dampened, a very pale gray was brushed on in successive layers in the *bokashi* technique to create a light shading (see the demonstration of the *bokashi* technique, page 202–203). After the palest petals were covered with wax, the darker areas of gray were brushed on to provide a feeling of depth. The area around the flower stamen and pistils was waxed to allow the strong yellow dye to be brushed in and define those parts. At the final stage, all the wax was removed and the piece was steamed and then washed to remove any excess dyestuffs. To complete the work, some stamens were enhanced with *gofun* (shell pigment) to increase their whiteness and the contrast.

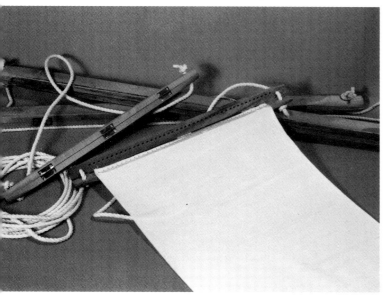

Figure 37 *Harigi* (also called *harite*) or needle-toothed wooden stretcher bars, come in a variety of lengths for narrow-width kimono fabric as well as wider Western-width cloth. The cloth is hooked over the needles to stretch the cloth length-wise.

Figure 38 *Shinshi*, or bamboo tenterhooks, are available in various lengths and diameters, from those that are 40–44 cm. long (15³/₄–17¹/₄ in.), which are used for stretching kimono-width fabric, to those 102–160 cm. long (40–63 in.), used for Western-width fabrics.

Figure 39 *Shinshi* are attached to the reverse of the fabric and used to stretch the cloth from selvage to selvage for dyeing.

Figure 40 Thin nails are embedded in the tip of the *shinshi*, to catch the edge of the fabric.

Frames and Stretching Equipment

Some artists build large wooden frames to stretch the fabric during the wax application and dyeing processes. In Japan, this kind of frame is often used by those dyeing standard-size folding screens of about 160 by 180 centimeters (5¹/₄ by 6 feet). However, artists who want greater flexibility, as well as those rōzome artists with a background in kimono production, often choose the traditional stretching equipment known as *harigi*[123] and *shinshi*. *Harigi* (tension sticks) are needle-toothed stretcher bars that are attached at the ends of the fabric length (Figure 37). *Shinshi* are flexible bamboo tenterhooks with a pin in the tip that stretch fabric across the width (Figures 38–40). This method of stretching narrow-width kimono fabric has been used in Japan since the seventeenth century and possibly earlier.[124] *Harigi* and *shinshi* come in various lengths; for wide, Western fabrics (101 or 121 centimeters/40 or 48 inches in length) as well as for kimono widths (39 centimeters/15 inches long).

Harigi come with and without hinges and can be made at home using wooden bars and stainless steel or brass nails. *Shinshi* are more difficult to make, and there are few alternatives resilient enough to replace the traditional bamboo. However, guidelines for making both types of stretching equipment are given below.

To use *harigi*, the cloth is placed between the stretcher bars and hooked over the protruding nails, and the bars are closed. The *harigi* are then tied securely to a nearby hook or post with additional rope, and the fabric is suspended across the room hammock-style. Traditional dyeing studios all have posts 15 centimeters (6 inches) in diameter running floor to ceiling at both ends of the dyeing room for this purpose. Fabric that has just been dyed can stay stretched and can be slid up the post to dry overhead while another piece is spread below for working. *Shinshi* are attached to the under- or reverse side of the fabric every 10 to 15 centimeters (4 to 6 inches; Figure 39). Newly purchased *harigi* and *shinshi* are usually coated with wax along the bar and the tips. This is to prevent any dye from staining the tools and later being transferred to clean fabric.

MAKING TOOLS

Harigi

Harigi can be made from fir or pine boards 1–2 cm. ($^3/_8$–$^3/_4$ in.) thick and cut 10 cm. (4 in.) longer than your cloth is wide. Hammer stainless steel or brass nails through two lengths of the wood, spacing the nails no more than 2 cm. ($^3/_4$ in.) apart. Pry the two boards apart and enlarge the holes created by the nails with a drill. Drill holes through either end of the bars and attach a length of sturdy cotton rope half again as long as the *harigi*.

Shinshi

The traditional tenterhooks used to stretch fabric from selvage to selvage are inexpensive and available in Japan and the United States where dye supplies are sold (see Suppliers, page 206). As a result, artists rarely make them themselves. However, Nakano and Stephan do describe the method in *Japanese Stencil Dyeing*:

> To make *shinshi* from bamboo poles stocked by garden or import stores . . . choose a thick-walled, uncracked pole. Save the lower, thicker sections for long *shinshi* and cut the thinner-walled segments into pieces for Japanese width fabric. Split with a knife and mallet and then drive a pin or nail into the ends, cutting the excess off in a point. The pin will penetrate more easily if the ends of the bamboo are first immersed in boiling water. If the bamboo cracks, the pin or nail can be secured with a combination of glue and thread.
>
> Pare and sand the bamboo stretchers smooth but do not remove the outer "bark" or skin, since this is a major factor in contributing to bamboo's flexibility. When bending *shinshi*, always make sure the skin is on the outside of the curve, or the stretchers may snap. Large-diameter *shinshi* from Japan may be so unyielding that they must be heated over a gas or electric burner before they can be flexed to a curve (66–67).

ADVANCED WAX-RESIST TECHNIQUES

Sekidashi (Barrier resist)

Barrier resist is the most popular wax-resist technique in Japan. In the *sekidashi* process, large areas of cloth are covered with wax, setting up a barrier that prevents penetration. In complex pieces, this means covering a dyed area with wax to preserve that color and then dyeing additional areas and waxing. In many cases, the background is waxed to stay white while the foreground is dyed with multiple colors. After removing all the wax the white background can then also be dyed, to create a finished wax painting in various colors (Plate 55).

Rōgaki (Wax drawing)

This process uses a brush to apply wax to fabric as if you were drawing, and thus its name, which literally means "wax writing." For this technique, a new, well-shaped brush with a pointed tip is essential; the tip is the part used to draw with. Delicate, subtle line quality can be achieved by varying the pressure placed on the brush, the speed of the stroke and the wax temperature. Wax should be hot enough to penetrate the fabric but not so hot as to spread uncontrollably. The brush commonly used in this technique is the pointed *rō-fude*, which is similar to the brush used in *sumi-e* ink painting (Figure 41).

Men-fuse (Wax surface)

This technique of double coating with wax provides a strong resist. In the sample shown, the area at the bottom was waxed once, while the top received a double coat (Figure 42). If complete blockage of dye penetration is desired, it is always best to cover the area with a double layer of wax. Care must be taken when applying the second coat not to dissolve the first layer, by using a light touch with the brush.

Figure 41 *Rōgaki* (wax drawing) In this technique the *rō-fude*, or pointed brush, is used as a drawing tool, producing both thick and thin lines of resist.

Figure 42 *Men-fuse* (wax surface) In the sample at right, the fabric at the top was covered with two layers of wax, which repelled dye. The area below received just one layer, allowing dye to penetrate. The fabric is shown from the back, to emphasize the difference.

Han-bōsen (Half-resist)

This delicate technique shows the shading that is possible with thick and thin wax application. The variables are the amount of wax on the surface of the fabric, wax temperature and the combination of waxes. A wax with a low melting point, with little resistance to dye, is ideal for this process (see Wax and Synthetic Resist Formulas, page 188). For a continuous, soft flow of color, wax must be applied very quickly; otherwise a seam will be created between the hot and the cooled wax. This means applying the second layer before the first hardens (usually in less than twenty seconds, depending on room conditions). The wax should be hotter than usual (180°C/355°F), but never smoking. For this technique, wax is applied to the back of the fabric and dye to the front. The first application of wax should be thin and even. A second layer can be applied quickly to create shapes or density in desired areas. Tilting the fabric frame to make wax puddle and flow more easily into areas where heavy resist is desired is also possible (Figure 43). A second section can be started once the first has cooled. After applying the wax and before dyeing, rough up the front of the fabric with a coarse brush to break some of the wax surface (Figure 44). Silk requires a light touch. In this technique a few drops of a penetration oil such as *rōto-yu* (turkey red oil) are usually added to the dye before that mixture is brushed onto the fabric (Figures 45–46). The interview with Mitsuo Takaya gives further information.

Figure 43 *Han-bōsen* (half resist) Apply hot wax to the reverse of the fabric. Tilt the stretched fabric allowing the "puddling" of wax in some areas for an effective block-out.

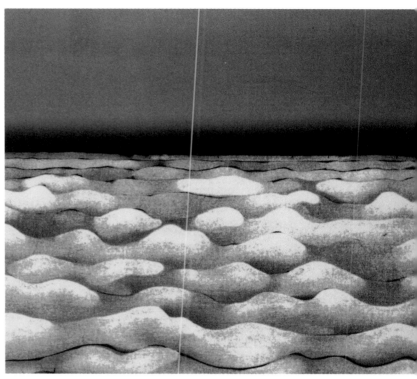

Figure 44 Rough up the front of the cloth with a stiff brush.

Figure 45 Apply dye to the front surface after adding a few drops of penetrating oil to it. This will help the dye to break through the wax surface.

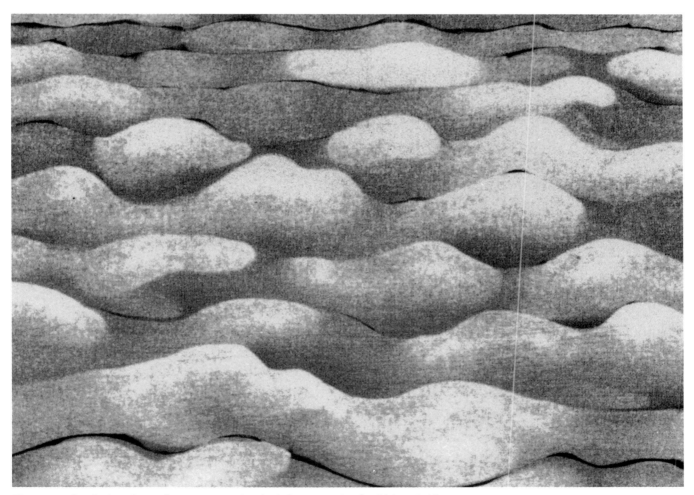

Figure 46 After dyeing, the surface appears to be shaded, as a result of a thick-and-thin wax application and the *han-bōsen* effect.

Rōkata (Wax stencil)

In this technique, wax is applied with a stencil or brush. While traditional stencil dyeing (*katazome*) is done using *shibugami* paper and *nori* paste, the stencils for *rōkata* can be made with heavier stock paper. *Kentōshi* or *bōrugami* (glossy card stock or thin cardboard) work especially well. Trace the desired pattern on the stencil paper, then place the paper on a plastic cutting mat or piece of cardboard and cut out the pattern with an Exacto knife, changing blades as needed (Figure 47). The stencil can then be taped carefully to the cloth and wax sprinkled over it, as in the *fubuki* process (Figures 48–50); alternatively, wax can be dabbed over it with any of a variety of applicators. A wax applicator, or *tanpo*, can be made by covering a wooden block with sponge, cloth, felt, and/or cotton toweling (Figures 51–52). Attaching a handle makes the wooden applicator easier to use. All wax tools must be heated well in the wax pot and the excess wax squeezed out before they can be used on the stencil (Figure 53). The results *of rōkata* created with a *tanpo* and the *fubuki* technique can be quite different (Figure 54). In addition to cut stencils, artists like Shigeki Fukumoto also use a nonsticky tape as a quick stencil to mask off areas before applying wax.

Figure 47 Cut stencils for wax application from cardstock or thin cardboard.

Figure 48 Sprinkle hot wax over the surface by tapping the brush against a dowel.

Figure 49 Remove the stencil carefully before the wax hardens completely (20 seconds).

Figure 50 After dyeing, the negative image of the stencil pattern is readily visible.

Rō-fubuki (Wax snowstorm)

Sprinkling or splattering wax onto fabric can be done with a variety of tools.[125] This technique requires a flip of the tip of the wax brush to create a fine spray of wax. The wax should be hotter than usual for good penetration, since airborne wax cools quickly. Tap the wax brush across a dowel stick or the handle of an additional brush to create fine droplets of wax. Shizu Nakajima suggests working with three wax brushes taped together in a row to cover a larger area quickly (57–59). For a consistent cover and wax dots of a uniform size, care must be taken to wipe off the brush properly and to use the same amount of force and a regular tapping rhythm while working over the entire area. A dynamic variation on the process using a bamboo or hemp palm broom is also done in Japan. To splatter large drops in random patterns, cut a broom (*hōki*) to shape and dip in wax. When using a broom, wax must be very hot and must be flicked with a forceful motion of the wrist to get it onto the fabric quickly. Waiting a number of seconds for the wax to harden each time before continuing gives the best results. Dye can be applied between layers of dots for an interesting, textured effect. Shigeki Fukumoto often uses this technique coupled with his hand-cut stencils.

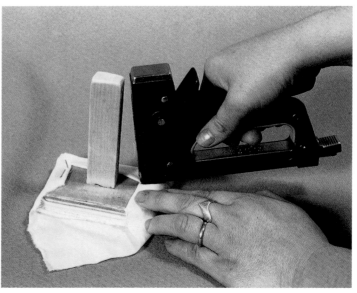

Figure 51 A piece of felt, toweling and cotton cloth are used to make a wax applicator.

Figure 52 The edges are stapled to the wooden base.

Figure 53 First the applicator is thoroughly heated in a wax pot. Then the excess wax is stamped out and the applicator pressed quickly onto the stencil and cloth.

Figure 54 The completed piece.

Figure 55 *Rō* etching is produced by breaking through the wax surface with a blunt needle or nail while being careful not to cut the fabric.

Figure 56 A few drops of penetrating oil mixed with the dye will allow the color to come through, showing the etched design.

Rō Etching (Scrafitto)

Wax etching is done by cutting through a layer of wax with a blunt tool, breaking the wax surface, and allowing dye to penetrate the line. The engraving tool can be a nail, a woodblock carving tool (an engraving needle, a triangle or a round point) or a handmade tool. In Japan, a large sewing needle is often slipped into a soft, disposable wooden chopstick (*waribashi*) and then filed to the correct point. A *shinshi*, or bamboo tenterhook consisting of a short needle embedded in a wooden stick, may also be used. To create the etching, brush wax onto the fabric as evenly as possible. Next, place the sketch and the waxed fabric on a linoleum square or wooden board and trace the design onto the fabric with the needle tool (Figure 55). Care must be taken, when scratching through the wax, to avoid cutting or damaging the fabric. A dark dye with a few drops of *rōto-yu* (penetrating oil) added should then be brushed on the fabric (Figure 56). A thin but densely woven fabric is best for good results with this technique.

Figure 57 For *rō-shibori*, sew running stitches to define a pattern or shape and then pull them up tightly and knot. Wrap the additional thread around the point to compress the end well.

Figure 58 Dip bound cloth into wax twice, being sure not to go above the stitched line.

Figure 59 Remove the stitching and open the cloth carefully before dyeing. Wax-covered areas resist the dye and produce patterns different from cloth dyed only with *shibori*. Often the reverse side is more interesting than the top.

Rō-shibori (Wax tie-dye)

Cloth may be folded, bound or stitched using the various *shibori* techniques and then dipped into wax and dyed to create unusual patterns (see Plate 25).[126] In the case of *nui* (stitched) *shibori*, a pattern of stitched lines is sewn in a simple running stitch with strong cotton thread. Next the stitches are pulled up and tied tightly (Figure 57). Binding the excess fabric is an option. The piece is then carefully dipped into wax (120–130°C/250–265°F), up to the stitched line (Figure 58). The wax creeps up the cloth quickly, so watch it carefully and remove it as soon as it has penetrated the sewn area. This process should be repeated two or three times. Nakajima suggests lowering the temperature of the wax after the first dip to 90–100°C/195–210°F to thicken the part where the hot wax has penetrated and create a thin, even coat (60). After the wax is cooled, the cords should be cut and the cloth carefully spread out and attached to *shinshi* and *harigi* or a frame for dyeing (Figure 59). Often, the reverse side of the fabric is the more interesting. (For wax blends used in *rō-shibori*, see page 189.)

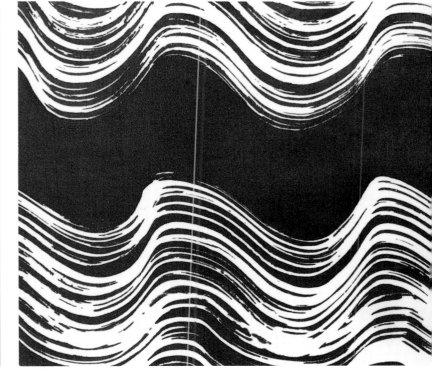

Figures 60a/60b/60c A *shike-bake*, or trailing brush, can produce patterns and dry brush effects on fabric.

Shikebiki (Coarse brush-trailing)

This technique is done with a *shike-bake*, a special brush made of deer hair and imported from Southeast Asia. Due to current restrictions, this brush is more costly than most others. It is a stiff, long-bristled, flat brush that can, with practice, be used to produce a fine, dry-brush effect. The brush is heated in the wax, wiped off well on the edge of the pot and then dragged lightly across the fabric surface (Figure 60a). Interesting qualities can result from layering wax and dye and trailing the brush at right angles, creating cross patterns (Figures 60b–60c).

Figure 61 For paste/wax resist, first apply paste to the fabric through a cut stencil.

Figure 63 Soak the fabric in water and dissolve the paste areas; a stiff brush will help to remove these areas. What remains is a negative wax stencil that will resist the dye.

Figure 62 After the paste has dried, lightly brush hot wax over the entire surface.

Figure 64 The finished dyed piece.

Gyaku-rō (Backward resist)

This interesting technique involves applying paste to fabric through a squeeze cone or stencil (Figure 61) and, after the paste has dried, applying a coat of wax to the surface (Figure 62). When the work is placed in water, the paste will dissolve, lifting the wax as well from the stenciled areas (Figure 63). Dye can then be applied to areas where the paste had been. The result is a controlled, yet soft-edged design that cannot be produced with wax stencils alone (Figure 64). Nozaki suggests adding a little sodium alginate (*fu-nori*) to the paste to make removal easier (258). (For directions on how to mix paste, see Wax and Synthetic Resist Formulas, pages 188–191).

Figure 65 Blocks for stamping wax on fabric can be made from wood, metal or clay.

Figure 66 Wax-stamped cloth after dyeing and wax removal.

Han (Stamps)

Wax stamping has been done since the Nara period (710–794) in Japan and earlier in India, Egypt and China. The stamps used for the Shōsōin *rōkechi* work are believed to have been wooden, but contemporary artists have successfully reproduced the designs seen in that ancient collection with stamps made of metal. Stamps made from wood, fired clay and metal all work well with wax. Traditional *hō* wood (magnolia) and cork are good for carving patterns. To use a stamp with wax, the block should be thoroughly heated and excess wax shaken or stamped off in a preliminary printing. A pad of smooth newspapers beneath the cloth gives a good stamping base. Traditional metal Indonesian *cap* are especially complex and wonderful to use, although many improvised metal tools such as kitchen utensils, nails, sieves and hardware can also be used to produce interesting patterns (Figures 65–66).

Figure 67 Cloth-wrapped rollers can produce unusual resists. To begin, heat the roller in the wax pot; roll the wax on in small sections.

Figure 68 Patterns or lines in roller-applied wax resist come from the thread that binds the cloth to the roller.

Wax Rollers

Wax can be applied with a roller in addition to brushes and stamps. A traditional linoleum or block printing roller is usually used. Some Japanese also create their own wooden rollers, 14 centimeters (5½ inches) long by 4 centimeters (1½ inches) in diameter, attaching a thick wire handle. Yasuhiko Tanaka, however, works with commercial gum rollers that he wraps with a thin cotton cloth and secures with fine thread (Figure 67). With this technique, wax must be quite hot in order to be rolled onto the fabric (150°C/300°F). It is important to heat the roller thoroughly before beginning. The wax will roll onto the fabric with some variations in thickness, so Tanaka suggests working in small sections and returning the roller to the wax source often for good coverage (see Wax and Synthetic Resist Formulas for roller blends). Heavier cotton cord and felt shapes wrapped around a roller also produce interesting patterns (Figure 68).

Figure 69 *Dakku* resist applied through a stencil on the reverse side of the fabric and then brush dyed from the top.

Dakku Resist

Various techniques can be used to apply this new synthetic cold resist: hand-painting with a brush, stamping, squeeze-cone application, spraying and screen printing. Yuki Katō often uses *dakku* with hand-cut stencils to create elaborate wallpaper-like patterns (see Figure 69 and also Plate 45). With this product, resist application is done from the front of the cloth, while dyeing is done from the reverse side.

Dakku can also be used as a color carrier resist; in other words, it can be mixed with color so that it resists and dyes at the same time. Then, once the *dakku* mixture has dried, another color may be applied to the background from the back of the fabric. Tanaka Nao Company has three products designed with various viscosities appropriate for different methods of applying wax.

Karāzoru T-100   For application by brush or sprayed as a resist, or mixed with dye for color detail work; also used to dilute the stickiness of other *dakku* products; not viscous.

Dakku 202   For application by brush or stamp; moderately adhesive.

Dakku 204   For screen printing of line drawing with a squeeze cone (*tsutsugaki*), use alone or mixed with Karāzoru T-100. Thick and highly viscous.[127]

Wax and Synthetic Resist Formulas

Many artists have their own personal wax formulas adapted to the particular wax application process and fabric type they like to use. The following is a sample of the variety of formulas created by contemporary rōzome artists for different wax-resist techniques.

Basic Wax Formula

mokurō	60–70%
or *hakurō*	
paraffin	40–30%

This is a basic formula, but Shūji Asada suggests including 20% microwax if you want a stronger resist and no cracks (Asada 118). Always adjust the proportions according to the materials and techniques used. If your wax peels off easily, add more *mokurō*. If you want some dye penetration, as for instance in *han-bōsen*, etching, *fubuki* or *rō-shibori*, avoid microwax altogether.

Tange Cover Wax

Winter		Summer	
paraffin	40%	paraffin	70%
microwax	60%	microwax	30%
HM wax	some		
ryūdō	some		

In the course of his work in kimono production, Tange has developed a wax formula that allows for excellent coverage with no cracking. He is able to roll or even fold waxed fabric without cracking the surface. His addition of *ryūdō* to slow the cooling of the wax on the brush in wintertime is innovative. *Ryūdō* has medicinal properties and is available at pharmacies under the names liquid paraffin or mineral oil. Tange cautions that varying climatic locations may necessitate changes in wax formulas.

Takaya *Han-bōsen* (Half-resist)

Winter		Summer	
paraffin	50%	paraffin	70–60%
mokurō	30%	*mokurō*	30–40%
microwax	20%		

When doing half-resist, Takaya uses very high temperatures (150–180°C/300–355°F) to create unusually thin wax.

Tanaka Roller Wax

paraffin	70%
microwax	30%

Wax must be quite hot (150°C/300°F) before being rolled onto the fabric. It is important to heat the roller thoroughly and to work only in small sections, returning to the wax source frequently.

Nakajima *Rō-shibori* Wax

paraffin	70–80%
mokurō	30–20%
pine resin	about 1 teaspoon per wax pot

Wax should be heated to 120–130°C (250–265°F) for the initial dipping of the *shibori* bound areas. Later, for the final dipping, the temperature should be lowered to 90 to 100°C (195–210°F) to allow for a good coating (Nakajima 60).

Basic Paste for *Gyaku-rō*

To prepare about 500 cc (2½ cups) of nori paste for application to fabric.

rice flour (*mochikō*)	120 g (1 cup)
rice bran (*nuka*)	150 g (1½ cups)
cold water	about 120–175 ml (½–¾ cups)
hot water	about 80 ml (⅓ cup)
salt	about 40 g (2 tablespoons) dissolved in a little hot water
calcium hydroxide	20 or more g (2 or more tablespoons) dissolved in 120 ml (½ cup) water

1. Sift rice flour and bran; mix well.
2. Add the cold water a little at a time while kneading.
3. Shape dough into doughnut shapes.
4. Wrap doughnut shapes in a damp cloth and steam 50–60 minutes.
5. After steaming and while they are still are hot, pound doughnuts into paste.
6. Add the hot water and the salt solution, beat well.
7. Skim some water from the top water of the calcium hydroxide solution and add just enough to turn the paste a glossy mustard yellow. Do not add any calcium hydroxide powder.

Apply the paste through a stencil with a wooden spatula (*hera*) or through a squeeze cone (*tsutsu*). The mixture can be covered with a film of plastic wrap and refrigerated for a number of weeks, but fresh paste is best to work with.

Dakku Resist

1. Mix *dakku* with Karāzoru to lessen the stickiness or with water to thin. It can also be used directly from the bottle. Shake well before using, as it is known to separate.
2. Apply to fabric using brush, stamp, spray, squeeze cone or silk screen.
3. Allow to dry thoroughly.
4. Apply dye from the reverse side of the fabric with *dakku* added (a one-to-one ratio); use care when rubbing over the resist areas as this is not a strong resist.
5. Steam to set dyes if necessary for dye group. Soak in fixer if required.
6. Rinse with water and line dry.

To use *dakku* for *irosashi* or as a color carrier

Prepare dye solution to desired color; add *dakku* in equal parts (a one-to-one ratio).

To thin, add water; to lessen the stickiness, add Karāzoru; for deeper color, add dye or pigment.

Application

1. Prepare drawing on fabric.
2. Paint colors on desired areas; never use a penetrating oil with *dakku*.
3. Dry thoroughly and steam for 30 minutes.
4. After steaming, turn cloth over and apply background color that has been mixed with *dakku* (in a one-to-one ratio). Be careful not to rub excessively onto areas already dyed. Some background dye may cling to the original dye but the top side should remain clear.
5. After dyeing, rub cloth (front) lightly with a dry brush.
6. Dry thoroughly; steam for 30 minutes, or for deeper shades, 60 minutes.
7. Rinse with water and line dry.

For ground pigments (resin *ganryō*) using brush application or stamps:

Dakku 202	40% (mix with *ganryō* pigments)
Karāzoru T-100	40%
Haipuren A (binder)	20%

For screen printing:

Dakku 204	60–80% (mix with dye)
Karāzoru T-100	20–0%
Haipuren A (binder)	20%

Wax Removal

Having a professional dry-cleaning company remove your wax is ideal. If cost or other considerations force you to deal with this yourself, here are some guidelines

1. Iron your fabric between layers of unprinted, absorbent paper, removing the layers, top and bottom, as they become saturated with wax. Always do this in a well-ventilated area, working in front of a window exhaust fan or outdoors.

2. For cotton and linen fabrics dyed with fiber-reactive dyes that have been set, add some washing soda (sodium bicarbonate) to boiling water, dip the fabrics in once and then remove them. Cool the water, skim the surface free of cold wax, reheat and dip the fabrics again.

3. After you have repeated this step a number of times, the piece may be washed in hot, soapy water and rinsed. Always collect the cold wax by skimming it off. Never pour wax down a sink drain.

4. For silk and other dyes that cannot withstand boiling, wax can be ironed out between sheets of plain paper and the fabric then may be carefully soaped in very warm water. Further wax removal requires the use of solvents and should, ideally, be done by a professional dry-cleaning establishment. White gas, kerosene and the dry-cleaning solvent perchloroethylene have all been used but require extreme care. These solvents are highly toxic solvents and are flammable. Ventilation equipment, solvent storage and required fire protection should be available in the studio before beginning. In Japan, many art colleges have outdoor facilities where N-11 solvent is heated in special trays to 40°C/105°F for wax removal.

DYES AND PIGMENTS

Before the development of synthetic dyes made from coal tar by William Perkin in 1850, all coloring of fabric was done with natural dyes. Even today, the more traditional *katazome* and *shibori* artists continue to use natural dyes, while the more experimental rōzome artists choose from chemical and dyes as well as pigments for their color. Teiji Nakai works only with indigo dye for his large rōzome screens (see Plate 20), but Kageo Miura uses natural dyes in the background of his panels and pigment in the foreground, and chemical dyes for the art that he does on kimono. Kohrow Kawata and Yuki Katō combine chemical and natural dyes in a single piece. Many of the artists enjoy the vibrancy of the new chemical dyes, but Katō says she uses natural dyes when she wants "a quieter, more restrained effect."

The majority of work by contemporary rōzome artists, however, is done with chemical dyes such as acid, pre-metalized, fiber-reactive or direct dyes (Figure 70). Since the introduction of such dyes in Japan from Germany in the early twentieth century, artists have appreciated the variety of intense colors as well as the permanency of these dyes. The following is meant to be a short introduction to the various dyes and pigments used to create rōzome in Japan. Each fiber group (plant, animal and synthetic) has a specific dye used to color it permanently. Often a chemical (such as salt, carbonate of soda, acetic acid, etc.) is needed to assist in penetrating the fiber. In addition, steaming may be necessary to "set" the dyes and bond them to the fiber. Detailed instructions on preparation and usage of chemical dyes can be obtained at the time of purchase or can be requested from the sources listed under Suppliers in the Appendix (page 206).

Acid Dyes (*Sansei senryō*)

Acid dyes are used with protein fibers such as silk and are the main dyes of the kimono industry. They are bright, intense dyes with a wide color range and moderate resistance to fading. They are only fairly washfast, and for this reason acid-

Figure 70 Acid dyes used for silk fabric. Clockwise from left: dry powdered dyes, dyes added to water to form a stock solution, a spray pump for applying water to keep fabric damp during dye application, dye color charts, a test strip of prepared colors, dyes prepared for use on work with one brush for each color, a pipette for taking small amounts of dye from stock solution bottles.

dyed silk fabric is usually dry cleaned. Often pre-metalized dyes (brand names: Cibalan and Irgalan) are blended with acid dyes, extending the color range into deep, muted colors and giving better washfastness. To prepare, mix a stock solution of 1–4 percent (10–40 grams per liter, or about $1/2$ to 2 ounces per quart) and thin as needed for application. Make the dye into a paste by dissolving it in a small amount of hot water in an enamel or stainless-steel container. Add the required amount of water, stir well and bring it to a boil. Allow the dye to reduce in volume by simmering for 5–10 minutes. Cool and pour into glass storage jars that can then be closed tightly. If the dye should become cloudy or coagulate, as some colors do, reheat the dye and it will clear. Steaming is necessary to set the dyes. The brand names available are Deluxe, Miyako and Kiton.

Fiber-reactive Dyes (*Hannōsei senryō*)

These dyes are unique in that they react with the fiber molecule and create a chemical bond. They are more fast to light and washing than are acid dyes and bond best with cellulosic fibers such as cotton and linen. Used in a 1–6 percent solution as a rule, some deep colors, such as navy and black, may require as much as 8 or 9 percent. During the dyeing process, an alkali (salt) and a fixer (such as washing soda, soda ash or sodium bicarbonate) are added to make the dye react with the fiber. Because of their reactive nature, these dyes must be mixed fresh each time and discarded after six hours, so stock solutions cannot be prepared. It is best to dye the cloth slightly darker than the shade that you actually want, since some excess dye comes off during rinsing. The color can be set by applying the gel RC Fixer to the surface of the fabric; next, cover the fabric with plastic for three hours and then rinse it thoroughly until no more color is released. Fiber-reactive dyes are produced under the brand names Remazōru, Han'nōru-F, Procion, Abacron and Dylon).

Direct Dyes (*Chokusetsu senryō*)

Direct dyes are strong dyes that work well with cellulosic fibers such as cotton and linen and less well with silk. One advantage of direct dyes is that the intensity of color is obvious when it is first applied, and very little is removed during the steaming and rinsing process. The colors, however, are not as bright as those obtained with acid or fiber-reactive dyes, and certain colors have been connected with cancer-causing benzidine dyes that make up this dye class. Direct dyes dissolve easily in water and prepared stock solutions can be kept for later use. The German Sirius brand (Bayer), available in Japan, has a good reputation for fade resistance. Washability can be improved if treated with a fixer (such as Fixanol ICI, Lyofix Ciba-Geigy, MS Powder and the Japanese products Ami-fix Seiwa and Amigen Tanaka Nao). Stock solutions can be prepared in the same way as acid dyes but are used in a concentration of 1 to 2 percent (10–20 grams per liter, or about $1/2$–1 ounce per quart). Direct dyes require steaming to set the color. Sirius, Roapas D, Miyako and Ciba Chlorantine are the brands available.

Naphthol Dyes (*Nafutōru senryō*)

These dyes (also called azoic) are extremely fast on plant fibers such as linen and cotton, and so are used on textiles that may require repeated washing or exposure to the elements, such as flags, door hangers (*noren*), tablecloths and cushion covers. Because the dye is a two-step process using a colorless napthol solution and "fast color salt," it is not possible to know the final color without consulting a color chart.[128] The dye bath can be reused for approximately six hours but requires the use of caustic soda (sodium hydroxide), which can be dangerous if not used carefully. Dyes that are easier to use have all but replaced naphthol dyes in Japan.

Vat Dyes (*Batto senryō*)

Vat dyes, like naphthol, are extremely fast to light and washing but are rarely used anymore except in a few rural areas of Japan. They are insoluble in water with no affinity to fibers until they are reduced or "vatted." After the fabric has been saturated, exposure to air will develop the color. Indigo is one type of vat dye. Brand names that are available are Cibanone, Soledon, Durindone, Caledone and In-kodye.

Indigo (*Ai*)

Indigo is one of the oldest dyestuffs and is more technologically complex than any other. It is also one of the world's most widely used dyes (Balfour-Paul 98). Indigo produces a strong bond with plant fiber (cotton, linen, flax, hemp) in its soluble state. The name is commonly used to refer to more than fifty varieties of herbaceous shrubs containing indican, and it comes from the Greek word *"indikon,"* which refers to a substance from India, the land that exported indigo to the classical world. Indican is a colorless substance that turns blue when oxidized and is found in the fresh leaves. The need to create a stable, long-lasting dye bath forced dyers to learn how to ferment the leaves in vats, removing the oxygen and thereby converting it into a colorless leuco-form of the dye called indigotin. This is then soluble in an alkaline (lye) solution. The *Indigofera tinctoria*, native to India and found on Egyptian textiles as early as 2500 B.C., was introduced to Japan in the nineteenth century. In prehistoric Japan, blue was initially found in the *yama ai* (mountain indigo; *Mercurialis leiocarpa Sieb. et Zucc.*) applied to fabric by rubbing the cloth with fresh leaves. It was considered a sacred dye and is reported to have been used on the purified ceremonial garments worn by emperors at their enthronement.[129] In the fourth or fifth century, a true indigo, *tade ai* (buckwheat or Japanese indigo; *Polygonum tinctorium Lour.*) was imported from China. *Tade ai* is used as fresh leaves (*namahazome*), in a fermented vat or as composted dried leaves (*sukumo*) in a vat of lye water. Other materials such as saké and bran may be added to encourage fermentation and the growth of the necessary bacteria. Indigo was one of the last dyes to be synthesized by dye chemists in 1897.

Vegetable Dyes (*Shokubutsu senryō; kusakizome*)

Before the development of synthetic dyes in 1850, all dyes came from natural sources. Over one hundred different plant varieties are listed in ancient records, which suggests how long a history natural dyeing has had in Japan. Materials for dyes come from trees (such as logwood as well as *suō*, or sappanwood; *shibuki*, or wax myrtle); flowers (*benibana*, or safflower); leaves and stems (*kihada*, or philodendron inner bark; *katekyu*, or cutch); roots (*murasaki*); as well as nuts (*kuri*, or chestnuts; *fushi*, or gall). Each material has to be gathered at a particular time of year, and the manner of preparation of dye stocks varies with different plants.[130] As a rule, the materials are chopped or crushed, mixed with water and brought to a boil to extract the dye. With the exception of the strong yellow *kihada*, most dyes need next to be mixed with mordants or metallic salts to bond the dye chemically to the fiber. During the Nara period (710–794) the mordants in use were iron (*tetsu*), ash lye (*aku*) and vinegar made from plums and rice (*umekawa shu, yonezu*) (Maeda 87). Alum, tin, copper, chrome and iron are the most popular mordants used for contemporary natural dyeing work (for a list of natural dyes, see the Appendix, page 206).

Ganryō (Pigments)

Pigments are insoluble powders and granules that are bound to cloth through the use of *gojiru* (soybean juice), which, after steaming, forms a protein-based binder.

Figure 71 Powdered and granular pigments are prepared in a mortar with a pestle. In the foreground are some additional pigments in stick form.

Unlike dyes that penetrate the cloth and in some cases the fiber molecules, *ganryō* sit on the top surface, requiring several thin layers to create dense color. They are usually opaque in nature when compared with the translucent dyes. Pigments for textiles are made from organic sources (such as vegetable dyes mixed with mineral salts to create a dye concentrate) or inorganic pigments derived from minerals. Minerals such as *ōdo*, yellow ochre (iron oxide), *bengara*, Indian red (red iron oxide) and *shu*, a vermilion (mercuric sulfide) are among the earliest colorants of cloth in Japan and date from prehistoric times. Most pigments come in powder form and are easily mixed with a soybean-based binder; however, some granular pigments need to be ground with a mortar and pestle before adding *gojiru* for painting on cloth (for a list, see the Appendix, page 206). Pigment also comes molded into a stick form (*bō*) with an animal glue (*nikawa*) base. The sticks are rubbed on the bottom of a shallow saucer with a little *gojiru* added to release the color. *Aibō*, or indigo stick, is prepared by skimming the purple bubbles from the oxidized "flower" that collects on the bath, drying and crushing and binding them into stick form (Nakano and Stephan 89–92). Indigo wax (*airō*), imported from India and mentioned in dyeing texts written during the Edo period, was probably prepared in the same way (Figure 71).

Binding Pigments

To make about 250 milliliters (1 cup) of soybean juice (*gojiru*) to be used as a binder for pigments, soak approximately fifteen dried soybeans in 250 milliliters of water overnight. In the morning, pour off the water and place the swollen beans in an electric blender with 250 milliliters of water and blend on high speed until the mixture has the consistency of a milkshake, or for about fifteen minutes. Strain the liquid through a damp cloth to get out any bean solids. Mix with pigments to paint on fabric as needed. This mixture will spoil quickly in hot weather, even if stored in the refrigerator, and should be prepared fresh every few days.

Setting Dyes and Pigments

Indigo, vat naphthol and reactive dyes can be set without steaming. Acid, direct and pigments benefit from a steam-setting. In essence, the heat and moisture

Figure 72 Professional cleaning establishments in Japan remove wax in solvent machines, then use large steam cabinets to set dyes.

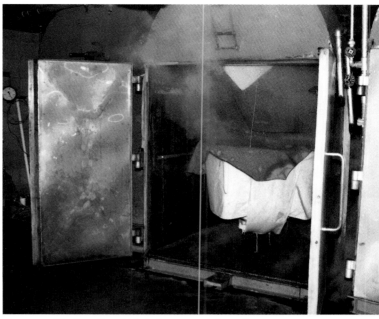

Figure 73 The bundle of fabric is removed from the steamer.

Figure 74 This kimono length of fabric is rinsed in running water for ten to twenty minutes to remove all residue dyestuff.

Figure 75 Finally, the fabric is hung in a heated-air drying room.

released during the steam process create an environment for the fiber and dye to form a permanent bond. Steaming will melt wax, but it is best to use solvents or hot soap to remove it completely.

Textile artists in the large cities in Japan have the advantage of professional *mushiya* (steaming factories; Figures 72–75). In Kyoto alone there are more than sixteen factories where waxed and dyed cloth can be brought for processing. The plant will remove wax or paste, steam and wash the fabric. In the case of kimono lengths, they will additionally press it and put it back on rolls. In a number of

Western countries, dry-cleaning establishments cooperate by removing wax from fabric for batik artists. The cleaning machines at such companies use an excellent wax-removing chemical on a daily basis. Some artists iron their waxed pieces between layers of newsprint, in a well-ventilated area, before bringing them to the cleaners. Steam frames that are used to set pinch pleats in curtains or drapes at dry cleaners can also be used to steam dyed fabric. A number of dye companies and individual artists also offer professional steaming service. For those who must do this themselves at home, some basic information follows:

1. For small pieces, a large pot or kettle will suffice. For larger fabrics, a piece of stovepipe 20 cm/8 in. in diameter and either 60 cm/24 in. or 150 cm/60 in. in length can be fitted on top of the largest pot available.

2. Fill the pot with about 8 cm/3 in. of water. Bring to a boil. Set a wire rack 10 cm/4 in. above the bottom of the container and cover the rack with a small towel.

3. Roll the fabric to be steamed in porous paper such brown wrapping paper or newsprint. Additional paper is necessary if the piece is heavily waxed. Tie loosely with string.

4. Hang the rolled bundle from the top of the stovepipe, suspended on crossed sticks, and above the towel-covered wire platform in the pot. Do not allow the paper to touch the sides or the boiling water to reach the platform.

5. Cover the top with a pile of newspapers to act as an absorbent pad and then put a small towel over that. Put the lid on the pot and weigh down the top. A fabric weight or a brick can be used for weighting, but be sure the length of stovepipe is well-balanced beforehand.

6. Steam for at least 20 minutes and as much as one hour or more depending on the amount of cloth, dye concentrations and fabric weight. A small test piece can be clipped from the piece and rinsed after steaming to see if more time is needed for your particular fabric. While steaming, add more water from a heated teakettle to maintain moisture and heat.

DYE TECHNIQUES

Japanese dyeing techniques are among the most refined in the world. The ability of dyers in that country to control the medium, producing special luminous effects that can be repeated at will, are envied by many professionals in other countries. The current extraordinarily high level of dyeing skill was encouraged, within the kimono industry, by the masters who taught the young apprentices. Yet there is no doubt that the *toiya*, or kimono wholesalers, to whom the masters sold the finished products were in many cases the harder taskmasters. The slightest flaw, wax crack or dye streak in a 12 meter (13 yard) kimono length was grounds for rejecting the entire bolt or drastically discounting the price paid, after days of tedious work. Because of this built-in quality control, the expertise of the traditional dyers grew to heights, some would say, unparalleled in modern times.[131]

Dye Brushes

Japan produces a number of brushes developed specifically for various dye application uses. These handmade brushes are made to withstand heavy use and constructed to last. Many Japanese dyeing brushes are made to be used in a circular, rubbing style, rather than a stroking motion. Below are a few of the typical brushes found in every dye studio (see also Figure 76).

■ *Surikomi-bake* (color gradation brush)
This wide, square, fully packed brush is used to create the graded shading that is so widely admired. It is flat on one end and used in a circular motion, which helps to push dye into the fabric and blend colors. Sizes from $1/2$ to 4 centimeters ($1/8$–$1^1/2$ inches) are available.

■ *Irosashi-bake* (detail brush)
The *irosashi* brush is a thin, flat brush made of soft badger hair and used for color

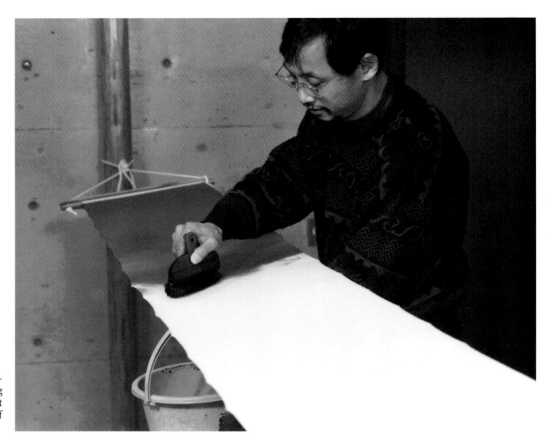

Figure 76 *Hikizome* background dyeing is done using a *jizome* brush, working it quickly down the length of the fabric in sections.

details. *Irosashi* brushes are constructed to stroke on color in the style of a watercolor brush, rather than in a circular motion. Beveled brushes are used in the *yūzen* industry for fine detail shading.

■ *Maru-bake* (circular brush)

The *maru-bake* is a round brush made of badger hair that comes in sizes from 2 to 8.5 centimeters (³/₄ to 3³/₈ inches) in diameter. It is used after color has been applied, to blend and even penetration.

■ *Jizome-bake* or *hikizome-bake* (ground color brushes)

The *jizome-bake* is a wide, tightly packed badger-hair brush ideal for dyeing large areas a consistent shade. It ranges in size from 9 to 16¹/₂ centimeters (3¹/₂ to 6¹/₂ inches) and was developed to hold a large amount of dye without dripping and to provide coverage without streaking. It too is used in a circular, scrubbing motion and is excellent for larger-scale work and background color application.

Basic Techniques

Hikizome (background dyeing) and *bokashi* (graduated shading) are two techniques that are widely used and basic to Japanese dyeing. The directions are given for use with traditional *harigi* and *shinshi* stretchers but can easily be adapted for dyeing with a frame for stretching fabric.

■ *Hikizome* (background dyeing)

To dye a background one consistent shade:

1. Prepare enough dye for brushing on the length of fabric and pour it into a bucket that will accommodate the width of the *hikizome-bake*. Wet your dye brush thoroughly with water and shake off any excess.

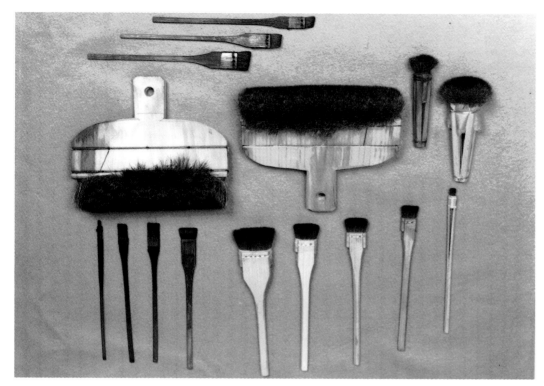

Figure 77 A variety of brushes are used for applying dye including, clockwise from left: the large *jizome-bake* brush for background dyeing, the beveled *irosashi-bake* brush for *yūzen*, the *maru-bake* circular brush for blending, the *surikome* for shading, and the flat *irosashi-bake* detail brush.

2. Position yourself at the right end of the work (left-handed dyers, at the left end). Put your brush into the dye and shake off any excess with two or three quick shakes. To stabilize the artwork, grasp two *shinshi* below the piece in your left hand, and, with the brush in your right hand, begin.

3. Using the brush in a circular motion, move across the fabric from the opposite side over toward yourself, vigorously rubbing the dye in within a 10–15 centimeter (4–6 inch) row without stopping at the selvage. At the edge closest to you, continue by moving back and across to the far side, always in a tight circular manner and slightly overlapping the previous row (Figure 77). You should be able to cross the fabric four to six times (depending on the width) before needing more dye. End just in front of yourself.

4. Recharge the brush. Remember to shake it vigorously two to three times to remove excess dye that may otherwise drip. Overlap the previous row slightly and continue from left to right, and then right to left, to the end of your length

> **Do not hold your fabric by the edge**, since your fingers can leave marks there and, should they become soiled with dye, can wind up transferring unwanted color from one area to another. Always hold the *shinshi* below, or the frame edge, as needed.

5. After all areas have been dyed, use the damp dye brush to go back over the length in light, sweeping motions, evening out any irregularly dyed areas. Pay special attention to selvages. Wipe the surface of the dyed cloth and any waxed areas carefully with a clean towel.

6. Allow the fabric to dry naturally and **in a level position**. Tilting the fabric or forcing it to dry quickly can cause dye to migrate from dry to wet areas, leaving streaks.

7. Finally, wash your brush thoroughly.

Because the *hikizome* brush holds so much dye, it can sometimes be difficult to clean completely. Many artists have a different brush for each color because of problems removing dye. However, if a brush is first rinsed thoroughly with clean water, and placed in a container with water changes for a few days, most of the residue color will eventually discharge. The brush should then be shaken vigorously and hung in a well-ventilated place to dry thoroughly.

■ *Bokashi* (Graduated shading)

This technique is used to created shaded backgrounds as well as smaller areas or details. It can involve the blending of two or more colors or the graduated shading of one color from a pale to a deep tone. It is a wet dyeing technique, so fabric must be kept damp throughout the process. This is a nonstop process, and so all materials should be assembled before you begin.

1. Prepare dye in a container. Have an additional container of fresh water and a water brush nearby as well as a clean towel. Soak the dye brush in clean water before using. Dampen well the entire area to be shaded.

2. To dye a graded shade of one color: dip a wet brush in the dye solution, shake two or three times to remove excess, grasp two *shinshi* below the cloth and begin applying the dye from the upper left-hand corner of the area you are shading. As with *hikizome*, the motion should be a circular, scrubbing application. If you pick up too much dye with your brush at first, wipe the brush on the side of the dye container or blot it with a rag before you start.

3. Continue across the fabric with a continuous motion, left to right and then back, right to left. **Cover about one-third of the entire area** in this manner, and then pause.

4. Make sure your fabric is still damp all over. Quickly dip into your dye again, shake the brush and begin **at the top once more**, applying a second layer of color over the top part and **continuing about two-thirds of the way down**. As you progress, the color should decrease in the brush, mixing with the water on the cloth and creating a thinner shade.

5. Next, using the brush set aside only for water, quickly dampen the bottom area quite well with water. Look at it from an angle. It should **not** be shiny with water, but should be quite damp. Now start again at the top, applying a third layer of color. Work in the same circular, rubbing motion across the fabric without stopping. You will be applying an additional coat of dye to the top third. In the second, you will be deepening the shade. In the final area you will be mixing what color is left on the brush with the ample amount of water that

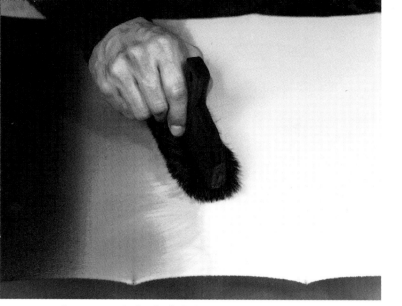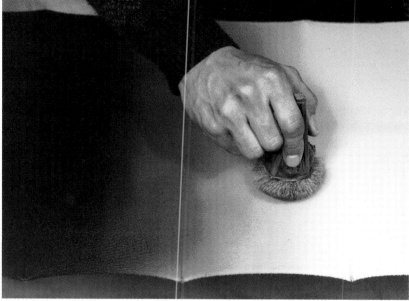

Figure 78 *Bokashi* shaded dyeing is done on dampened fabric, using the large brush in a circular motion and blending the dye into the fabric in overlapping sections.

Figure 79 The *maru-bake* brush is used to blend in the color for a smooth graduated shade.

Figure 80 The *bokashi* technique can also be used to shade smaller areas.

has soaked into the fabric. The result should be a very light shade (Figure 78).

6. You should now have an area of beautiful shading from dark to light without any lines or streaks, as if the fabric had been air-brushed. If some areas need additional blending, go back over them with a fairly dry dye brush. Don't be afraid to brush vigorously on places that need work. The *maru-bake* is excellent to use for blending from the light areas up into the darker (Figure 79).

7. Finally, with a clean towel, carefully wipe off waxed areas and any excess dye. It is best to work from light to dark, to avoid smudging the dye.

The *bokashi* process can also be used to blend two colors, beginning at either end of the piece and creating a pale blend in the middle, or blending in the same area. This process can also be done to shade small areas between waxed shapes, by using smaller brushes and the same instructions (Figure 80). If you like the luminosity of Japanese artists' work, control your dyeing and leave some white. The most important points of *bokashi* are:

1. **Always work with dampened fabric.** The water in the fabric mixes with the dye as you go, thinning the color and creating lighter shades. This helps to control the application of color.
2. **Always begin with a medium color dye.** The layering of dye will create a dark color for you. You can always go back and darken the color, if needed, but taking color out is impossible.
3. **Work quickly, without stopping.** Interruptions will allow the dye to begin drying and leave a line of color or a streak.
4. **Always work in thirds.** Do not try to dye the entire fabric at once. It would be very difficult to get a good shading without layering the color.
5. **Choose the correct size brush for the area you want to cover.** Small areas or fabric of a narrow width (33 centimeters/13 inches) may allow you to use a 4 centimeter (1½ inch) brush, but for larger areas a 13 centimeter (5 inch) *jizome-bake* brush is best.

Other materials can be substituted in some cases for the Japanese brushes mentioned here. A firm, dense sponge (cello or natural) can also work, and allows for the circular, rubbing motion. Always wear rubber gloves if you are working with a sponge and be careful to clean the gloves often. A sponge brush is good simply for stroking on the dye, though some artists may be able to use one successfully for this entire shading process, with practice.[132]

APPENDIX

Microscopic Analysis of Resist Textiles

Identifying the various resist materials used to pattern texitiles is never easy, and most scholars reserve judgment. However, resists do have characteristic qualities: the liquid line, strong block-out and occasional veining of wax, and the softer edge and thinner resist of paste or mud. Under magnification, each resist shows distinct qualities.

Hot wax is a liquid resist which penetrates fabric easily and provides a strong block to dye. When the wax is applied hot, penetration is complete and the reverse of the fabric shows a clear image of the top. Under a magnifying glass the edge looks sharp and shows a strong break between the resist and dyed areas of the fibers. Occasionally the wax may break in cooling and show veining or crack lines where dye has seeped in before the wax was removed. But these breaks are not necessary to identify fabric as wax resist.

Paste is a thicker resist that is applied cold and rests on the top surface of the fabric. Dampening the reverse of the fabric while the paste is still wet will "pull" the resist into the cloth only slightly. Under magnification the resist edge shows a soft block-out, with some dye moving into the fibers of the resist areas. The reverse side of the fabric will show a shadow image where dye has colored the resist.

Mud is also a thick resist, and its adhesive and block-out qualities may vary, depending upon its source. Mud resist is used in India to reserve areas that are later to be printed. Under magnification the resist qualities of mud look similar to the soft edge of paste resist, and the reverse of the fabric will show dye coloring the resist area. In lesser quality mud- and paste- resist textiles, a smudge may be evident where the resist was accidentally brushed while still wet.

Figure 80 Three cotton woven fabrics from the seventeenth through the nineteenth centuries. When magnified five times, the wax textile at left shows the hard edge of wax resist, while the edges of the paste- (top right) and mud-resist (above) samples are softer.

Pigments (*Ganryō*)

ai	indigo	(powdered and granular forms)
aibō	indigo	(stick form)
bengara	Indian red; red brown	(powdered)
bero; berensu	Prussian blue; deep blue	(granular)
gofun	shell white	(powdered)
gofunbō	shell white	(stick)
gunjō	azurite; clear bright blue	(powdered)
gunseibō	bright blue	(stick)
honshubō	vermilion	(stick form)
miaibō	ultramarine; indigo	(stick)
ōdo	yellow ochre	(powdered)
ryokuseibō	green	(stick)
sekiō	King's yellow; arsenic yellow	(powdered; granular)
sumi	black	(liquid and stick)
taishabō	brown	(stick)
yamabukibō	bright yellow	(stick)
yoko	carmine; bright purplish red	(granular)
yokobō	carmine; bright purplish red	(stick)

Natural Dyes

ai; tade ai	Japanese indigo	blue
yama ai	mountain indigo	light green blue
akane	madder	red
aobana	dayflower; spiderwort	pale blue
asen; katekū	catechu; cutch	burnt umber; dark red; dark brown
benibana	safflower	yellow; lavender; pink
cha	tea	beige; gray; terra-cotta
chōji	clove	tan; terra-cotta
enji	lac	deep red
fushi	gall	tan; brown; gray; black
gennoshōko	geranium, cranesbill	yellow; green; gray
gereppu	old fustic; Cuba wood	beige; tan; brown
kariyasu	miscanthus	deep yellow; green
kihada	philodendron	lemon yellow; olive
kochiniiru	cochineal	pink; red; purple; green gray
kuchinashi	gardenia	yellow
kuri	chestnut	pale yellow; green; gray
kurumi	walnut	tan; gray; green
murasaki	gromwell	purple; lilac gray
rogguuddo	logwood	purple; black; green
shibuki	wax myrtle	tan; brown; black
shikon	purple root; gromwell	purple; gray
suō	sappanwood	crimson; red; purple
tsurubami	acorn	tan; brown
ukon	turmeric	pale yellow; green; gray
ume	plum	red; tan; gray
yamamomo	mountain peach	gold; olive; gray; brown; black
yasha	pine cone	pale yellow; green; gray
yashabushi	alder	yellow; brown; black

Suppliers

The following suppliers are listed for readers' convenience. Most of these sources do mail-order business and will supply a catalog on request. The Japanese companies do not have English catalogs, but the photographs are helpful.

JAPAN

Small Japanese retail firms are not always accustomed to doing business abroad, and in some cases correspondence may be difficult. Credit cards are not accepted for payment of mail-order goods and shipping. In ordering please specify air or sea mail. Prepare a postal money order in yen after being advised of the total cost plus shipping charges.

Seiwa, Inc.
1-1-1 Shimo-ochiai, Shinjuku-ku, Tokyo 169
Tel (03) 3364-2112   Fax (03) 3364-2115

Extensive catalog, Japanese language only. Wax, dyes, Japanese brushes (including *rō-fude*), paste-resist supplies, fabric, *shinshi* and *harigi* stretchers, thermostatically controlled wax heaters.

Tanaka Nao Dye Supplies
Sanjō-dōri Ogawa Nishi-iru, Nakagyō-ku, Kyoto 690
Tel (075) 221-4112   Fax (075) 221-0276;

Takara Building 3F, 1-26-30 Higashi, Shibuya-ku, Tokyo 150
Tel (03) 3400-4894   Fax (03) 3400-4969

Extensive catalog, Japanese language only. Send orders (by fax) to Kyoto branch only. Wax, dyes, Japanese brushes (including *rō-fude*), paste-resist supplies, cloth, *shinshi* and *harigi* stretchers, fabric steamers, thermostatically controlled wax heaters.

UNITED STATES AND CANADA ———————————

With the closing of Cerulean Blue, Inc., in Seattle, the most extensive selections of traditional Japanese brushes and equipment for the rōzome artist of any shops in North America are to be found at Maiwa Handprints in Vancouver and Aiko's Art Materials of Chicago.

Maiwa Handprints
1666 Johnston Street, Vancouver, British Columbia
Canada V6H 3S2
Tel (604) 669-3939   Fax (604) 669-0609

Catalog and information sheets. Japanese brushes (including *rō-fude*), dyes, wax, paste-resist supplies, chemicals, *shinshi* stretchers.

Aiko's Art Materials
3347 North Clark Street, Chicago, Illinois 60657
Tel (312) 404-5600

Catalog. Wax, dyes, paste-resist supplies, Japanese brushes, *shinshi* stretchers.

Pro Chemical and Dye, Inc.
Post Office Box 14, Somerset, Massachusetts 02726
Tel (508) 676-3838   Fax (508) 676-3980

Catalog, free technical laboratory service and consultation for customers. Wax, dyes, pigments, chemicals, dye equipment, safety equipment.

Aljo Manufacturing Company
81 Franklin Street, New York, New York 10013
Tel (212) 966-4046   Fax (212) 274-9616

Catalog, dyer's manual. Wax, dyes, chemicals, tools, safety equipment.

Dharma Trading Company
Post Office Box 150916, San Rafael, California 94915
Tel (415) 456-7657   Fax (415) 456-8747
(Toll-free) 800-542-5227

Catalog. Wax, dyes, Chinese brushes, fabric, steamers, tools, safety equipment.

Ruppert, Gibbon and Spider
Post Office Box 425, Healdsburg, California 95448
Tel (707) 433-9577   Fax (707) 433-4906
(Toll-free) 800-442-0455

Wax, dyes, cloth, Japanese brushes, chemicals, fabric, steamers.

UNITED KINGDOM ———————————

Hays Colours, Ltd.
55–57 Glengall Road, London, England SE15 6NQ
Tel (171) 639-2020

Dyes, pigments, indigo, chemicals.

R A Smart Screen Supplies, Ltd.
Clough Bank, Grimshaw Lane, Bollington, Macclesfield, Cheshire, England SK10 5NZ
Tel (1625) 576-255

Fabric steamers.

George Weil and Sons, Ltd.
18 Hanson Street, London, England W1P 7DB
Tel (171) 580-3763

Wax, dyes, fabric, frames for waxing, equipment.

Wild Barfield, Ltd.
Delegation Road, Diglis, Worcester, England WR5 3BT
Tel (1905) 352-440

Thermostatically controlled wax heaters.

AUSTRALIA ———————————

Batik Oetoro
203 Avoca Street, Randwick 2031
Tel (02) 398-6201

Catalog, information sheets. Wax, dyes and batik supplies.

NEW ZEALAND ———————————

C C G Industries, Ltd.
33 Crowhurst Street, Post Office Box 9523
Newmarket, Auckland
Tel (09) 524-8208   Fax (09) 522-0635

Wax, dyes, batik tools and chemicals.

Textile Requisites
Box 45081, Epuni Lower Hutt
Tel & Fax (04) 569-8834

Dyes and chemicals.

NOTES

1. Jack Lenor Larsen. Keynote lecture, International *Shibori* Symposium. Nagoya, November 21, 1993.

2. Bughler, cited in Larsen 35, Robinson 39, Barber 225.

3. Cited in Schaefer 915.

4. Megasthenes, *Travels*, fourth century; Bernier, *Travels in the Mughul Empire*, 1670; cited in Robinson, 17.

5. Barber 226; Gittinger 43; Rutschowscaya 28.

6. The original fabric color of some cotton-indigo-dyed resist fragments of the thirteenth and fourteenth centuries A.D. found at Quseir Al-Qadim look similar to the orange-buff wool and may suggest a natural color for the Kertch piece. Dye analysis would clarify this. See Vogelsang-Eastwood 1990, cat. #80-262, #80-270, #80-271.

7. Vogelsang-Eastwood suggests that the indigo blue color was most likely from woad (*Isatis tinctoria*), the indigo-bearing plant native to Europe. More than fifty plants contain the blue chemical indican, but the plant that gave the dye its name, indigo, is native to India (*Indigofera tinctoria*). This dye is thirty times greater in concentration than most other indican species and was exported to the classical world through mid-Eastern ports. Woad and indigo cannot be distinguished chemically from one another with the technology available at present. See Vogelsang-Eastwood 16; Barber 234; Balfour-Paul 98–105.

8. Many of these geometric patterns and palmetto motifs can be seen in Chinese as well as Japanese resist textiles dating from a thousand years later.

9. According to Gerziger, the fleeing women are related to Onus and Dinos Greek vase painting.

10. In addition, Arynea, Jocasta, Phaidra, Iolaos, Mopos and Hippomedon can be deciphered.

11. Such water women are seen in vase painting of 460–440 B.C. by the *eretria* painters of Athens.

12. Barber cites Peroni's unpublished find as "sembra attestare l'uso di tessuti 'stampati' mediante l'impresione di sostanze forse resinose" (175). Barber surmises that numerous clay "pintadera" found all over Neolithic Europe might have been used for cloth printing with resinous substances (175).

13. Victoria and Albert Museum, inventory number 1522–1899.

14. Vogelsang-Eastwood suggests Syria because of the construction. Letter to author, July 12, 1994.

15. Kendrick cited in Rutschowscaya, 46.

16. See Gervers, "Early Christian Curtain" 68–75, for information on linen curtains with tapestry and applied decoration from the same period used in Christian churches and meeting rooms.

17. Cited in Weibel, 32.

18. Most of the Coptic textiles were found in tombs of wealthy individuals, who were generally buried wearing as many as four embroidered tunics. Corpses were dressed in these tunics before they were wrapped in one or two white shrouds with a layer of palm fiber and a final shroud was placed over all. The Veil of Antinoopolis was found twisted into a rope and used to secure this last shroud.

19. *Adoration of the Magi* (or *Shepherds*), *Miracles of Christ* and *Jonah and the Fish* (98 x 104 cm.) accn. # 51.400.

20. Possibly Dionysus Infancy (55.9 x 44.5 cm., 42 x 26 cm. and 29.2 x 26.7 cm.) accn. #72.178A, 72.178B.

21. See Beckwith 5 and Shepherd 67.

22. Cited by Gittinger 13.

23. Sir Aurel Stein (British), 1900, 1907, 1914; Sven Hedin (Swedish), 1890, 1894, 1895, 1899, 1926; Albert von Le Coq (German), 1904, 1905, 1914; Paul Pelliot (French), 1908; Rev. Kozui Ōtani (Japanese) with Zuichō Tachibana and Shōichirō Yoshikawa, 1902, 1908, 1910; Langdon Warner (American) with Horace Jayne, 1923, 1925

24. Min Wu. Letter to author, January 20, 1994. Cited by Aikawa 11.

25. Zhou Qufei, ed. *Ling wai daida*.

26. The Miao are originally from north central Asia, but through centuries of migration have dispersed to the mountainous regions of Guizhou, Yunnan, Hunan, Sichuan and Guangxi provinces of China, as well as to northern areas of Burma, Thailand, Laos and Vietnam (Rossi II, 30).

27. See Rossi, I and II, for description of contemporary *laran* production by minority peoples.

28. Min Wu. Letter to author, January 20, 1994.

29. Riboud, ii in Vogelsang-Eastwood, *Resist Dyed Textiles from Quseir Al-Qadim Egypt*.

30. Dr. Wu believes that the cotton resist pieces could not have come from the area since raw cotton was not locally produced until the eleventh century and blue-and-white

resist dyeing was not done until after the Qing dynasty. Wu feels the Niya fragments are early Indian wax-resist pieces, and she is supported in this belief by Xia Ting, the late Chinese archaeologist. Indian textile scholars, however, feel that the iconography is consistent with a Central Asian origin. Letter to author. Min Wu, January 20, 1994. Ruth Barnes, January 24, 1994.

31. 1993 studies by Dr. Victor Mair of the University of Pennsylvania on discoveries by Chinese archaeologists of the late 1970s have revealed more than a hundred corpses with distinct Caucasian characteristics found in the Xinjiang desert, carbon-dated from the Yin-Shang dynasty (1523–1028 B.C.). This confirms the theory that the area was inhabited very early by racial groups other than ethnic Chinese.

32. Found in an ancient Nanyue Kingdom site; cited by Riboud, iii in Vogelsang-Eastwood, *Resist Dyed Textiles from Quseir Al-Qadim Egypt*.

33. Prof. Kōgi Kudara, Ryūkoku University. Conversation with author, February 4, 1994.

34. Cited in *Archaeology of the Western Regions*, K. Nagasawa, "*Ōtani Tanken-tai*," 21.

35. Illustrated in *Senshoku no bi* 30, 1984, p. 55 fig. 52, p. 63 fig. 64; Yamanobe 1979, p. 141 pl. 80 (L.L. 02), p. 143 pl. 82 (Ast. vi 3.07), p. 145 pl. 83a 83b (Ast. ii 1.020), National Museum, New Delhi.

36. Ast. ix 2.012, National Museum, New Delhi.

37. Reported by Uighur Autonomous Museum personnel in *Xinjiang*, 185.

38. Additionally, some tabby-woven silk fabrics from the Tang dynasty are thought to be stencil printed with colored paste, possibly a process similar to the Japanese *iro-nori* technique.

39. Dr. Min Wu, director of textile research at the Uighur Autonomous Region museum, feels that the wax-resist process could not have been done on silk during the Tang dynasty and believes that the known resist pieces on silk from this era were probably all done with an alkaline-based block or stamp. She explains what look like crack lines and veining as breaks between the printed blocks (Wu 1972: 1; pers. comm.).

40. *Textiles in the Shōsōin*. Asahi p. xxxv

41. *Textiles in the Shōsōin*, vol. 2 (1964), p. xxv.

42. See "Architecture of the Shōsōin" in Hayashi, *The Silk Road and the Shōsōin* for additional information on construction and preservation. The Shōsōin building, located behind the Daibutsuden, the Great Buddha Hall of Tōdaiji, may be viewed from outside by the public from 10 A.M. to 3 P.M. weekdays excluding national holidays.

43. Many of these textiles were re-created from ancient source material under the supervision of Tsuneo Yoshioka for a special rededication of the Daibutsu in 1980 following major restoration work at Tōdaiji Temple.

44. From the closing lines of Empress Kōmyō's petition to Tōdaiji, *Kokka chinpō-chō* (Catalog of Rare National Treasures). 756. Shōsōin.

45. See "The Shōsōin Legacy" and "The Tōdai-ji and the Shōsōin" in Hayashi, *The Silk Road and the Shōsōin*, pp. 34–36 and 54–65.

46. The Hōryūji treasures were presented to the Imperial Household in 1878 and transferred to the national government following World War II. They are housed in a special gallery on the Tokyo National Museum grounds that is open to public viewing every Thursday when it is not raining and when the humidity does not rise above 70 percent.

47. The *Wo-jen-chuan* says of the Japanese that "they plant rice and ramie. They raise silk worms and mulberry trees. Thus they have fine ramie, and silk." *Wo-jen-chuan* [Accounts of Japanese People] found in the *Wei-shin* [History of the Wei Kingdom], often cited as the earliest account of Japanese textiles and compiled in the third century.

48. See Matsumoto, *Jōdai-gire*, pp. 203–207 for further information on weaving of the Shōsōin.

49. Also called *samit façonne* in French. See Yokohari for an extensive discussion of *samet* in Astana, China, and a comparison of it to the Shōsōin collection.

50. *Textile Designs of Japan*, vol. 3, p. 26.

51. See Matsumoto, *Jōdai-gire*, p. 214 for reference to these woven, embroidered, crocheted and dyed leather pieces.

52. Kaneo Matsumoto. Conversation with author, April 28, 1993.

53. A possible error in the translation of an early article on ancient textiles by Sanjōnishi (1940) and repeated in Alfred Steinmann's well-known 1947 *Ciba Review* article on world batik has allowed some to assume that wooden stencils, rather than wooden blocks, were used on *rōkechi*. Steinmann records that, "Thin sheets of wood were laid on the silk and wax poured into the cut-out spaces" (2107). While such a process is suggested in Chinese texts, stamps and brushes are the only tools used with wax, according to all Japanese-language sources and confirmed by curator Kaneo Matsumoto. The Steinmann description and the incorrectly captioned photograph in his article (p. 2104) both seem to relate to *kyōkechi*, where dye, not wax, was poured through holes in wooden templates. An ancient Chinese source refers to poured wax, but, at this point, it is not assumed to have been part of resist dyeing in Japan. At least three later sources have continued what seems to have been an error in translation (Sanjōnishi, 1940; Steinmann, 1947; Robinson, 1969; Dyrenforth, 1988).

54. Conversations with author. Shigeki Kawakami, March 25, 1994. Ken Kirihata, October 9, 1993. Kaneo Matsumoto, April 28, 1993.

55. The Kyoto National Museum has three additional small pieces of this popular lattice mist motif. The Kyoto fragments are each a different color and are not from the same original piece. All seem to have an indigo overdye. One shows eight different small bird stamps within the lattice, rather than alternating fish stamps.

56. *Treasures of the Shōsōin. North, Middle and South Sections*. Vol. 1, North Section. 1962, p. xi.

57. Additional examples of this flowering grass stamp on smooth weave rather than *aya* figured twill are in the collections of the Kyoto National Museum and the Brooklyn County Museum.

58. Illustrated on p. 111, *Textile Designs of Japan*. 1961.

59. See Matsumoto, "Stamped *Rōkechi* Fabrics" 1973, p. 1. Applying wax through several layers of fabric is practiced by contemporary minority tribes in China, but there is no evidence at present of a historical layered application of wax in Japan.

60. For additional information in English on dyes used in ancient Japan, see Bethe, pp. 58–76 and 202–209; Sanjōnishi, pp. 114–116; and ancient source material in Japanese: *Engishiki* and *Ryō no shūge*.

61. See Matsumoto, *Jōdai-gire*. Pl. 84, pp. 97–99 for a detail of this piece.

62. Also seen in *The Treasures of the Shōsōin*. 1965, pl. 106. Description on p. 99.

63. See *Saikō sannen rokugatsu nijū-go nichi zatsu zaibatsu jitsu-*

roku [Record of the Various Treasures Held as of June 25th, year 3 of the reign of Saikō, or 856 A.D.]. Record of the North Section. 856. Shōsōin.

64. The remounting took place in the Meiji period, again in the late 1920s and finally in Heisei 2 (1990).

65. Mark shows inscription reading "Tenth month, Tenpyō–Shōhō 3rd year" (751). *Treasures of the Shōsōin. North, Middle and South Sections.* Vol. 1, North Section. 1987, p. xxxiv. Matsumoto cautions in *Jōdai-gire* that this inscription could relate to something other than tax payment but in personal communication uses it as validating the native province of the screen.

66. See *Textile Designs of Japan*, vol. 3, pp. 26–27.

67. Reference is made to similarities seen in a Sassanid *nishiki* cloth with ram design discovered at Antinoe, Egypt. *Treasures of the Shōsōin. North, Middle and South Sections.* Vol. 1, North Section. 1987, p. xxxiv.

68. First, the form lacks the fluidity normally associated with freehand brushwork. Second, the very graphic design of the ram and the thin, even wax coverage are not usually seen on pieces that have been brush-waxed. However, if this regal ram figure truly were applied with a stamp, the stamp would have measured approximately 60 x 50 cm. (20 x 24 in.) and been quite challenging to use.

69. Ogata in *Treasures of the Shōsōin: Furniture and Interior Furnishings*. p. 53.

70. Ogata also thinks the rock in the foreground of the hawk screen is the same as the tree trunk in the ram version.

71. Matsumoto. *Treasures of the Shōsōin: Musical Instruments, Dance Articles, Game Sets*. p. 69.

72. Ibid., p. 69.

73. Seen in *Shōsōin Exhibition Catalog* 1991, #29, 131 (96 x 150 cm./38 x 59 in.). Other costumes measure 130 x 199 cm./51 x 78 in.

74. The Tang fragment was discovered by Paul Pelliot and is now in the Musée Guimet, Paris. See discussion on the differences between the Shōsōin and Tang *nishiki* prototype in Matsumoto, *Jōdai-gire*, pp. 225–226. The phoenix with outstretched wings can also be seen in the Tang resist fabric *Hermits Riding Cranes* found in Astana in 1973.

75. Small clay stamps (*pintadera*) have been found throughout Europe, dating from Neolithic times (Barber 226), and elaborately patterned vessels and funerary figures of clay are part of Japan's ancient heritage; however, it has never been suggested that the Shōsōin stamps were made of clay.

76. *Jōdai-gire* 208.

77. For research by Kaneo Matsumoto on the development of the *karahana* in the *nishiki* and *aya* fabrics of the seventh and eighth centuries with some reference to *rōkechi* stamps, see pp. 219–221 of *Jōdai-gire*.

78. Found in Antinoe, Egypt, and now located in the Musée Historique des Tissus, Lyons (26812/10), and illustrated on p. 69 of *Textiles: 5000 Years*.

79. Illustrated in Hayashi, pl. 131, p. 120. Tokyo National Museum.

80. Figure #158, found in *Treasures of the Shōsōin. Middle Section*, 1988.

81. Figure #156, found in *Treasures of the Shōsōin. Middle Section*, 1988. Matsumoto also cites the document entitled *Awanokuni no meihōgun zue* [Surveyor's Map of Awanokuni]. *Senshoku to seikatsu* [Dyeing and Lifestyle] 23 (1978).

82. Matsumoto. "Pattern Dyeing of the Shōsōin." pp. 16–17.

83. Conversations with author. Ken Kirihata, October 9, 1993. Kaneo Matsumoto, April 28, 1993.

84. See pages 158–159 for further information on the origin and production of wax in ancient times.

85. Ken Kirihata. Conversation with author, October 9, 1993. There does seem to be a characteristic smell in older resist pieces when wax was not completely removed. Reports say that many centuries later, the Dutch struggled to market imitation batik printed with resin for the Indonesian market that "lacked the proper wax scent so greatly characteristic of original batiks" (Kroese 17).

86. India, Indonesia, Egypt, Greece, Persia.

87. The *Engishiki* is a fifty-volume collection of regulations for palace ceremonies, customs of the provinces and details on the costumes, dyes and supplies that were available during the tenth century. The work was revised and ten more volumes were added in 1818.

88. Two Chinese wax-rubbed cloths discovered in the Gansu Mogaoku Caves, China, are said to be locally produced pieces and show a weaker resist than other pieces found with them (*Wenwu* 12, 1972).

89. Cited in Yoshioka, p. 89.

90. The Dutch were at the same time also importing resist-dyed cloth, called *inkafu*, or "imitation batik," from China.

91. Rouffaer. Appendix III, xii.

92. Suntory Museum, Tokyo.

93. See Yoshioka 1993, pl. 100, 101 and 103.

94. Cited in Cort 1989: 34.

95. See Yoshioka, pl. 75, 76 for the *sarasa* of the Minami-kannonyama float with ink inscription and an additional hanging for the Koiyama float.

96. Kefukigusa, cited in Yoshioka, 91.

97. Cited in Gittinger, p. 167.

98. See "Traditional Wax Production," page 160.

99. Later in 1872, an imitation batik (resin plate print) machine was developed to produce fabrics for the Indonesian and West African markets. See Kroese, *The Origin of Wax Block Prints on the Coast of West Africa* for information on this development.

100. The Dutch artist Chris Lebeau established his own batik studio in Haarlem and was teaching the technique at the Haarlem School of Fine Arts. French artist Madame Marguerite Pangon visited this school in 1905 and returned to Marseilles, where she set up her own batik studio in 1908. She later exhibited her work in Paris in the Salon des Artistes Decorateurs, becoming the most celebrated European batik artist. The Kyoto Costume Institute has a tiger batik–dyed evening coat in purple and red by Madame Pangon from 1920. Interest in wax resist soon spread beyond Europe as well when one of America's foremost artist-embroiderers, Marguerite Zorach, returned to the United States in 1911 after a period of study in Paris. She traveled by way of China, Indonesia and Japan, carrying Indonesian batik tools. Zorach worked in New York City during the era known as the "batik craze" of 1918–20 and produced wax-resist wall-hangings that are now held in the collections of New York's Metropolitan Museum and Boston's Fine Arts Museum (Shilliam 36).

101. From the application by Toshimichi Ōkubo, Minister of Home Affairs, Meiji 9. *Textiles in the Shōsōin*, vol. 2, 1964, p. XXXVI.

102. Tsurumaki later became president of Kyoto Kōgei Sen'i Daigaku, the predecessor of the Kyoto Institute of Technology.

103. In 1924, a fourth division—*kōgei* (craft)—was included in the Teiten National Exhibition, but it was actually 1927 before any pieces were accepted. In that year the judges selected came from the fields of painting, sculpture, lacquer, ceramics and metalworking, but no textile judges were included. To be accepted for exhibition by this non-textile jury, *senshoku* artists had to create work that would appeal to judges from the field of painting and so were forced to go beyond their usual work. It was not until two years later that a *senshoku* artist was regularly included among the judges. In 1927, Sakurai's work was accepted and in 1929 Yamagata and Hirokawa won awards.

104. Maruyama Shijō-ha was an Edo-period school of *sumi-e* painting based on sketching and realistic interpretation of nature.

105. The volumes were published by the Nishiki Orimono Museum under the series title *Ayanishiki*.

106. See Liddell, pp. 136–139, for information of the development of the Mitsukoshi store in the eighteenth century.

107. Criteria for nominating a craftsperson or artist in the fields of ceramics, textiles, lacquerwork or metalwork for the title of "living national treasure" are that the person's technical skill is sufficient to create a body of work that has especially high artistic value or particular importance to the history of applied arts or, alternatively, one that has either artistic value or historical importance. In this last case, the work must also have a conspicuous local flavor or be representative of a particular school. Finally, a person may be nominated not for ability in, but for profound knowledge of these same areas (Harada 15). No *rōzome* artist has ever been declared a living national treasure.

108. Takeo Sano. Conversation with author, July 24, 1992.

109. In 1940, Ogō, Koga, Inagaki, Kanō and Sano started this group. (*Moyurasō* combines *moyura*, a little-known word evocative of the sound made by a collection of precious stones as they jostle against one another, with *sō*, meaning "villa" or "inn." The name suggests that the group acts as a kind of haven and that the artists inspire each other to produce beautiful work. See Sano, 1990, p. 126, for a narrative on the founding and purpose of Moyurasō.

110. Conversations with author. Takeo Sano, July 24, 1992. Kageo Miura, February 13, 1992. Yoshizō Nakamura (third-generation candle maker of Nakamura Rōsoku Company, Kyoto), February 20, 1992.

111. In 1946, the year after the end of World War II, the name of this exhibition was changed from the Teiten ("Imperial exhibit") to the Nitten (lit., the "Japan exhibit") to create a greater sense of modernity and openness.

112. "Lighting equipment." In *Kodansha Encyclopedia of Japan* (Tokyo: Kodansha, 1983), 5: 8–9.

113. Documents say that *haze* workers had their children drink wax root with their milk so that they would grow up to be good *haze* pickers. Such early exposure could also ward off natural allergies to this species of the sumac family.

114. Yoshizō Nakamura. Conversation with author, February 20, 1992.

115. In 1985, 246 tons of fruit were collected, but this figure had declined to 109 tons by 1990, as a result of competition from China. Nakamura explains that there are fewer typhoons and volcanic eruptions in China to destroy harvests than in Japan, and more people who were willing to climb trees to harvest the fruit.

116. It is interesting to note that the color of *mokurō* is not stable but changes due to oxidization when the wax is stored for long periods. Also, if *mokurō* is heated too long or at too high a temperature, it can turn black and stain cloth.

117. *Ibota* wax is such a hard wax that a number of thin layers on fabric can crack spontaneously in very cold weather (Takahashi 40).

118. *Han-bōsen* can also be done by blending lard, beef tallow or coconut oil with wax, but this must be done carefully, since wax tends to penetrate the cloth very quickly.

119. Other types of fluorocarbon polymers go by brand names such as Teflon (Dupont) and Furuon (ICI) and are used as low-friction coating materials.

120. Additional information on Threshold Limit Values (TLV) is available from American Conference of Governmental Industrial Hygienists, 6500 Glenway Avenue, Building D-7, Cincinnati, Ohio 45211. The Center for Safety in the Arts, 5 Beekman Street, Suite 1030, New York, New York 10038, and the monthly newletter on Arts, Crafts and Theatre Safety titled *ACTS Facts*, edited by Monona Rossol and available from 181 Thompson Street #23, New York, New York 10012, also supply important information on wax and health.

121. A #8 brush is recommended, or one with a base the diameter of your smallest finger (approximately 0.2 cm./5/8 in.).

122. Room temperature can greatly influence work with wax. Although Japanese wax combinations are formulated for seasonal variations in temperature, wax resist should never be done with a fan or air conditioning vent blowing on the work. The wax can cool on the brush before it reaches the fabric. Additionally, working in direct sunlight outdoors on a hot day can cause wax to melt on the fabric and destroy any fine edges.

123. *Harigi* are also called *harite* in some areas of Japan.

124. *Six-fold Screen with Pictures of Craftsmen* by Yoshinobu Kanō (1522–1640) shows this process of stretched fabric with *shinshi* attached. (Kitain Temple, Kawagoe City, Important Cultural Property)

125. Hand-held electric wax-spray machines, as well as automated machines with bristled rollers, have been developed to spray wax onto 12 meter (13 yard) lengths of silk for kimono in large Japanese dyeing companies.

126. Various *shibori* techniques that could be adapted to work with *rō-shibori* are illustrated in Wada Yoshiko, Mary Kellogg, and Jane Barton, *Shibori: The Inventive Art of Japanese Shaped Resist Dyeing* (Tokyo: Kodansha International, 1983).

127. For information on the *tsutsugaki* squeeze cone process see Brandon, *Country Textiles of Japan*, pp. 29–37.

128. Noel Dyrenforth's *The Technique of Batik* has an excellent section of on naphthol dyes for those interested in trying these Indonesian dyes (67–71).

129. Kiichi Tsujimura. "*Injigo o fukumanai shinpi no yama ai*" [Mysterious Mountain Indigo, Containing No Real Indigo]. *Senshoku Alpha*. 49 (April 1985): 63–64.

130. For information in English on early dye making in Japan as well as a description of the preparation of *murasaki*, *benibana* and indigo, see Bethe, "Colors, Dyes and Pigments," in Amanda Mayer Stinehecum, *Kosode: 16th–19th Century Textiles from the Nomura Collection*, 58–76.

131. Gai Nishimura. Conversation with author, October 2, 1993.

132. For information on how to do shaded dyeing with a sponge brush, see Susan Louise Moyers' *Silk Painting* (pp. 76–77).

GLOSSARY

aibō: Indigo in stick form prepared from oxidized dye. See also indigo.

airō: Indigo mixed with wax.

acid dyes (*sansei senryō*): Dyes derived from sodium salt of organic acids and having a direct affinity to protein fibers such as silk and wool.

aizome: Dyeing with indigo.

aobana: A fugitive blue tint derived from the spiderwort (*tsuyukusa*) plant and used for temporary sketching on fabric; disappears in water.

asa: Specifically, hemp; also a general term for bast (plant-stem) fibers and the cloth made from them, including hemp, linen and ramie.

ashiginu: Plain weave silk.

aya: Figured twill weave.

azekura: The architectural style of the Shōsōin repository of Tōdaiji Temple in Nara, in which large triangular timbers are laid horizontally one on top of another; a log construction in which corners of the building join in a lap-joint style.

ban: Buddhist ritual banners.

batik (from Javanese *ambatik*, "to mark with spots or dots"): A resist-dye process in which wax is applied to the cloth's surface with a brush, stamp or stencils, creating a resist to subsequent dyeing that results in a reserved pattern of the cloth's original color.

bingata: Paste-resist dyed textiles of Okinawa that use *ganryō* pigments for coloration.

board-jamming: See *kyōkechi*.

bokashi: Graduated shading or blending dyes from dark to light shades or color into color; also called *ombre* (French).

bōsen: A resist material such as wax or paste.

byōbu: A traditional Japanese folding screen containing two or more panels.

canting (Javanese; also *tjanting*): A bamboo-handled tool with a copper bowl and spout, used to apply wax in a linear manner. Similar to the *kalam*, an Indian tool for wax drawing.

cap (Javanese; also *tjap*): Metal stamps for printing patterns in wax. These stamps are distinguished by being fabricated, not cast.

carnauba wax: A Brazilian palm wax (*Copernicia cerifera*) that is very fragile and lacking in adhesive qualities; used in blended wax formulas to raise the melting point.

chay: A strong red dye produced from the roots of the plant (*Oldenlandia umbellata*) of Sri Lanka and Southern India; known as Indian madder.

chintz (from Hindi *chitta*, "spotted cloth"): Mordant printed and dyed cotton textiles; in many cases these also incorporate wax resist.

color carrier: A resist that can be mixed with dye to color fabric and, at the same time, create a resist area into which other dyes cannot penetrate. See also *dakku, ironori*.

dakku: A fluorocarbon polymer resin that can be used alone as a cold resist or together with dye as a colored resist. See also color carrier, *ironori*.

damor gum (also dammar gum): A gum suspended in volatile oil and used as a cold resist on fabric.

direct dyes: Dyes named for their direct affinity to plant fibers; salt is added as a dye assistant and steaming is necessary to fix the color.

dye assistant: A substance added to dye to aid in the chemical bonding of fiber and dye (e.g., salt, acetic acid).

dyebath: A solution of water, dye and assistants in which fabric is immersed.

ekirō: An oil-based fluorocarbon substance used on fabric as a cold resist.

fiber-reactive dyes: Dyes that react chemically in an alkaline solution with plant fiber molecules to produce a permanent bond, resulting in exceptional washfastness.

fubuki: Literally, "blizzard"; a splattering of fine dots of wax on fabric.

fude: A long-handled, pointed brush used for wax application and *sumi* brush painting.

funori: Sodium alginate. A seaweed-based thickener used to thicken dye solution and sometimes to size fabric.

furoshiki: A square piece of fabric used to wrap and carry packages.

ganryō: Opaque, water-soluble pigments.

gasenshi: Paper used by ink painters; originally from China.

gigaku: A masked theatrical dance of the seventh and eighth centuries; wax-resist textiles were created for *gigaku* performers.

gofun: Opaque, white (oyster shell) pigments used with binder on fabric.

gojiru: Soybean liquid used to bond dyes and pigment to fabric.

gomu nori ("gum paste"): The modern resist line used in *yūzen* dyeing.

gum arabic: Yellowish white or amber gum from the genus *Acacia*; used to draw fine resist lines on fabric in a modern version of the traditional rice paste line. See also *itomeya, yūzenzome*.

hake: A general term for any brush other than the narrow pointed brush called *fude;* when the term is used as a suffix, the "h" is voiced, e.g., *shike-bake.*

hakurō: A bleached form of a natural plant wax from the *haze* sumac tree. See also *mokurō.*

han-bōsen ("half-resist"): An advanced technique in which hot wax is brushed onto fabric for a shaded application.

harigi (also, *harite*): Wooden bars with needlelike teeth used to stretch fabric lengthwise.

haze: The sumac tree (*Rhus succedanea*) native to Japan, which produces a waxlike oil used in *rōketsuzome;* also *hazenoki.* See also *mokurō, hakurō.*

hera: A spatula used to apply paste through a stencil.

hibi: A crack or fissure; in this case, a break in the wax surface.

hikizome: Application of background color using a large brush.

hikizome-bake: See *jizome-bake.*

hikizomeya: A professional dyer of background fabric, usually for the kimono industry.

hiinagata-bon: Design catalogs of women's *kosode* or other textile products published between the late seventeenth and the nineteenth centuries.

HM wax: The brand name of a blended wax produced by the Tanaka Nao Company containing paraffin, microcrystalline wax and other waxes.

hōki: A palm fiber brush similar to a common kitchen (brown fiber) whisk broom; used to splatter large dots of wax onto the fabric in the technique known as *fubuki.*

hyōguya: Makers of traditional Japanese screens.

ibota wax: A wax derived from the secretions of an insect, used in blended wax formulas for its unusual crack patterning.

ikat (Malay/Indonesian): bound warp or weft threads used to resist dye.

indican: A blue coloring substance found in more than fifty varieties of herbaceous shrubs. The term is from Greek *indikon*, meaning a substance from India. See also indigo.

indigo: One of the oldest and most important dyestuffs in the world. The dye is found in the leaves of the plant *Indigofera tinctoria* and was first synthesized in 1897. An insoluble blue vat dye, indigo is made to adhere to cloth through a chemical change occurring at the molecular level, called reduction. When reduced, the dye is soluble in alkali. Indigo has a strong affinity to plant fibers including cotton, linen, flax and hemp and contains a colorant similar to woad. See also indican, woad.

ironori: Paste into which dye has been mixed to color the fabric and which is used in the *katazome* process. Products such as *dakku* are used for *rōzome* instead of paste. See also color carrier, *dakku.*

irosashi (also, *irozashi*): The application of detail dye with a small brush, often done in *yūzen.*

irosashi-bake: The flat brush used in *irosashi*, or the application of color detail.

itome: The fine paste line of *yūzen* resist dyeing; the "fine thread" paste line.

itomeya: Workers who outline designs in paste or gum. See also *yūzenzome*, gum arabic.

jiajie: (Chinese) board-jamming or clamp resist, similar to the ancient Japanese process of *kyōkechi.*

jinbaori: Campaign coats worn over armor; some seventeenth-century coats include *sarasa* (wax-resist fabrics from India).

jizome-bake (also, *hikizome-bake*): The wide, wooden-handled badger hair brush with short, dense bristles used for dyeing large background areas.

jōdai gire (also, *kodai gire*): Ancient textile fragments; cloth from the Shōsōin and Hōryūji collections of the seventh and eighth centuries and earlier.

Jūyō mukei bunkazai hojisha: See *Ningen kokuhō.*

kalam: A wax drawing tool used in India. The *kalam* is composed of a ball of fibers, such as hair or thread, wrapped around a stick core that acts as a reservoir to hold wax; pressure is applied in order to squeeze the liquid out to the drawing point. The *kalam* is used to draw with dyes or mordants, as well as with wax and is similar to the Indonesian wax tool the *canting.*

karahana: Literally, "Chinese flower"; a term coined in the twentieth century to refer to the large floral patterns peculiar to *jōdai gire* fabrics. These imaginary flowers similar to tree peonies or lotus blossoms were popular in the art of Nara-period Japan and Tang-dynasty China.

katazome: Resist dyeing done with stencils and rice paste.

keman: Buddhist floral decorations placed before statues or images; also, cloth pendants made with wax-resist fabric and used in place of flower garlands in Buddhist ceremonies.

kesa: A Buddhist priest's shawl or stole worn over robes.

kihatsu: Solvents used to remove wax from fabric.

kimono: Literally, "something to wear"; the traditional full-length garment of Japan worn by males and females alike. Strictly speaking, indicates a long, one-piece garment that wraps around the body. The term *kimono* was popularized during the eighteenth century and, by the Meiji period, had replaced *kosode*, used for a similar garment that was its precursor.

kōgei: Crafts.

kōkechi: Ancient term for *shibori* or tie-dye; one of the three resist processes (*sankechi*) known to date from the Nara period or even earlier.

kosode: An outer garment worn by men and women from the Muromachi period through recent times. During the Heian period, the *kosode* (lit., "small sleeves") served as daily wear for commoners and was worn beneath the *ōsode* ("great sleeves") by members of the Heian Imperial court.

kusakizome: Natural or vegetable dyeing.

kyōkechi: The ancient term for the clamp-resist process done in Japan of the Nara period. One of the *sankechi*, or three ancient Japanese resist processes and the most popular form of resist dyeing during the Nara period. In this technique, fabric was clamped between perforated carved wooden boards and dye was poured through to create patterns.

labi: A wax application tool of the Miao minority tribe of Asia, consisting of a homemade brush of hair inserted in a knob of cold wax to which a quill is attached.

ladao: wax application tool of the Ge and the Buyi minority tribes of Asia, consisting of two small, triangular pieces of metal to which a wooden handle is attached.

la-jie: (Chinese) wax-resist printing.

laran: Batik of the Asian minority tribes (the Ge, Miao and Buyi).

madder: A brilliant red dye similar to the common bedstraw plant (*Rubia tinctorum*), madder is cultivated extensively in Turkey and throughout Europe. See also chay.

maru-bake: The round, flat-bottomed brush used to blend dye into fabric.

Maruyama Shijō-ha: *Sumi-e* painting style of the Edo period.

meibutsu gire: Literally, "celebrated cloth"; special *sarasa* cloth imported during the Edo period for use as cases for tea ceremony utensils.

microcrystalline wax: A synthetic substance derived from petroleum, also called microwax. It is used in wax formulas as a substitute for paraffin and beeswax.

men-fuse ("wax surface"): Varying the number of layers of wax applied to fabric in order to allow for varying amounts of dye penetration.

mitsurō: Beeswax. The material used in ancient Japan for *rōkechi*, or wax resist.

mokurō: Natural plant oil from the *haze* or Japanese sumac tree (*Rhus succedanea*).

monozukuri: Literally, "the making of things"; a term frequently used in the Taishō and early Shōwa periods to refer to the attitude of care and responsibility necessary for creating craft pieces or art works individually, rather than by the traditional Japanese method of group production.

213

mordant: Any chemical that serves to fix a dye on fabric by combining with the dye to form an insoluble compound (and including iron, tin, alum, etc.).

mordant printing: The process, popular in India, of applying mordants with stamps, often to show a dark outline of a design after dyeing.

mushi: Steam (used to fix dyes on fabric).

mushiya: Workers at professional textile steaming and processing factories.

naphthylene: A derivative of the white, solid aromatic hydrocarbon $C_{10}H_8$ obtained from coal-tar distillates and crystallized to white platelets.

naphthol dye: A dye that develops color on fibers after the cloth is first impregnated with naphthylene (a coal-tar distillant) and then immersed in a "fast-color" salt dyebath.

nageshi: Ceiling beams. During the Nara period, decorative cloth covers made with wax resist were often prepared for beams of this kind in temples.

nihonga: Japanese traditional painting using pigments on paper.

Ningen kokuhō: Individual craftspeople and artists officially designated by the government as *Jūyō mukei bunkazai hojisha* (Bearers of Important Intangible Cultural Assets). *Ningen kokuhō* (Living National Treasures) is the unofficial but more popular term.

nikawa: Glue prepared from animal and fish byproducts, used to bind pigments to fabric.

nishiki: Silk polychrome patterned weave.

Nitten: The Nippon Bijutsu Tenrankai, or All Japan Art exhibition, was sponsored by the government until 1954, when a private association took over sponsorship. The Nitten exhibition was launched as the Buten in 1906; it was renamed the Teiten in 1919, the Shin-buten in 1934 and the Nitten in 1946.

noren: A traditional fabric curtain, generally of two or more narrow cloth segments, hung over a doorway.

nori: Paste used as a dye resist on fabric, traditionally composed of glutinous rice powder, rice bran, salt and calcium hydroxide.

ōshi: An outer garment or coat, usually padded for winter wear; examples of the wax-resist *ōshi* coats in the Shōsōin collection are unlined, however, and were worn by musicians and dancers.

ōshi-rōkechi ("pressed wax resist"): A term used in ancient texts to refer to a process of creating dyed patterns on cloth.

overdye: To dye one color over a previously dyed color without reserving the original with a resist such as wax. Also, to mix two colors through successive dyeing. See also top-dye.

paraffin wax: A translucent white wax derived from petroleum. This inexpensive wax has a low melting point but is brittle and less dye-resistant than its usual substitute, microcrystalline wax.

pine resin: A solid oil from the pine tree. Used in wax formulas to increase adhesiveness, this resin has a very high melting point.

pre-metalized dyes: Acid dye and chromium complex in a soluble form that can be applied directly to fiber without further treatment.

ra: Twist-weave silk gauze; a complex construction of threads entwined with adjacent warp threads in a continuous, sometimes irregular pattern.

ramie: A glossy bast fiber cloth woven from the nettle-family shrub; also called China grass cloth.

rinzu: Figured satin-faced silk or damask.

rō: Wax.

rōgaki: Literally, "wax drawing"; the application of hot wax to fabric with a brush, as if one were writing (alternatively known as *sengaki*, "line drawing").

rōkechi ("wax-resist dyeing"): This term for resist wax was used during the Nara period but is now obsolete. See also Definitions, pages 13–14.

rōkechi-dokoro: The ancient name for workshops that produced wax-resist fabric; often appears in Nara-period documents.

rōketsu ("wax-resist"): See also *rōkechi*, *rōzome* and *rōketsuzome*.

rōketsuzome ("wax-resist dyeing"): See also Definitions, pages 13–14.

rōsoku: Candle.

rōsokuya: A candle maker.

rōto-yu ("turkey-red oil"): An oil mordant sometimes mixed with dyes in small amounts to assist with penetrating wax in such techniques as *rō* etching and *han-bōsen*. Mineral oil can be substituted for *rōto-yu* when necessary.

rōzome ("wax dyeing"): See also Definitions, pages 13–14.

rōzuri: Wax rubbing; an ancient resist process of rubbing or daubing wax on the surface of white cloth; and then rubbing the cloth with crushed grass or flowers; references are made in ancient literature to *rōzuri*, but no specimens survive.

sankechi: The three resist-dyeing methods of the Nara period. These are *rōkechi* ("wax-resist dyeing," now known as rōketsuzome), *kōkechi* ("tie-dye," now called *shibori*) and *kyōkechi* ("clamp-resist dyeing").

sansei-senryō: Acid dye used for protein fibers such as silk and wool.

sarasa: Wax-resist cotton fabric from India included in the seventeenth-and eighteenth-century trade lists throughout Asia; batik as in *jawa sarasa*. (Alternatively called *sarassah* in Malay, *saraza* in Spanish and *serasah* in Javanese).

Seiryukai: A group developed to promote *senshoku* art created with fabric and dye; their first exhibition was held in 1991.

sekidashi ("barrier resist"): An advanced technique in which certain areas of the cloth are covered with wax to create barriers to dye penetration.

sengaki Literally, "line drawing.": See *rōgaki*.

senshoku: A general term meaning dyeing, printing and coloring of fabric using direct hand-painting, as well as resist methods.

senshokusha: People who work with dye; surface designers of fabric.

serigraphy: A printing process that produces colored prints on cloth or paper by pushing color (inks or dyes) through a stencil that has been affixed to a screen frame made of thin silk or synthetic thin fabric. See silk-screen process and split-font technique.

sha: Twist weave silk gauze; the fabric is made by entwining warp threads with successive weft threads in a regular manner.

shamuroshi: Japanese dyers who imitated the resist-dyed cloth (*sarasa*) of India in the Edo period; from the Japanese *Shamu* ("Siam").

shiborizome: Tie-dye. In this method of resist dyeing, patterns are reserved by pressing, stitching or binding before immersion in a dyebath.

shifuku: Cloth cases used to protect tea caddies. During the Edo period, these were often made of fine, imported wax-resist cloth.

shike-bake: A long-bristled brush made of deer hair used in the brush-trailing technique.

shikebiki: The brush-trailing technique of wax application.

Shin-kōgei (Nihon Shinkōgei Renmei): Japan New Craft Artist Association, the sponsor of one of Japan's largest crafts exhibitions, the Shin-kōgeiten.

shinshi: Stretchers or resilient bamboo rods set with a pin or nail in each end and positioned from selvage to selvage to stretch fabric along its width.

silk-screen process: A printing process that forces ink or dye through the mesh of a silk screen on which a pattern or design has been imposed. See also serigraphy, split-font technique.

sodium alginate: See *funori*.

someru: to dye. The noun form ("dyeing") *some*, or *-zome* is used in such compounds as *rōketsuzome* or *katazome*.

split-font technique: A method of printing multiple colors on fabric or paper using the serigraphy process; a number of colors of inks or thickened dyes are poured onto the font or printscreen and then drawn across the screen with a squeegee, creating a polychrome print.

stearin wax: A wax derived from animal and plant oils; used in blended wax formulas for its distinctive crack patterning and as an aid in easy wax removal.

stock solution: A concentrated solution of dye powder and water. Dye colors can be stored for long periods in this form. They are then diluted and mixed just before being applied to fabric.

sumi: Japanese carbon black ink available in stick and liquid forms.

sumi-e: Ink drawing.

surikome-bake: A square brush with a flattened end, used in color gradation.

tegaki-yūzen: Freehand dye painting; a technique often used in the *yūzen* industry.

tjanting: See *canting*.

tjap: See *cap*.

toiya (also, *tonya*): A draper or kimono wholesaler.

tokusen: The top prize in the Nitten exhibition; at present, receiving this award twice eliminates the need for future jurying for the annual exhibition.

top-dye: To dye one color over another in order to produce a third shade (e.g., top-dyeing blue with yellow produces a green color). See also overdye.

tsutsugaki: A method of applying a cold resist or paste using a paper squeeze cone.

turkey-red oil: See *rōto-yu*.

vat dyes: Dyes that are insoluble in water and must be chemically dissolved before they will adhere to cloth; their color develops when they are exposed to the air or to an oxidizing agent. Vat dyes have a strong affinity to cotton and silk. Indigo is one example of a vat dye.

warp: Parallel threads or fibers that run longitudinally on a loom or in fabric.

weft: Traverse threads that cross and interwork with warp threads to form woven fabric.

woad: An indican-bearing plant (*Insatis tinctoria*) native to ancient Europe and providing the only blue dye of substance prior to the introduction of indigo in the seventeenth century. A member of the mustard family, this vat dye is also referred to as "dyer's weed."

yūzenzome: A refined style of dyeing combining fine lines of paste-resist applied through a paper cone with delicate hand painting; named for a Kyoto fan painter. See *itomeya*, gum arabic.

BIBLIOGRAPHY

Adachi, Barbara Curtis. *The Living Treasures of Japan*. Tokyo: Kodansha International, 1973.

Aston, W. G., trans. *Nihon Shoki: Chronicles of Japan from the Earliest Times to A.D. 697*. From the original Chinese and Japanese. Rutland, Vt., and Tokyo: Tuttle, 1972.

Balfour-Paul, Jenny. "Indigo in the Arab World." *Hali: The International Magazine of Fine Carpets and Textiles* 61 (Feb. 1992): 98–105.

Barber, E. J. W. *Prehistoric Textiles: The Development of Cloth in the Neolithic and Bronze Ages*. Princeton: Princeton University Press, 1991.

Barnes, Ruth. "Indian Resist-dyed Textiles: The Newberry Collection." *The Ashmolean* 22 (Spring/Summer 1992): 10–12.

——. *Indian Block-Printed Cotton Textiles in the Kelsey Museum, The University of Michigan*. Ann Arbor: University of Michigan Press, 1993.

Beckwith, J. "Coptic Textiles." *Ciba Review* 12, no. 133 (1959): 2–27.

Bender Jorgenson, Lisa. "Mons Claudianus." *Acta Hyperborealia: Archaeological Textiles Newsletter* 10 (1990): 10.

Bennett, Wendell. *Ancient Arts of the Andes*. New York: Museum of Modern Art, 1954.

Bethe, Monica. "Colors, Dyes and Pigments." In *Kosode: 16th–19th Century Textiles from the Nomura Collection*, by Amanda Mayer Stinchecum, 59–76. Exhibition catalog. New York: Japan Society and Kodansha International, 1984.

Bonavia, Judith. *The Silk Road*. London: Harrap, 1988.

Brandon, Reiko Mochinaga. *Country Textiles of Japan: The Art of Tsutsugaki*. New York and Tokyo: Weatherhill, 1986.

Cort, Louise Allison. "Gen'ya's Devil Bucket." *Chanoyu Quarterly* 1982: 30: 31ff.

D'Harcourt, Raoul. *Textiles of Ancient Peru and Their Techniques*. Trans. by Sadie Brown; ed. by Grace G. Denny and Carolyn H. Osborne. Seattle: University of Washington Press, 1962. (first pub. in Paris: 1934).

Dunn, Charles J. *Everyday Life in Traditional Japan*. Rutland, Vt., and Tokyo: Tuttle, 1969.

Dyrenforth, Noel. *The Technique of Batik*. London: B. T. Batsford, 1988.

Elliott, Inger McCall. *Batik: Fabled Cloth of Java*. New York: Clarkson Potter, 1984.

Exhibition of Shōsō-in Treasures. cat. Nara National Museum, 1976, 1979, 1992, 1993.

Fukumoto Shigeki. "Japan and the Art of Dyeing." *Japan ECO Times: For Environmental Awareness* [newsletter] 2, no. 5 (May 5, 1993): 14; 2, no. 6 (June 1993): 13. Tokyo: Asia Pacific News.

——. "Rōketsuzome." Unpublished workshop notes. n. d.

Geijer, A. "A Silk from Antinoe and the Sassanian Textile Art." *Orientalia Suecana* 12 (1963): 3–36.

Gervers, Veronica. "An Early Christian Curtain in the Royal Ontario Museum." In *Studies in Textile History*, edited by Veronika Gervers. Toronto: Royal Ontario Museum, 1977.

Gittinger, Mattiebelle. *Master Dyers to the World: Technique and Trade in Early Indian Dyed Cotton Textiles*. Washington, D.C.: The Textile Museum, 1982.

Harada Hiroshi. "Japanese Traditional Crafts and the Government Administration for Their Protection." *Living National Treasures of Japan*, exhibition catalog. Boston: Museum of Fine Arts, 1983.

Hayashi Ryōichi. *The Silk Road and the Shoso-in*. Trans. by Robert Ricketts. New York: Weatherhill; Tokyo: Heibonsha, 1975.

Hopkirk, Peter. *Foreign Devils on the Silk Road*. Amherst: University of Massachusetts Press, 1984.

Hsio-yen Shih. "Textile Finds in China." In *Studies in Textile History*, edited by Veronika Gervers. Toronto: Royal Ontario Museum, 1977.

Japan Textile Color Design, comp. *Textile Designs of Japan*. Revised ed. 3 vols. Tokyo: Kodansha International, 1961, revised ed., 1980.

Kendrick, A. F. *Catalog of Textiles from the Burying Grounds in Egypt*. 3 vols. London: Victoria and Albert Museum, 1922.

Kroese, W. T. *The Origin of the Wax Block Prints on the Coast of West Africa*. Hengelo: N.V. Utitgeverij Smit van 1876, 1976.

Larsen, Jack Lenor, Alfred Bühler, Bronwen Solyom, and Garrett Solyom. *The Dyer's Art: Ikat, Batik, Plangi*. New York: Van Nostrand Reinhold, 1976.

Liddell, Jill. *The Story of the Kimono*. New York: E. P. Dutton, 1989.

"Lighting equipment." In *Kodansha Encyclopedia of Japan*, vol. 5, 8–9. Tokyo: Kodansha, 1983.

McDowell, Joan Allgrove. "The Mediterranean." "Sassanian Textiles." In *Textiles: 5000 Years*, edited by Jennifer Harris, 57–65, 68–70. New York: Harry N. Abrams, 1993.

Minnich, Helen Benton, in collaboration with Shōjirō Nomura. *Japanese Costume and the Makers of Its Elegant Tradition*. Rutland, Vt., and Tokyo: Tuttle, 1963.

Moyer, Susan Louise. *Silk Painting: The Artist's Guide to Gutta and Wax Resist Techniques*. New York: Watson-Guptill, 1991.

Nakano Eisha and Barbara B. Stephan. *Japanese Stencil Dyeing: Paste Resist Techniques*. New York and Tokyo: Weatherhill, 1982.

Nara National Museum. *Exhibition of Shōsō-in Treasures*. Exhibition catalog. Nara, 1976, 1979, 1992, 1993.

Noma Seiroku. *Japanese Costumes and Textile Arts*. Trans. by Armins Nikovskis. The Heibonsha Survey of Japanese Art, no. 16. New York and Tokyo: Weatherhill, Heibonsha, 1974.

Philippi, Donald, trans. *Kojiki [A Record of Ancient Things]*. Tokyo: University of Tokyo Press, 1968.

Pires, Tome. *The Suma Oriental of Tome Pires: An Account of the East*. Ed. and trans. by Armando Cortesao. London: Hakluyt Society, 1944.

Plinius the Elder. *Natural History*. 10 vols. Trans. by H. Rackman. Cambridge: Harvard University Press, 1940; reprinted 1983.

Riboud, Krishna. "A Closer View of Early Chinese Silks." In *Studies in Textile History*, edited by Veronika Gervers. Toronto: Royal Ontario Museum, 1978: 252–280.

Robinson, Stuart. *A History of Dyed Textiles: Dyes, Fibers, Painted Bark, Starch Resist, Discharge, Die Dye, Further Sources for Research*. Cambridge: Massachusetts Institute of Technology Press, 1969.

Rodrigues, Joao. *This Island of Japon: Joao Rodrigues' Account of Sixteenth-Century Japan*. Ed. and trans. by Michael Cooper. Tokyo and New York: Kodansha International, 1973.

Rossi, Gail. "The Laran Artists of the Mountains of China's Guizho Province." *Surface Design Journal* 10, no. 3 (Spring 1986), Part I: 18–22; 10, no. 4 (Summer 1986), Part II: 20–22.

Rossol, Monona, ed. "All About Wax." In *ACTS FACTS: The Monthly Newsletter From Arts, Crafts and Theatre Safety (ACTS)* 7, no. 10 (October 1993). New York.

Rutschowscaya, Marie-Helene. *Coptic Fabrics*. Paris: Adam Brio, 1990.

Saitō Shōji. "Bees and wasps." In *Kodansha Encyclopedia of Japan*, vol. 1, 149. Tokyo: Kodansha, 1983.

Sakamoto Kazuko. "Silk Fabrics of the Silk Road." In *Nara Symposium '91 Report*, 48–57. Nara: The Nara International Foundation, 1993.

Sanjōnishi Kinwosa. *Cultural Nippon*, vol. 8, no. 1 (1940): 101–126.

Sansom, George. *A History of Japan*. 3 vols. Rutland, Vt., and Tokyo: Tuttle, 1963.

Schaefer, Gustav. "The Earliest Specimens of Cloth Printing." *Ciba Review* 26 (October 1936): 914–917.

Shepherd, Dorothy S. "An Egyptian Textile from the Early Christian Period." *The Bulletin of the Cleveland Museum of Art* (April 1952): 66–68.

Shilliam, Nicola J. "Emerging Identity: American Textiles in the Early Twentieth Century." *Early Modern Textiles: From Arts and Crafts to Art Deco*. Exhibition catalog. Boston: Museum of Fine Arts, 1993.

Stein, Sir Aurel, and F. H. Andrews. "Ancient Chinese Figured Silks Excavated by Sir Aurel Stein." *Burlington Magazine*. Vol. xxxvii, no. 208 (July 1920): 3–10; (Sept. 1920): 147–152.

Steinmann, Alfred. *Batik: A Survey of Batik Design*. London: F. Lewis Publication, 1958.

—. "Batik Work, Its Origin and Spread." *Ciba Review* 58 (July 1947): 2102–2107.

Takeda, Sharon Sadako. "Clothed in Words: Calligraphic Designs on *Kosode*." *When Art Became Fashion*. Exhibition catalog. Los Angeles: Los Angeles County Museum, 1992.

Textiles: 5000 Years. Ed. by Jennifer Harris. New York: Harry N. Abrams, 1993.

Tokyo National Museum. *Masterpieces of Japanese Art: Special Exhibition*. Exhibition catalog. 1990.

Trilling, James. "The Roman Heritage: Textiles From Egypt and the Eastern Mediterranean 300 to 600 A.D." *Textile Museum Journal* 21 (1982): 102.

Vogelsang-Eastwood, Gillian. *Resist Dyed Textiles from Quseir Al-Qadim Egypt*. Paris: A. E. D. T. A., 1990.

—. "Unearthing History." *Hali: The International Magazine of Fine Carpets and Textiles* 67 (15 Aug. 1992): 85–89.

—. "The Textiles From Quseir Al-Qadim, Egypt." In *Proceedings of the Archaeological Textile Meeting, 1989*. Leiden: Rijksmuseum van Oudheden, 1990.

Wada Yoshiko, Mary Kellogg and Jane Barton. *Shibori: The Inventive Art of Japanese Shaped Resist Dyeing*. Tokyo: Kodansha International, 1983.

Weibel, Adele Coulin. *Two Thousand Years of Textiles: The Figured Textiles of Europe and the Near East*. New York: Pantheon, 1952.

Wessel, K. *Coptic Art in Early Christian Egypt*. New York: McGraw Hill, 1965.

Whitfield, Roderick, and Anne Farrer. *Caves of the Thousand Buddhas: Chinese Art from the Silk Route*. Exhibition catalog. London: British Museum, 1990.

Yokohari Kazuko. "An Essay on the Debut of the Chinese 'Samit' Based on the Study of Astana Textiles." *Bulletin of the Ancient Orient Museum*, XII (1991): 41–101.

Chinese

Dunhuang wenwuyenjiusuo kaoguzu. *Mogaoku faxian de Tang-dai sizhiwu ji qita* [Tang Silk Textiles and Other Finds from the Mogao Caves at Dunhuang, Gansu Province] *Wenwu* 2 (1972).

Hunan sheng bowuguan. *Changsha Mawangdui yihao Hanmu* [The Han Tomb I at Mawangdui in Changsha]. Beijing, 1973.

Gao Hanyu. *Zhong'guo lidai zhi ranxiu tulu* [Chinese Dyeing and Embroidery Patterns Through the Ages]. Hong Kong: Commercial Press, 1986.

Ling wai daida ["Written in Reply from the South"; a Tang-dynasty document detailing various aspects of life and culture]. In *Baibu congshu jizhen*, edited by Zhou Qufei. 10 vol. Taipei: Yiwen Yinguan, 1964–1970; vol. 6: 11.

Shou Ming. *Sichou zhi lu—Han Tang zhiwu* [Silk Road—Silk Fabrics in the Han and Tang Dynasties]. Beijing: Wenwu, 1973.

Wu Min. *Tangdai jiaban yinhua—Jiajie* [Wooden Plate Dyeing—Jiajie —in the Tang Dynasty] *Wenwu* 8 (1979).

——. *Tulufan chutu sizhiwu zhong de Tangdai yinran* [The Printing and Dyeing Techniques of the Tang Dynasty as Indicated by the Silk Fabrics Unearthed at Turfan, Xinjiang] *Wenwu* 10 (1973).

Xinjiang Weiwuer zizhiqu bowuguan. *Tulufan xian Astana—Helahezhuo gumuqun fajue jianbao* [A Brief Report on Finds from the Ancient Necropolis at Astana and Kharakhojo in Turfan County] *Wenwu* 10 (1973).

Xinjiang Weiwuer zizhiqu bowuguan. Xinjiang Minfeng xian Beidashamo zhong guyiji muzangqu Dong Han hezangmu qingli jianbao [A Brief Report on the Clearing of an Eastern Han Double-burial Tomb in the Necropolis of an Ancient Site in the Northern Great Desert of Minfeng County, Uighur Autonomous Region, Xinjiang Province] *Wenwu* 6 (1960).

German

Gerziger, Dora. *"Eine Decke Aus Dem Sechsten Grab Der 'Sieben Bruder.'"* *Anttike Kunst* 18 (1975): 51–55.

Rouffaer, G. P., and H. H. Juynboll. *Die Indische Batikkunst und ihre Geschichte*. Haarlem: von H. Kleinmann, 1900.

Stephani, Ludolf. "Erklärung einiger Kunstwerke der Kaiserlichen Ermitage und anderer Sammlungen." In *Compte-Rendu de la Commission Imperiale Archéologique pour les Années 1878 et 1879*. St. Petersburg, 1881.

French

Benazeth, Dominique. *"Un rare exemple de tissu copte a fil d'or."* In *Tissage, corderie, vannerie–IXe Rencontres Internationales d'Archeologie et d'Histoire*, 219–228. Antibes octobre 1988, Éditions A.P.D.C.A., Juan-les-Pins, 1989.

Gayet, Albert. *Catalogue Sommaire*—Société Française des Foilles Archéologiques, First edition, June/July 1905, Petit Palais des Champs Elysées.

Pfister, R. *"La decoration des etoffes d'Antinoe."* *Revue des Arts Asiatiques* 5 (1928): 215–243.

——. *Nouveaux textiles de Palmyre*. Paris: Les Editions D'art et D'histoire, 1937.

——. *Les Toiles Imperimees de Fostat et l'Hindoustan*. Paris: Les Editions D'art et D'histoire, 1938.

Riboud, Krishna, and Gabriel Vial. *Tissus de Touen-Houang*. Paris: Mission Paul Pelliot, 1970.

Japanese

Aikawa Kayoko. *"Rōketsuzome no rekishi"* [Rōketsuzome History]. *Senshoku to seikatsu* [Dyeing and Lifestyle] 31 (May 1981): 10–15.

Akashi Someto. *Senshoku shi kō* [History of Textiles]. Kyoto: Shimonkaku, 1927, reprinted 1977.

Asada Shūji. *Gendai no some* [Modern Dyeing]. Tokyo: Shibundo, 1989.

Chūka Jinmin Kyōwakoku shutsudo bunbutsu-ten [Archaeological Treasures Excavated in the People's Republic of China]. Exhibition catalog. Tokyo National Museum, Kyoto National Museum. Tokyo: Asahi Shimbun, 1973.

Engishiki [An ancient law, the compilation of which began during the Engi period and was completed in 927]. 3 vols. Tokyo: Yoshikawa Kobunkan, 1972.

Fuji Yoshiyuki. *"Rōketsuzome o gendai ni yomigaeraseta isai—Kitano Tsukio"* [The Genius Who Gave Birth to Modern Rōkechi: Kitano Tsukio]. In *Kitano Tsukio sakuhin-shū* [Collected Wax-resist Works of Tsukio Kitano]. Tokyo: Kyuryudo, 1993.

Fujii Kenzō. *Japanese Modern Textiles*. Trans. by A. Shimoyama, C. Furutani and J. Clancy. Ed. by Shikosha Publishing Co., Ltd., and GEN Editorial Studio. Kyotoshoin's Art Library of Japanese Textiles Series, vol. 17. Kyoto: Kyotoshoin, 1993.

Fukumoto Shigeki. *"Kata ni yoru rōketsuzome"* [Patterns of Wax Dyeing]. *Senshoku Alpha* 97 (April 1989): 18–23.

Genshoku gendai Nihon no bijutsu [Modern Japanese Art: The Full-Color Volume]. Ed. by Suzuki Kenji. Vol. 14, *Kōgei* Section. Tokyo: Shogakukan, 1979.

Genshoku senshoku daijiten [Illustrated Encyclopedia of Dyeing]. Ed. by Itakura Hisarō, Nomura Kihachi, Motoi No, Yoshikawa Kiyobei and Yoshida Mitsukuni. Tokyo: Tankosha, 1977.

Harada Yoshito. *Kan rikuchō no fukushaku* [Chinese Dress and Personal Ornaments of the Han and Six Dynasties]. Trans. by Harada Jirō. The Tōyō Bunko, 1937, revised as vol. 49, 1967.

Inuzuka Mikishi. *"Yamagata-ken Shōnai chihō no rō tsukuri"* [Wax Production in Shōnai, Yamagata Prefecture]. *Senshoku to seikatsu* [Dyeing and Lifestyle] 31 (1980): 43–44.

Kaneko Kenji. *Katazome, komon, chūgata*. Trans. by A. Shimoyama and J. Clancy. Ed. by Shikosha Publishing Co., Ltd., and GEN Editorial Studio. Kyotoshoin's Art Library of Japanese Textiles Series, vol. 15. Kyoto: Kyotoshoin, 1994.

Kan-Tō no senshoku: Shiruku Rōdo no shin shutsudo-hin [Chinese Textiles Discovered Along the Silk Road from the Han Through the Tang Dynasties]. Tokyo: Shogakukan, 1973.

Maeda Ujō. *Nihon kodai no saishiki to some* [Color and Dyeing in Ancient Japan]. Tokyo: Kawade Shobō, 1975.

Maruyama Nobuhiko. *Yūzen Dyeing*. Trans. by A. Shimoyama and J. Clancy. Ed. by Shikosha Publishing Co., Ltd., and Karinsha Co., Ltd. Kyotoshoin's Art Library of Japanese Textiles Series, vol. 5. Kyoto: Kyotoshoin, 1993.

Matsumoto Kaneo. *"Shōsōin kire to Asuka Tempyō no senshoku"* [*Jōdai-gire*: Seventh-and-Eighth-Century Textiles in Japan from the Shōsōin and Hōryū-ji]. Trans. by Shigetaka Kaneko and Richard Mellott; ed. by Sachio Yoshioka. Kyoto: Shikosha, 1984.

——. *Shōsōin rōkechi no hangata ni tsuite* [Stamped Rōkechi Fabrics in the Shōsōin]. Shoryōbu Kiyo no. 25. Tokyo: Imperial Household Agency, 1973.

——. *"Shōsōin no katazome: Kyōkechi to rōkechi o chushin ni"* [Pattern Dyeing of the Shōsōin: Thoughts on *Kyōkechi* and *Rōkechi*]. *Senshoku to seikatsu* [Dyeing and Lifestyle] 23 (Fall 1978): 13–17.

Muramatsu Hiroshi. *"Ogō Tomonosuke—Sono jidai, sono sakuhin"* [Tomonosuke Ogō—His Times, His Work]. In *Ogō Tomonosuke sakuhin-shū* [Collected Works of Tomonosuke Ogō]. Kyoto: Yushodo, 1972.

Nagasawa Kazutoshi. *"Kan-Tō no senshoku to sei iki e no denpa"* [The Textiles of the Han and Tang Dynasties and Their Diffusion to the Western Region]. *Senshoku no bi* [The Beauty of Dyeing] 30 (Summer 1984): 65–72.

Nakajima Shizu. *Kimono no rōketsuzome* [Dyeing Kimono with Wax Resist]. Bijutsu Shuppansha, 1978.

Nihon bijutsu [Arts of Japan]. Ed. by Eiko Kamiya. *Kosode* Issue, no. 67. Tokyo: Shibundo, 1971.

Nihon bijutsu zenshū [Arts of Japan series]. Ed. by Sae Ogasawara. *Sarasa* Issue, no. 175. Tokyo: Shibundo, 1981.

Nihon bijutsu zenshū [Arts of Japan series]. Ed. by Shōichi Gotō. Shōsōin Issue, Vol. 5. Tokyo: Gakken, 1978.

Nihon no senshoku: Bi to giryō [Japanese Dyeing: Beauty and Skill]. Ed. by Kyoto National Museum; essay by Ken Kirihata; trans. by Sachiko Usui. Kyoto: Kyotoshoin, 1987.

Nihon Orimono Shinbunsha, comp. *Senshokujiten* [Dictionary of Dyed Textiles]. Osaka: Nihon Orimono Shinbunsha, 1931. Reprinted as *Zōho senshoku Jiten* [Expanded Dictionary of Dyed Textiles]. Kyoto: Kyotoshoin, 1976.

Nihon senshoku bunken sōran [Compendium of Sources on Japanese Dyeing]. Kyoto: Senshoku to Seikatsusha, 1980.

Nozaki Kunio. *"Rōketsuzome."* In *Tegaki yūzenzome no gijutsu to gihō* [Hand-dyeing: Technique and Process]. Ed. by Tatsuo Honma. Kyoto: Kyoto-shi Senshoku Shikenjo, 1974.

Ogasawara Sae. *"Rōzome no genryū to Nippon"* [The Origin of Wax Resist and Japan]. *Rōketsuzome Historical and Contemporary.* In the exhibition catalog. Tokyo: Suntory Art Museum, 1981.

"Ōtani tanken-tai, 1902–1914: Chūō Ajia no yume to bōken" [Ōtani Expedition, 1902–1914: Central Asian Dream and Adventure]. *The Sun Magazine* 360 (June 1991): 5–91.

Ryō no shūge [Explanatory companion volume to the *Engishiki*]. 4 vols. Tokyo: Yoshikawa Kobunkan, 1972.

Sano Takeo. *"Rōzome no ayumi"* [The History of Roketsu]. In *Rōketsuzome Historical and Contemporary.* In the exhibition catalog. Tokyo: Suntory Art Museum, 1981.

——. *"Rōketsuzome kagirinaki romansu"* [Roketsuzome Endless Romance]. *Senshoku Alpha* 29 (August, 1983), 8–12.

——. *"Ogō Tomonosuke, Inagaki Toshijirō: Sōsaku e no michi"* [Tomonosuke Ogō, Toshijirō Inagaki: The Path of Creation]. In *Senshoku no sōsaku: Ogō Tomonosuke, Inagaki Toshijirō* [Creativity in Dyeing: Tomonosuke Ogō, Toshijirō Inagaki]. Exhibition catalog. Kyoto: Museum of Kyoto, 1990.

Sato Taketoshi. *Chūgoku kodai kinu orimono shi kenkyū ge* [Chinese Ancient Silk Weaving History Study]. Vol. 2, section 4, chapter 1. Tokyo: Kazama Shobō, 1977–1978.

Takada Yamato and Yamanobe Tomoyuki. *"Senshoku shi ni nai senshoku shi"* [Unwritten Textile History]. *Nihon no bijutsu* [Japanese Art]. No. 263. Tokyo: Shibundo, 1988.

Takahashi Seiichirō. *"Rōketsuzome no kiretsu"* [The Cracks of Wax-dyeing]. *Senshoku to seikatsu* [Dyeing and Lifestyle] 31 (Fall 1980): 38–44.

Teraishi Shōsaku. *"Rōraa hiki-ki"* [Rōketsuzome Technique: The Roller]. *Senshoku to seikatsu* [Dyeing and Lifestyle] 30 (1980): 16–17.

Textiles in the Shōsōin (in Japanese). Vol. 1, comp. by the Shōsōin office. Tokyo: Asahi Shimbun, 1963.

Textiles in the Shōsōin (in Japanese). Vol. 2, comp. by the Shōsōin office. Tokyo: Asahi Shimbun, 1965.

Treasures of the Shōsōin (in Japanese). Comp. by the Shōsōin office. Tokyo: Asahi Shimbun, 1965.

Treasures of the Shōsōin: Furniture and Interior Furnishings (in Japanese). Ed. by Kimura Norimitsu. Kyoto: Shikosha, 1992.

Treasures of the Shōsōin: Musical Instruments, Dance Articles, Game Sets (in Japanese). Ed. by Matsumoto Kaneo. Kyoto: Shikosha, 1991.

Treasures of the Shōsōin. North, Middle and South Sections. 3 vols. Comp. by the Shōsōin office. Tokyo: Asahi Shimbun, 1960–1962.

Treasures of the Shōsōin. North, Middle and South Sections. 3 vols. Comp. by the Shōsōin office. Tokyo: Asahi Shimbun, 1987–1989.

Tsuchiya Yoshio. *"'The Origin of Rōketsu' Exhibition: From the Shōsōin to Modern Rōzome"* (in Japanese). *Senshoku to seikatsu* [Dyeing and Lifestyle] 2 (May 1981): 9–13.

Tsujimura Kiichi. *"Injigo o fukumanai shinpi no yama ai"* [Mysterious 'Mountain Indigo' Containing No Real Indigo]. *Senshoku Alpha* 49 (April 1985): 63–64.

Tsurumaki Tsuruichi. *Senshoku binran* [Handbook of Dyeing]. Tokyo: Hakubunkan, 1907.

Uchiko Town Office. *"Mokurō."* *Uchiko kikō* [Uchiko Travelogue newsletter], 8–9. Uchiko Town Housing Preservation Office, 1991.

Uemura Rokurō. "The Originator of Rōketsuzome: Memories of Professor Tsuruichi Tsurumaki" (in Japanese). *Senshoku to seikatsu* [Dyeing and Lifestyle] 31 (Fall 1980): 16–18.

Xinjiang Province, Uighur Autonomous Region Museum: Chinese Museum, Second Period (in Japanese). Vol. 1, comp. by museum staff. Japanese edition by Katsuhisa Kato. Tokyo: Kodansha and Wenwu, 1987.

Yamanobe Tomoyuki. *Fabrics From the Silk Road: The Stein Collection, National Museum, New Delhi* (in Japanese). Trans. by Akiko Murakata. Kyoto: Shikosha, 1979.

Yoshimoto Shinobu. *Jawa-sarasa* (in Japanese). Tokyo: Heibonsha, 1993.

Yoshioka, Sachio. *Sarasa: Printed and Painted Textiles* (in Japanese). Trans. by A. Shimoyama and J. Clancy. Ed. by Shikosha Publishing Co., Ltd. Kyotoshoin's Art Library of Japanese Textiles Series, vol. 20. Kyoto: Kyotoshoin, 1993.

ACKNOWLEDGMENTS:

Over the number of years it took to research and write this book, the list of important individuals who gave me help has grown quite long. At the heart of this book are the artists who continue the work of rōzome. They have been among my most enthusiastic supporters, discussing their work, sharing techniques and generously loaning many of the color photographs that are included. Their support, understanding of the process and eagerness to deal with my many questions are all greatly appreciated. Thanks also to Mr. Kiyoji Tsuji, an independent curator and professor of Seian University of Art and Design who, from the very beginning, was willing to help in any way necessary, from providing introductions to artists, to searching for research materials. Mr. Tsuji and I were fortunate to share some time with Mr. Takeo Sano, who despite ill health, graciously agreed to talk with us about his long association with rōzome. Mr. Sano's memories added a very personal dimension to my understanding of the history of rōzome's development in the twentieth century. Mr. Taizō Minakawa and Mr. Seiji Hirokawa also shared their perspectives. Mr. Ichirō Yamamoto, secretary of the Seiryū Association, spoke with me on the future of rōzome, and Mr. Motoharu Koyama kindly allowed us to photograph the work of Tomonosuke Ogō from his collection. Prof. Teiji Nakai of Kyoto City University of Arts gave me background information and searched his resources numerous times for answers to specific questions. In addition, Mr. Gai Nishimura illuminated additional points of Japanese textile history, discussed his collection of *sarasa* textiles and loaned precious samples to be photographed.

A number of curators and textile authorities have been important sources of information and knowledge. Mr. Kaneo Matsumoto, former curator of the Shōsōin Collection of the Nara National Museum, graciously met with me and later corresponded in reply to various questions on ancient rōkechi. Others who also assisted my research were Mr. Shigeki Kawakami of the Kyoto National Museum, Mr. Iwao Nagasaki of the Tokyo National Museum, Mr. Ken Kirihata of Otemae University, Prof. Kōgi Kudara of Ryūkoku University, Prof. Kayoko Aikawa of Nara Women's College, Ms. Kazuko Sakamoto of Kokushikan University, and Ms. Keiko Fujimoto of the Museum of Kyoto. In addition, Dr. Ruth Barnes of the Ashmolean Museum, Dr. Min Wu of the Uighur Autonomous Region Museum and Ms. Gillian Vogelsang-Eastwood were all very generous in sharing their expertise on ancient textiles. Thank you also to Ms. Hero Granger-Taylor of the British Museum, Ms. Linda Woolley of the Victoria and Albert Museum, Dr. Marie-Helene Rutschowscaya of the Louvre, Dr. James Watt and Ms. Joyce Denney of the Metropolitan Museum, Ms. Miyako Yoshinaga of the Brooklyn Museum, Ms. Anne Ward-

well of the Cleveland Museum of Art, Ms. Jessica Sloane of the Textile Museum, Washington, D.C., and Ms. Diane Mott of the Museum of Fine Arts Boston.

Researching English source materials while living in Japan was not easy; however, a number of institution libraries abroad were of great assistance. These included the British Museum, The Victoria and Albert Museum, the Museum of Fine Arts Boston, the Textile Museum, Washington, D.C., the Metropolitan Museum of Art and the Cleveland Museum of Art. Special thanks to Judy Rittersporn of the Royal Ontario Museum, Toronto, who came through with resources at a crucial time. Within Japan I received assistance from the following libraries: Kyoto University Oriental Center, Osaka Prefectural Industrial Design Research Center, Nara National Museum, Doshisha University, Kyoto Institute of Technology, International Research Center for Japan Studies, Kyoto Japan Foundation, Museum of Kyoto and the Kyoto Prefectural and Kyoto City Central libraries. Thanks to Mr. Hiroki Tomiyama, President of Senshoku to Seikatsu Publishing Company and Editor Yoshifumi Sato who knew exactly where to find many of the specialized books I needed within Japan.

A number of textile authorities and friends agreed to read portions of the manuscript and to give suggestions and comments during the writing process. I am indebted to Ms. Rachel MacAlpine, Mr. Andrew Hare, Ms. Gillian Vogelsang-Eastwood, Mr. Bill Morton, Ms. Monica Bethe, Ms. Saaraliisa Ylitalo and Mr. Chris Ward for their help.

Thanks also to Ms. Diane Durston for her encouragement and an early introduction. When Mr. Shigeyoshi Suzuki, executive editor at Kodansha International, appeared at my solo rōzome exhibition in Tokyo five years ago, he asked if I had considered writing about the process I have worked with for so many years. Mr. Suzuki's interest, expertise and guidance have been greatly appreciated through the long process leading to the final publication. I am also grateful to my editor Ms. Elizabeth Floyd, proofreader Mr. Keith Learmonth and all the Kodansha staff for the meticulous work that has gone into the many phases of the book's preparation.

Two individuals, Mr. Yusuke Tange and Ms. Yumiko Ueno, were key sources of inspiration and assistance in the writing of this book. They both have my deepest gratitude. Mr. Tange, an artist himself, has for many years felt strongly that a book solely on rōzome needed to be written. His encouragement in every facet of this book has been tremendous. Mr. Tange is responsible for all the monochrome photographs of techniques and of artists' studios and for drawing the wax-block reproductions. He also demonstrated the *sekidashi* and other dyeing processes. Certainly, I could not have found a better assistant than Ms. Yumiko Ueno who worked on many phases of the research, from translation and interpreting to searching for source materials. Her expertise with language, knowledge of the culture, enthusiasm for the work of the artists made working with her, every day, a very special joy. Others who are due thanks for translation or interpreting assistance are: Ms. Chie Koyama, Ms. Li Ping Fu, Ms. Kazuko Noro, Ms. Sueko Watanabe, Ms. Yuri Yamamoto, Dr. Wolfgang Ruttkowski, Ms. Yoshiko Wakui, Ms. Ling Gao, Dr. Reichi Kiga, Ms. Nobuko Sakurai, Ms. Noriko Tsuji, Ms. Hisako Fukui, Ms. Tomoyo Daidō, Mr. Philip Meredith, Ms. Judith Clancy and Dr. Maureen Robertson. For computer assistance, I owe great thanks to Dr. Hiroshi Ueno who always had an answer for this novice. Thanks also to Dr. Thomas Robb for his computer assistance with the index.

On the technical aspects of rōzome process and materials, a number of people were most helpful: Mr. Kunio Nozaki of Kyoto Textile Research Institute, Prof. Shūji Asada of Kyoto Seika University, Mr. Seiichirō Takahashi of Tanaka Nao Dye Supplies, Mr. Yoshizō Nakamura of Nakamura Rōsoku Co., Mr. Don Wiener of PRO Chemical and Dye Inc. and Mr. Hideshi Maejima, president of Rokujō Company, Ltd., who allowed us to photograph his textile processing plant. Ms. Seiko Yamade also worked with me to prepare many of the samples included in the technique section and Mr. Mitsuo Takaya, Mr. Yasuhiko Tanaka and Ms. Yuki Katō demonstrated processes and supplied samples of their specialized techniques for photographing.

Finally, sincere thanks to numerous friends in Japan, the United States and Europe who answered my pleas for help by locating and shipping books, copying source material at libraries and giving professional advice, especially: Ms. Lee Hubert, Dr. Frances Clegg, Mr. Brent Elliott, Mr. Ted Landry, Ms. Barbara Lee Smith, Ms. Marion Maule and Dr. Roberta Wollons. Grateful thanks also to Dr. and Mrs. Keiji Araki, Momoko and Biji Araki, Sean Murray and Amanda Benjamin-Murray, who have all come to my rescue.

INDEX

Abe, Midori 43 (Plate 39), 138, 146–147
acid dyes 117, 130, 135, 146, 192–193, 194
acorn, dye from 83, 85, 206
acrolein 167
ai 195, 205, 206
aibō (indigo stick) 196, 206
akane (Japanese madder) 82, 206
Akashi, Someto 102
alum 117, 195
ambatik. See batik.
analysis of resist textiles 58, 71, 73, 79, 89, 205
Annunciation, The 64 (Figure 3)
Antinoopolis. See *Veil of Antinoopolis, The*
aobana 135, 170, 206
apprenticeship 120–122, 130, 140, 155, 199
Arles 62
Artemis 64, 65 (Figure 4), 66
ash lye 82, 195
ashiginu (plain weave silk) 21 (Plate 6), 77, 80, 81, 83, 85
Ashmunein 65 (Figure 4)
Astana 18 (Plates 3–4), 70 (Figure 6), 71, 72 (Figure 7), 73, 87 (Figure 12)
At-tar 61
aya (figured twill) 61, 77, 81 (Figure 9), 82
azoic dyes. *See* naphthol dyes

banners, Buddhist 71, 76, 77, 84, 87 (Figure 13)
Barber, E. J. W. 60, 61
barrier resist. See *sekidashi*
batik. Indonesian/Javanese: 9, 10, 12, 13, 57, 97 (Figure 16), 100, 103, 165; Japanese: 10, 12, 13, 102, 107; of other cultures: 10, 13, 95, 101, 161, 198, 207
bees, keeping of 158–159, 163
beeswax (*rōmitsu*) 61, 68, 77, 93, 98, 158, 159, 160, 161, 163
Bender Jorgensen, Lisa 61
bengara (Indian red pigment) 117, 196, 206
benibana (safflower) 82, 94, 195, 206
binders 117, 119, 190, 191, 195, 196

Birds in a Cage 18 (Plate 4), 73
board-jamming. See *kyōkechi*
bokashi 126, 128, 129, 130, 131, 154, 170, 200; demonstration of 202–203
bound resist. See *shibori*
brushes. For dyeing, see *irosashi-bake, jizome-bake, maru-bake, surikomi-bake.* For applying wax, see *hōki, rō-fude, shike-bake*
Bühler, Alfred 57

candles 161 (Figure 30); allotment in wartime 108, 115; early production in Japan 142, 158, 159 (Figure 29), 160
canting (Indonesian wax writing tool) 10, 13, 99, 103, 165
cap (Indonesian metal stamp) 13, 89, 185
Caucasus 61
chay 98
carnauba 161 (Figure 30), 162–163 (Figure 31), 164–165
chintz 95, 97–98. See also *sarasa*
chokusetsu senryō (direct dyes) 192, 194
chronicles, ancient Japanese 77, 158
clamp resist. See *kyōkechi, jiajie*
climate, influence of on development of wax resist 68, 93
color carrier 166, 187; *dakku* as a 190
copper 120, 195
Coptic 62, 63, 66, 90, 100, 104, 110
Coromandel 95
corvée ("tax payment"), textiles produced in lieu of 79, 81, 86 (Figure 10), 20 (Plate 8)
costumes, held in the Shōsōin 75, 76, 77, 80, 84, 85–86, 87 (Figure 12), 90
cotton as resist ground in antiquity 61, 67, 68, 69, 71, 73, 77; of Edo 95, 96, 97, 98; artists' use of 118, 122, 129, 146, 159, 163; instructions on use of 173, 178, 180, 182, 186, 191, 193, 194, 205
cracks, in the surface of wax. Acceptability of 13, 161; as clue to resist method used 71, 73, 205; instructions on patterning with 161
cutch (*asen*) 195, 206

Daibutsu, dedication of the 76, 90
Daimaru 107
dakku, as new resist medium, 121, 135; general description 165 (Figure 32), 166, 187 (Figure 69); instructions for use 190–191
damaru (damor or dammar gum) 121, 165 (Figure 32)
Date 105
demonstrations, of dyeing techniques See *bokashi, hikizome* and *sekidashi*
design motifs. Abstract 106, 109, 115, 118, 122, 127, 129, 131, 140, 142, 147, 150, 151, 155; asymmetrical 84; classical 62, 66; geometric 62, 66, 67, 68, 69, 89, 97, 109, 116, 140, 150, 151; sawtooth 21 (Plate 10), 68, 96; symmetrical 21 (Plate 10), 68, 96. Of Persian Sassanid origin: animal under a tree 91; *renjū* collar 90. Of Chinese origin: *karahana* 19 (Plate 7), 88, 89, 90; phoenix 21 (Plate 9), 72 (Figure 7), 85, 87 (Figure 12), 91; dot matrix 18 (Plate 3), 61, 71 (Plate 3), 73. Seen among the Shōsōin treasures: arabesque 73, 81 (Figure 9), 90, 91; eight-lobed 87 (Figure 12), 90; elephant 84, 85; facing ducks 85, 86 (Figure 11), 89; floral lattice 19 (Plate 5), 80, 81, 89; fish, waves, and birds 19 (Plate 6), 83, 87 (Figure 13), 88, 89; grass 81 (Figure 9); *kirin* 21 (Plate 9), 85; lotus 90; parrot 19 (Plate 7), 21 (Plate 9), 84, 85, 88, 89; phoenix 21 (Plate 9), 85, 87, 89, 90; ram 20 (Plate 8), 84, 85, 90; vines 18, 61, 69, 90, 91, 97; scrolling vines 63, 79, 87, 89; zigzag 88 (Figure 14), 89
direct dyes 192, 194
Dunhuang temple caves 90
Dutch Haarlem School 100
dyes. Stock solutions of 193, 194; streaking of 199, 200, 201, 203, 204; to thicken 121, 182. *See also* fiber-reactive dyes, naphthol dyes, acid dyes, vat dyes, direct dyes, pre-metalized dyes and natural dyes. For techniques in applying, see *bokashi, hikizome* and overdyeing

221